POCKET ATLAS

Maps compiled and drawn by Collins Cartographical Department

First Published 1961
Reprinted 1963
Revised 1963
Revised 1964
Revised 1965
Revised 1967
Revised 1968
Revised 1969
Revised 1970
Revised 1972
Revised 1973

Printed and bound in Great Britain by
Collins Clear-Type Press
ISBN 0 00 447032 X

COLLINS POCKET ATLAS *of the World*

160 pages
96 pages of full colour
24 pages of other maps
Index of 5000 entries

COLLINS, *Glasgow, London, New York, Toronto, Sydney, Auckland, Johannesburg.*

LIST OF CONTENTS

FULL COLOUR MAPS

SPECIAL FEATURES

INDEXES

COUNTRIES OF THE WORLD

Map	Country	Area (sq.miles)	Population	Capital
	THE COMMONWEALTH			
36-47	UNITED KINGDOM	94,448	55,521,000	London
101, 104/5	CANADA	3,851,920	21,017,000	Ottawa
80-83	AUSTRALIA	2,968,030	12,713,000	Canberra
84-85	NEW ZEALAND	103,741	2,860,000	Wellington
74/5	INDIA	1,175,484	550,000,000	Delhi
74	SRI LANKA	25,332	12,748,000	Colombo
94	GHANA	91,850	8,546,000	Accra
78	SINGAPORE	224	2,975,000	——
63	CYPRUS	3,571	633,000	Nicosia
94	NIGERIA	356,679	66,174,000	Lagos
90	SIERRA LEONE	27,925	2,512,000	Freetown
95	TANZANIA	362,830	12,508,000	Dar-es-Salaam
87	WESTERN SAMOA	1,100	132,000	Apia
106	JAMAICA	4,230	1,893,000	Kingston
107	TRINIDAD & TOBAGO	1,979	1,010,000	Port of Spain
95	UGANDA	93,983	9,764,000	Kampala
92	MALAWI	46,067	4,530,000	Zomba
78	MALAYSIA	128,432	10,434,000	Kuala Lumpur
95	KENYA	224,966	10,890,000	Nairobi
60	MALTA	122	330,000	Valletta
92	ZAMBIA	290,600	4,054,000	Lusaka
90	GAMBIA	4,003	374,000	Bathurst
93	LESOTHO	11,716	970,000	Maseru
107	GUYANA	83,000	714,000	Georgetown
93	BOTSWANA	212,000	629,000	Gaborone
107	BARBADOS	170	254,000	Bridgetown
107	ANTIGUA	170	65,000	St. John's
19	MAURITIUS	810	834,000	Port Louis
93	SWAZILAND	6,700	451,000	Mbabane
106	BAHAMAS	4,400	169,000	Nassau
75	BANGLADESH	55,143	59,993,000	Dacca
18	Bermuda Islands	20	53,000	Hamilton
78	Brunei	2,225	130,000	Brunei
112	Falkland Islands	4,617	2,200	Stanley
87	Fiji	7,010	524,000	Suva
59	Gibraltar	2	28,000	——
106	Honduras, British	8,866	122,000	Belize
76	Hong Kong	398½	3,951,000	Victoria
86	Papua, and New Guinea	178,270	2,418,000	Port Moresby
92	Rhodesia	150,337	5,190,000	Salisbury
19	St. Helena	45	5,000	Jamestown
19	Seychelles	155	51,000	Victoria
87	Western Pacific	17,645	301,000	Honiara
106/7	West Indies Associated States	945	483,000	*on* Barbados
	OTHER COUNTRIES OF THE WORLD			
70	Afghanistan	250,000	16,516,000	Kabul
61	Albania	11,100	2,075,000	Tirana
62	Algeria	952,200	13,825,000	Algiers
59	Andorra	174	19,000	Andorra
111	Argentina	1,079,000	23,300,000	Buenos Aires
64	Austria	32,375	7,391,000	Vienna
73	Bahrain	230	207,000	Manama

Map	Country	Area (sq. miles)	Population	Capital
56	Belgium — — —	11,779	9,691,000	Brussels
110	Bolivia — — — —	424,175	4,931,000	La Paz
110	Brazil — — — —	3,286,570	93,200,000	Brasilia
61	Bulgaria — — —	42,730	8,524,000	Sofia
75	Burma — — —	261,796	27,584,000	Rangoon
95	Burundi — — —	10,747	3,475,000	Bujumbura
78	Cambodia — — —	69,900	6,701,000	Phnom Penh
90	Cameroon — — —	183,000	5,836,000	Yaounde
90	Cent. African Rep. — —	238,231	2,088,000	Bangui
90	Chad — — — —	495,767	3,510,000	Fort Lamy
111	Chile — — — —	286,405	9,144,000	Santiago
76	China — — —	3,691,616	732,000,000	Peking
106	Colombia — — —	439,525	22,000,000	Bogota
94	Congo (Brazzaville) — —	132,049	900,000	Brazzaville
106	Costa Rica — — —	19,575	1,685,000	San Jose
106	Cuba — — — —	44,219	8,553,000	Havana
65	Czechoslovakia — —	49,368	14,467,000	Prague
90	Dahomey — — —	44,697	2,640,000	Porto Novo
55	Denmark — — —	16,618	4,879,000	Copenhagen
30	Faeroe Islands — —	540	37,000	Torshavn
98	Greenland — — —	840,025	39,613	Godthaab
167	Dominican Republic — —	18,816	4,030,000	Santo Domingo
110	Ecuador — — —	109,490	5,890,000	Quito
90	Egypt — — — —	386,112	34,000,000	Cairo
91	Equatorial Guinea — —	10,830	300,000	Sta. Isabel
73	Ethiopia — — —	471,800	24,769,000	Addis Ababa
54	Finland — — —	130,123	4,779,000	Helsinki
77	Formosa (Tiawan) — —	13,884	14,746,000	Taipei
57/8	France — — —	212,827	50,770,000	Paris
107-110	Guiana & W. Indies, Fr.	36,247	652,000	Cayenne
90	Terr. of Afars & Issas —	8,495	125,000	Djibouti
91	Gabon — — — —	103,092	630,000	Libreville
64	Germany (total) — —	137,400	55,371,000	——
64	Eastern — — —	41,660	15,993,000	Berlin
64	Western — — —	95,740	59,378,000	Bonn
64	Berlin — — —	341	3,271,000	——
61	Greece — — — —	50,950	8,763,000	Athens
99	Guatemala — — —	42,042	5,014,000	Guatemala City
90	Guinea — — —	94,968	3,890,000	Conakry
101	Haiti — — — —	10,714	4,768,000	Port-au-Prince
106	Honduras — — —	43,280	2,535,000	Tegucigalpa
61	Hungary — — —	35,919	10,344,000	Budapest
4	Iceland — — —	39,770	204,000	Reykjavik
87	Indonesia — — —	735,350	118,000,000	Jakarta
72	Iran (Persia) — — —	636,312	28,448,000	Tehran
72	Iraq — — — —	173,270	9,465,000	Baghdad
48-51	Ireland — — —	27,136	2,944,000	Dublin
72	Israel — — — —	7,992	2,919,000	Jerusalem
60	Italy — — — —	116,306	54,683,000	Rome
60	Ivory Coast — — —	124,506	4,195,000	Abidjan
77	Japan — — — —	142,730	104,049,000	Tokyo
72	Jordan — — — —	37,740	2,300,000	Amman
77	Korea — — — —	84,600	45,038,000	——
77	North — — —	46,540	13,300,000	Pyongyang
77	South — — —	38,060	31,738,000	Seoul
72	Kuwait — — —	7,780	733,000	Kuwait
78	Laos — — — —	91,431	2,700,000	Vientiane
72	Lebanon — — —	4,015	2,700,000	Beirut
90	Liberia — — —	43,000	1,150,000	Monrovia
62	Libya — — — —	679,379	1,869,000	Beida
64	Liechtenstein — — —	60	22,000	Vaduz
57	Luxembourg — — —	998	343,000	Luxembourg
91	Malagasy Republic — —	229,230	6,777,000	Tananarive
70	Maldive Islands — —	114	114,000	Male

Map	Country	Area (sq. miles)	Population	Capital
90	Mali	476,500	4,929,000	Bamako
90	Mauritania	407,640	1,140,000	Nouakchott
99	Mexico	761,640	48,600,000	Mexico City
76	Mongolia	592,681	1,240,000	Ulan Bator
62	Morocco	172,421	15,525,000	Rabat
86	Nauru	8	7,000	——
75	Nepal	54,363	10,845,000	Katmandu
56	Netherlands	15,790	13,077,000	Amsterdam
101	Neth. Antilles	371	214,000	Willemstad
110	Surinam	55,146	350,000	Paramaribo
106	Nicaragua	53,940	1,984,000	Managua
90	Niger	489,210	4,033,000	Niamey
54	Norway	125,190	3,892,000	Oslo
74	Pakistan	310,403	48,051,000	Islamabad
106	Panama	29,210	1,417,000	Panama
111	Paraguay	157,051	12,314,000	Asuncion
110	Peru	496,236	13,600,000	Lima
79	Philippine Republic	115,710	39,079,000	Quezon City
65	Poland	124,670	32,889,000	Warsaw
59	Portugal	35,360	9,560,000	Lisbon
18	Azores & Madeira	1,236	620,000	Angra & Funchal
18	Cape Verde Islands	1,557	250,000	Praia
93	Mozambique	302,337	7,376,000	Lourenco Marques
90	Guinea, Portuguese	13,948	549,000	Bissau
91	Angola	481,365	5,430,000	Loanda
31	Romania	91,703	2,010,000	Bucharest
95	Rwanda	10,169	3,500,000	Kigali
99	Salvador	8,259	3,150,000	San Salvador
73	Saudi Arabia	870,044	7,200,000	Riyadh
90	Senegal	76,126	3,780,000	Dakar
73	Somalia Republic	246,208	4,500,000	Mogadishu
93	South Africa, Rep. of	471,470	21,282,000	Cape Town & Pretoria
93	South West Africa	318,270	610,000	Windhoek
73	Southern Yemen	112,560	1,500,000	Al Shaab
59	Spain	194,890	33,290,000	Madrid
90	Canary Islands	2,807	967,000	Las Palmas
90	Sahara, Spanish	102,705	55,000	El Aaiun
73,90	Sudan	967,528	15,312,000	Khartoum
54	Sweden	173,657	8,014,000	Stockholm
64	Switzerland	15,942	6,270,000	Berne
72	Syria	71,480	6,290,000	Damascus
78	Thailand (Siam)	198,461	34,738,000	Bangkok
90	Togo	21,853	1,857,000	Lome
62	Tunisia	63,380	5,027,000	Tunis
72	Turkey	308,388	35,667,000	Ankara
102-5	Untd. States of America	3,615,316	203,166,000	Washington, D.C.
56	Guam	211	79,000	Agana
56	Pacific Islands (Trustees)	690	94,000	——
106	Panama Canal Zone	552	56,000	Balboa Heights
107	Puerto Rico	3,435	2,750,000	San Juan
87	Samoa (American)	76	28,000	Pago Pago
107	Virgin Islands	132	63,000	Charlotte Amalie
90	Upper Volta	105,871	5,330,000	Ouagadougou
111	Uruguay	72,174	2,852,000	Montevideo
31,66/7,72	U.S.S.R.	8,649,937	241,748,000	Moscow
107	Venezuela	352,153	10,399,000	Caracas
78	Vietnam	127,250	39,207,000	——
78	North	59,935	21,340,000	Hanoi
78	South	65,950	17,867,000	Saigon
73	Yemen	75,290	5,000,000	Sana & Tiaz
61	Yugoslavia	98,770	21,500,000	Belgrade
94	Zaïre	905,609	17,100,000	Kinshasa

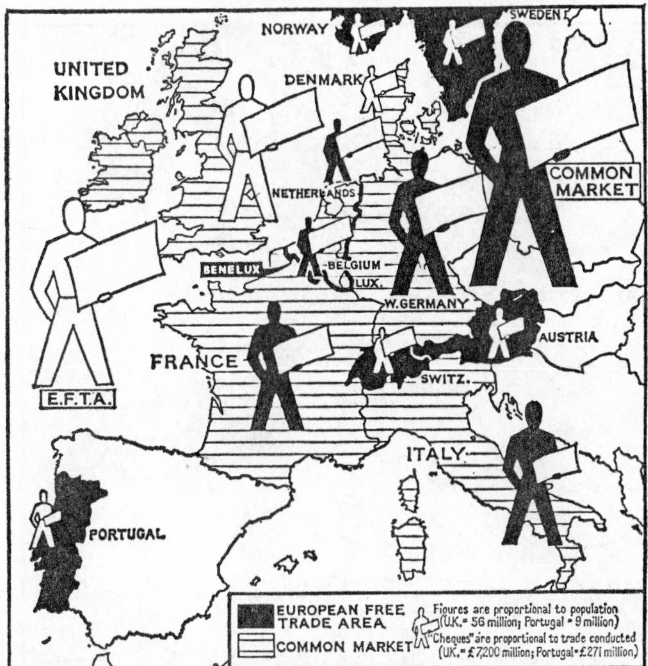

Since 1946 important international organisations have been formed. *Benelux:* economic (customs) union of Belgium, Netherlands, Luxembourg, formed in 1947.
European Coal and Steel Community: association formed in 1952 by France, Italy, W. Germany, and Benelux for planning coal and steel production, and for free trade in these goods within the Community. The same countries formed *Euratom* in 1958 for the common development of nuclear energy for peaceful purposes.
O.E.E.C., E.E.C., and E.F.T.A. The Organisation for European Economic Co-operation was formed in 1948 and eventually included all countries of Western Europe plus Greece, Yugoslavia, and Turkey. Economic co-operation between members was fostered as a corollary of American aid (ended 1952) and the Organisation had a great effect on the post-war recovery. It was superseded in 1960 by the Organisation for Economic Co-operation and Development (O.E.C.D.)

The European Economic Community (E.E.C.) and Free Trade Area (E.F.T.A.) developed from the O.E.E.C. The *E.E.C.* or *Common Market* comprised six countries when founded in 1959 and formed a customs union with common external tariffs, looking forward to eventual political federation. *E.F.T.A.* (*European Free Trade Area*) had seven members and while they promoted freer trade with each other, they maintained individual external tariffs. In January 1973 the United Kingdom and Denmark left E.F.T.A. and together with the Republic of Ireland, joined the E.E.C.

The notorious "Iron Curtain" descended in 1945 and cut off Eastern Europe (occupied by communist armies) from the Western countries including those areas of Germany occupied by British, France, and U.S., and thus the pattern of present-day Europe emerged.

Germany: division into Eastern (16 millions, communist state, low living standards), and Western (59 millions, prosperous, democratic), represents the greatest political problem in Europe to-day since the great powers disagree violently on the form any future government shall take and on the means of arriving at it. Russia is deeply suspicious of the possible orientation of a United Germany, whilst Poland is apprehensive about her undefined western boundary (the "Oder-Neisse line"). Both Russia and Western powers have bases, etc., in Germany. Berlin is also divided, although wholly within E. Germany access from West being by defined routes. Russia has unsuccessfully applied great pressure to dislodge Western powers from West Berlin and in 1961 built the Berlin Wall, preventing movement between eastern and western zones.

North Atlantic Treaty Organisation: a defensive alliance of European countries plus U.S. and Canada. Formed in 1949 at height of the "cold war," the alliance has withstood many internal strains and remains the keystone of Western defence policies. Has been highly effective in maintaining international balance of power. It has been countered in Eastern Europe by the "Warsaw Pact" organisation.

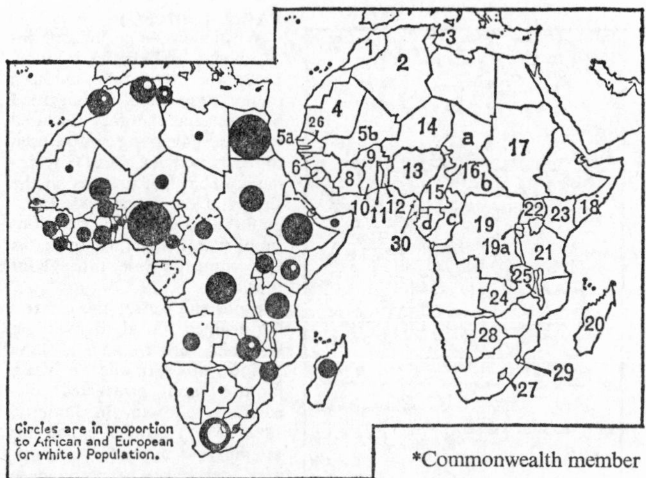

*Commonwealth member

1. Morocco (ex French, Spanish and Tangier) 1956
2. Algeria (ex French) 1962
3. Tunisia (ex French) 1956
4. Mauritania (ex French) 1960

5a Senegal (ex French) 1960 } Formed short lived "Mali
5b Mali (ex Fr. Sudan) 1960 } Federation."

6. Guinea (ex French) 1958
7. *Sierra Leone (ex British) 1961
8. Ivory Coast (ex French) 1960
9. Upper Volta (ex French) 1960
10. *Ghana (ex British—"Gold Coast") 1957
11. Togo (ex French trusteeship) 1960
12. Dahomey (ex French) 1960
13. *Nigeria (ex British) 1960 including Northern Cameroon 1961
14. Niger (ex French) 1960
15. Cameroon (ex French Trusteeship) 1960, including Southern Cameroon 1961

16a Chad.
16b Central African Republic
16c Congo
16d Gabon
} (all ex French) 1960

17. Sudan (ex Egyptian-British) 1956
18. Somali Republic (ex Italian plus ex British) 1960
19. Congo (ex Belgian) 1960 renamed Zaïre 1972

19a Rwanda. Burundi. (ex Ruanda-Urundi) 1962

20. Madagascar *or* Malagasy Republic (ex French) 1960
21. *Tanzania, comprising Tanganyika (ex British Trusteeship) 1961 and Zanzibar (ex British Protectorate) 1963; united in 1964
22. *Uganda 1962
23. *Kenya (ex British) 1963
24. *Zambia (formerly N. Rhodesia) 1964
25. *Malawi (formerly Nyasaland) 1964
26. *Gambia (ex British) 1965
27. *Lesotho (formerly Basutoland) 1965
28. *Botswana (formerly Bechuanaland) 1966
29. *Swaziland (ex British) 1967
30. Equatorial Guinea (ex Rio Muni, and Fernando Po) 1968

CENTRAL & SOUTH AFRICA

ZAÏRE (CONGO)

When the Congo became independent of Belgium in June, 1960, the very rich southern mining province of Katanga led by President Tshombe declared itself self-governing and refused to recognise the Central Government. The then premier of the Central Government, M. Lumumba, asked for United Nations support to help him impose his Government's rule throughout the Congo.

From the outset the Central Government failed to maintain law and order, and a long period of sporadic fighting, looting, and protracted discussions followed. In January, 1963, M. Tshombe ended his attempt at secession for Katanga, and agreed to recognise and co-operate with the Central Congolese Government. He did this only after a full-scale invasion of Katanga by U.N. troops. The Tshombe Government was dismissed by President Kasavubu in Oct. 1965, but he in turn was deposed by Gen. Mobutu, who assumed the office of Prime Minister in Oct. 1966. In 1972 the country was renamed Zaïre.

CENTRAL AFRICA

The Central African Federation was formed by the British Government in 1953, and comprised Northern Rhodesia, Southern Rhodesia and Nyasaland. The Federation was dissolved on December 31st, 1963, and Nyasaland became independent under the name of Malawi in July 1964. Northern Rhodesia became independent in October, 1964, and was renamed Zambia, Southern Rhodesia, now called Rhodesia, declared illegal unilateral independence in November, 1965. The U.N. imposed trade sanctions in December, 1966, while negotiations continue to find a settlement.

SOUTH AFRICA

The situation in this vast area is dangerously explosive between a backward African majority and a white minority (of British and Dutch origin) who at present hold almost all political and economic power.

In the Republic the official policy of Apartheid is designed to ensure permanent control by the three million whites, treating the fourteen million Africans as distinctly inferior socially and politically. However, Africans constitute most of the Republic's labour force. A head-on clash eventually seems inevitable and serious disturbances have already taken place—that at Sharpeville in 1960 being the worst. Plans were announced in January, 1962, to grant self-government to the Transkei which would thus become the first self-governing Bantu State. South Africa has been condemned for its racial policies by both Commonwealth and world opinion. On 31st May, 1961, it became a Republic and left the Commonwealth.

China: has made enormous disciplined efforts, under the most rigid communist system in the world, to increase agricultural and industrial production. Population about 740 millions increasing annually by 15-20 millions. Interfered actively in Korean War (1950-53), in S.E. Asia, and the subjugation of Tibet since 1957 has brought friction with India. Has sought to extend influence amongst under-developed countries; was admitted to the U.N. Organisation in 1971.

U.S.S.R.: the war stimulated development of the Asiatic industrial areas. Crop areas also extended especially in Kazakhstan where rainfall is uncertain.

India and Pakistan: Independent within Commonwealth since 1947. Hostility arising from boundary decisions of 1947 increased, in Sept. 1965, to a state of war over the ownership of Kashmir. Like China, both countries are making great efforts to increase production and fight poverty but under more democratic regimes. After a war between India and Pakistan at the end of 1971 the independent state of Bangladesh was formed. *S.E.A.T.O.:* defensive alliance of S.E. Asia countries, backed by Western powers, in face of communist threats.

Malaysia: a Federation formed on 16th Sept. 1963, consisting of the Federation of Malaya, the State of Singapore and the Colonies of Sarawak and North Borneo (re-named Sabah). Singapore seceded from the Federation in Aug. 1965.

Former French Indo-China: split into three independent states of Cambodia, Laos and Vietnam the last by the Geneva Armistice agreement of 1954 is split at the 17th parallel into Northern (communist) and Southern Zones. Fighting between Viet Cong (communist guerrillas) and the Southern Zone, backed by the U.S. continues.

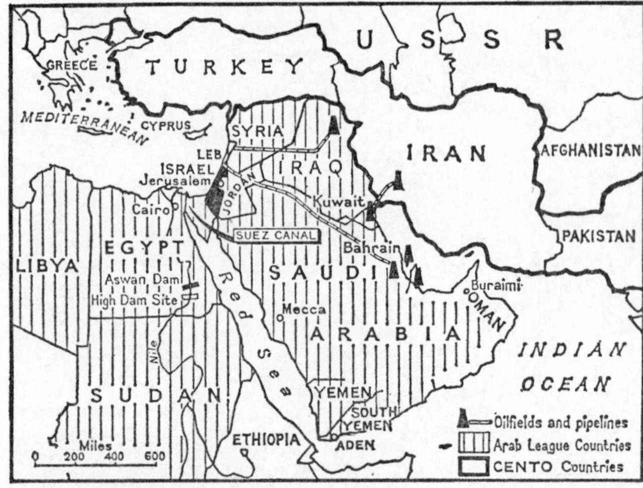

The Middle East is one of the key areas of the world—the bridge between Asia, Africa and Europe, the focus of three world religions, and the greatest oil reservoir. Britain and France have long associations with the area; U.S. has enormous financial interests in oil production, whilst Russia is a very active neighbour. Repudiation of the partition of Palestine is the one permanent unifying factor in the Arab world. Israel, created in 1948 and enriched by immigration and U.S. capital, is to-day a thriving but much threatened country. *Egypt*, populous but poor, with a military government under Colonel Nasser, formed a union with *Syria* in 1958. Syria seceded from the United Arab Republic on Sept. 28th, 1961. In June 1967, a lightning war, lasting six days, between Israel on the one hand, and Egypt, Jordan and Syria on the other, resulted in Israel gaining territory to the river Jordan in the East, and to the Suez Canal in the West. After Col. Nasser's death in September 1970, Anwar Sadat became president. In *The Yemen*, a military revolution in September, 1962, deposed the Imam. Egypt supported the revolution, but Saudi Arabia the Imam's regime. Bordering the Yemen is the former British Colony of Aden, an important fuelling station for shipping. The Colony, together with thirteen Arab States of the Western Protectorate formed, in February 1959, The Federation of South Arabia, but terrorist activities of rival political groups resulted finally in the Federation, together with the Eastern Protectorate, being given independence as the Republic of South Yemen, November, 1967.

Central Treaty Organisation: Successor (1958) to the Baghdad Pact and backed by West as buffer against Russia.

KASHMIR AND SINO-INDIAN BORDER

The dispute between India and Pakistan over Kashmir has been at times overshadowed by Chinese claims along India's northern frontier. The Chinese, who have never recognised the McMahon line in the N.E. Frontier Agency, invaded Assam in 1962, but after reaching the plains withdrew voluntarily to the border area. Incursions were also made in Ladakh. They then made proposals for a settlement which India rejected. Attempts between India and China to reach a settlement have so far proved inconclusive. In September, 1965, war broke out between India and Pakistan over the Kashmir dispute.

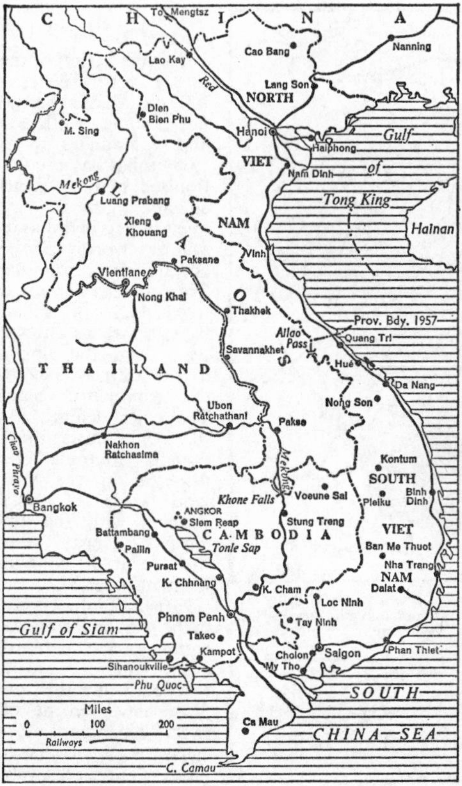

VIETNAM, LAOS AND CAMBODIA

Vietnam, Laos and Cambodia became independent within the French Union in 1949. During the Japanese occupation of 1940-45 Communist nationalist movements arose in all three countries. The strongest of these, the Viet Minh, launched several successful attacks in Vietnam, Laos and Cambodia. Following a Geneva Conference in 1954 French troops were withdrawn from the area and Communist rebels integrated into the individual governments. In Laos, which became neutral in 1961, there has been sporadic fighting between Government troops and Communist rebels (Pathet Lao). Also following the Geneva Conference a ceasefire line was established in Vietnam along the 17th Parallel with a Communist republic in the north. Since 1954 the Viet Cong, Communist guerrillas from North Vietnam, have made incursions into South Vietnam, whose defence is aided by the U.S.A. Negotiations for a peaceful settlement of the war by various nations, from both east and west, have proved unsuccessful. Withdrawal of U.S. troops from Vietnam began in September 1969 following President Nixon's pledge to end U.S. involvement in the war.

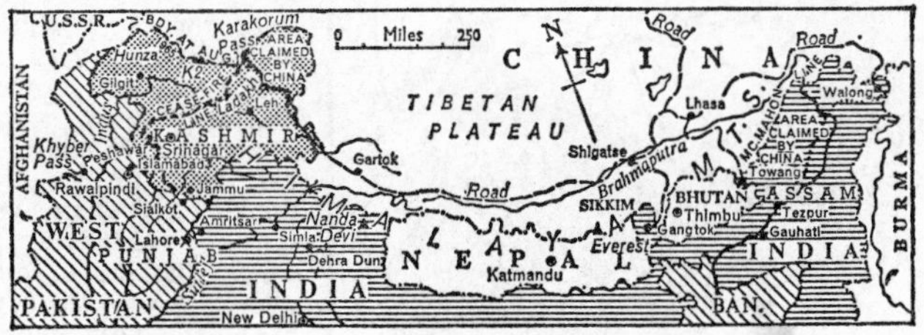

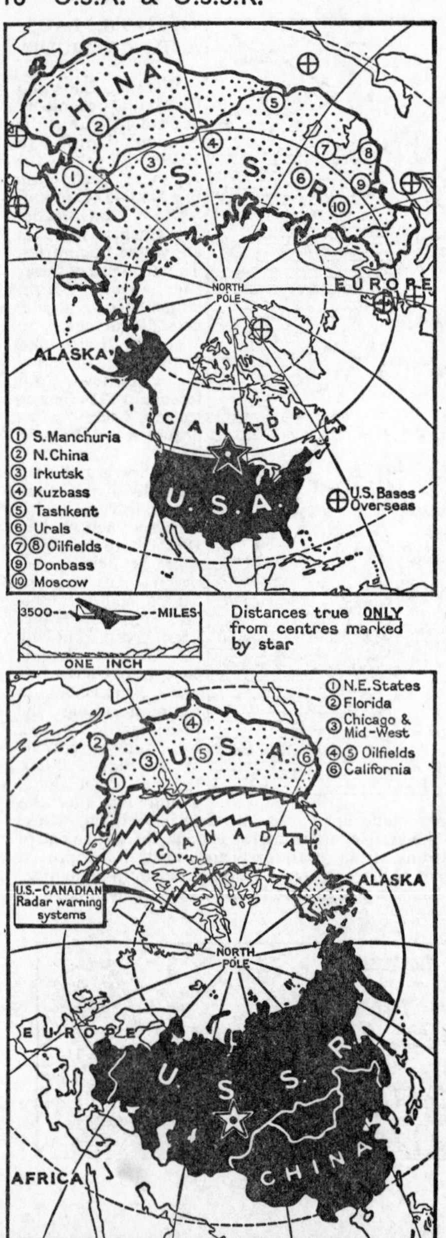

The perfection of the Inter-Continental Ballistic Missiles carrying atomic warheads and with ranges up to 5,000 miles has revolutionised military strategy and logistics.

Few targets in the communist world can be considered immune from attacks mounted from U.S. or allied bases which as can be seen from the upper map effectively encircle the communist bloc. The chief defence for the communists must therefore continue to be dispersal in the vast land areas of Asia coupled with the intensive security that their form of government affords.

Targets of importance in the U.S. and Western countries are perhaps even more easily reached, hence the fantastic development of radar defences. Because U.S. overseas bases are relatively much farther from 'home' than the Soviet bases in Eastern Europe the U.S. has much more to lose by agreeing to the abandonment of foreign bases—a constant theme of communist propaganda.

The advent of the nuclear-powered, missile-firing submarine has made further rethinking of defensive strategy necessary, whilst the threat of satellite-borne missiles has already been made.

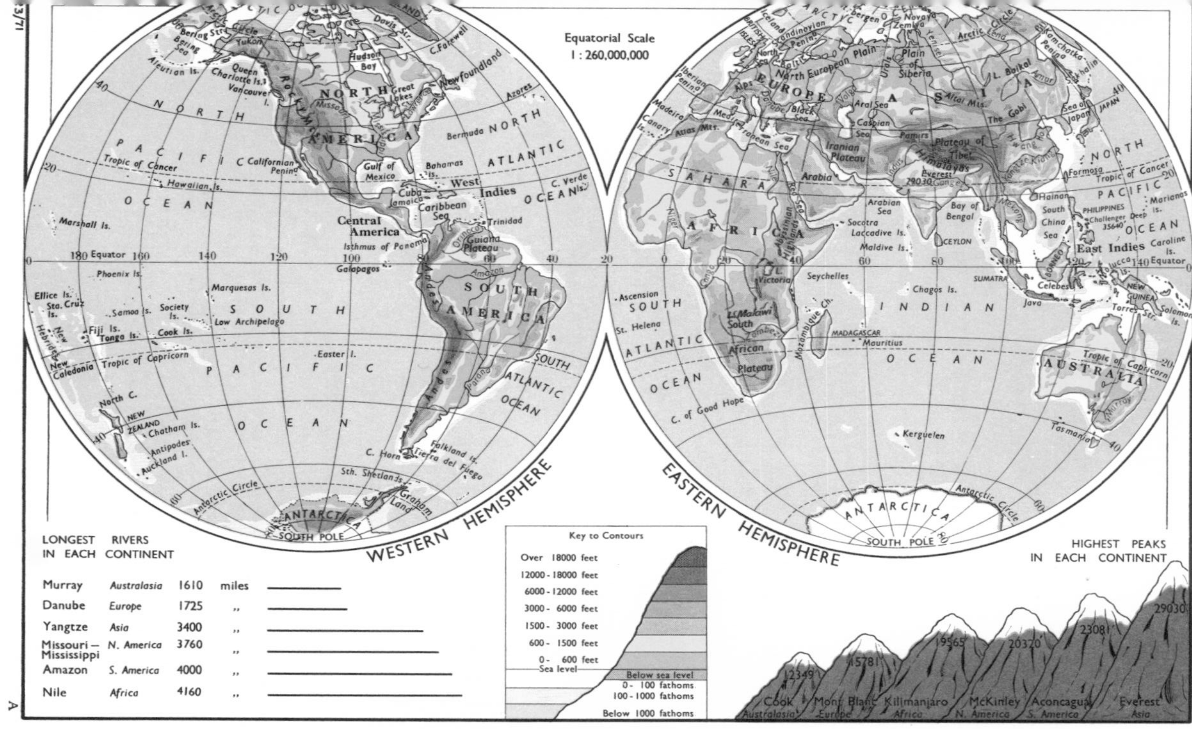

LONGEST RIVERS IN EACH CONTINENT

Murray	*Australasia*	1610	miles
Danube	*Europe*	1725	,,
Yangtze	*Asia*	3400	,,
Missouri – Mississippi	*N. America*	3760	,,
Amazon	*S. America*	4000	,,
Nile	*Africa*	4160	,,

23/71

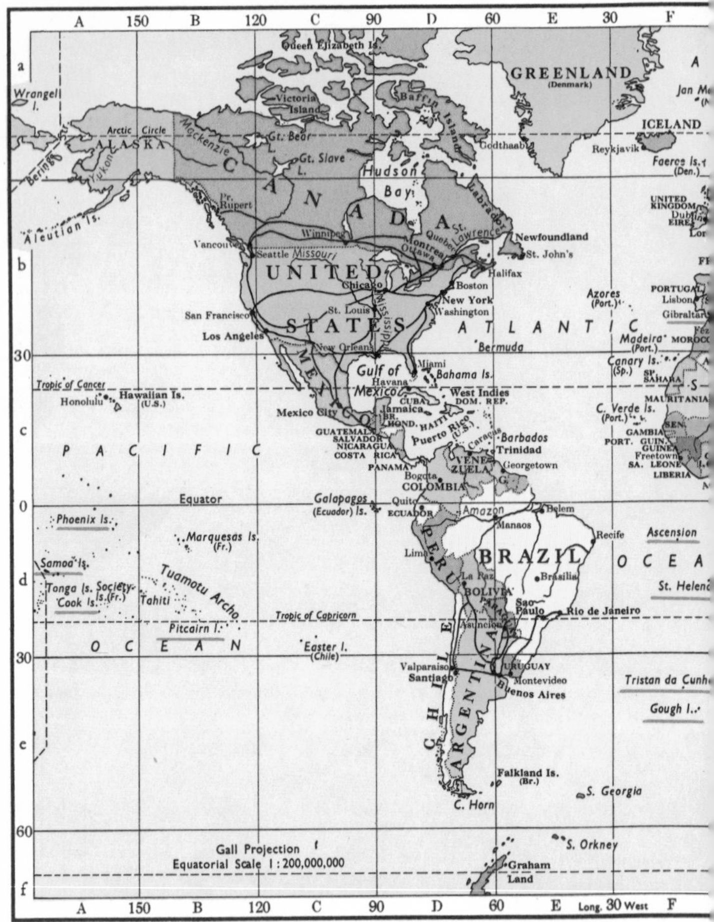

THE EARTH

Total AREA of Earth's surface is 196,940,400 sq. miles.
Total LAND AREA (*incl. inland water but excl. Antarctica*), 52,228,000 sq. miles.
Total WATER AREA is 144,712,400 sq miles. (*incl. Antarctica*)
The Equatorial Circumference is 24,902 miles; the Polar Circumference is 24,860 miles (42 miles less)

AREAS OF OCEANS *in square miles*

N. Pacific	28,000,000	Total 64,000,000
S. Pacific	36,000,000	
N. Atlantic	14,000,000	Total 32,000,000
S. Atlantic	18,000,000	
Indian		5,540,000

Greatest Ocean Depth is at Challenger Deep (36,204ft.) in square L c above

CONTINENTS (*Figures Approximate*)

Asia	16,500,000 sq. miles;	$56\frac{1}{2}$% of World's population.
Africa	11,725,000 sq. miles;	$9\frac{1}{2}$% ,, ,,
N. America	9,362,000 sq. miles;	9 % ,, ,,
S. America	6,870,000 sq. miles;	5 % ,, ,,
Europe	4,065,000 sq. miles;	$19\frac{1}{2}$% ,, ,,
Australasia	3,295,000 sq. miles;	$\frac{1}{2}$% ,, ,,
Antarctica	6,000,000 sq. miles;	(*Uninhabited*)

WORLD POPULATION

Total world population is about 3,552,000,000 giving an overall average DENSITY per square mile of about 68.

HIGHEST MOUNTAIN

Mt. EVEREST in the Himalayas is 29,030 ft. in height.

LONGEST RIVER

River Nile (Africa) is 4,160 miles in length.

LOWEST POINT ON LAND

On shores of the Dead Sea, Palestine, 1,292 ft. below sea level.

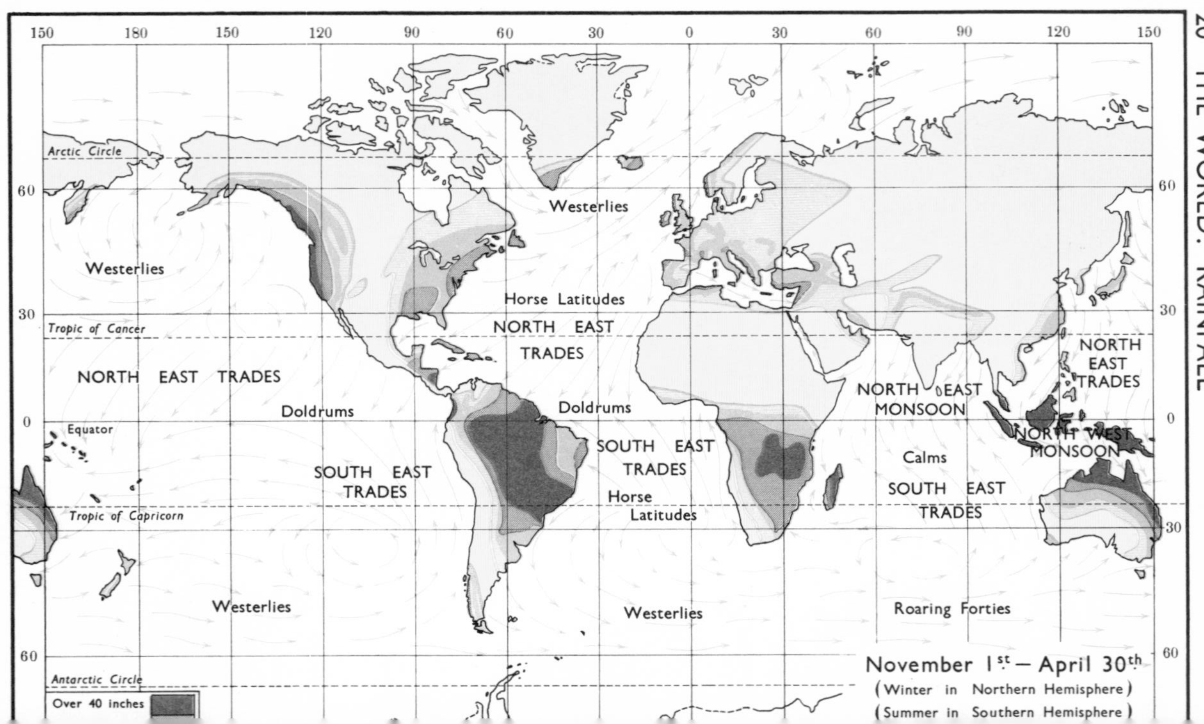

Arctic Circle
Tropic of Cancer
Equator
Tropic of Capricorn
Antarctic Circle
Westerlies
Horse Latitudes
NORTH EAST TRADES
Doldrums
SOUTH EAST TRADES
NORTH EAST MONSOON
NORTH WEST MONSOON
Calms
Horse Latitudes
Roaring Forties
November 1st. – April 30th.
(Winter in Northern Hemisphere)
(Summer in Southern Hemisphere)
Over 40 inches

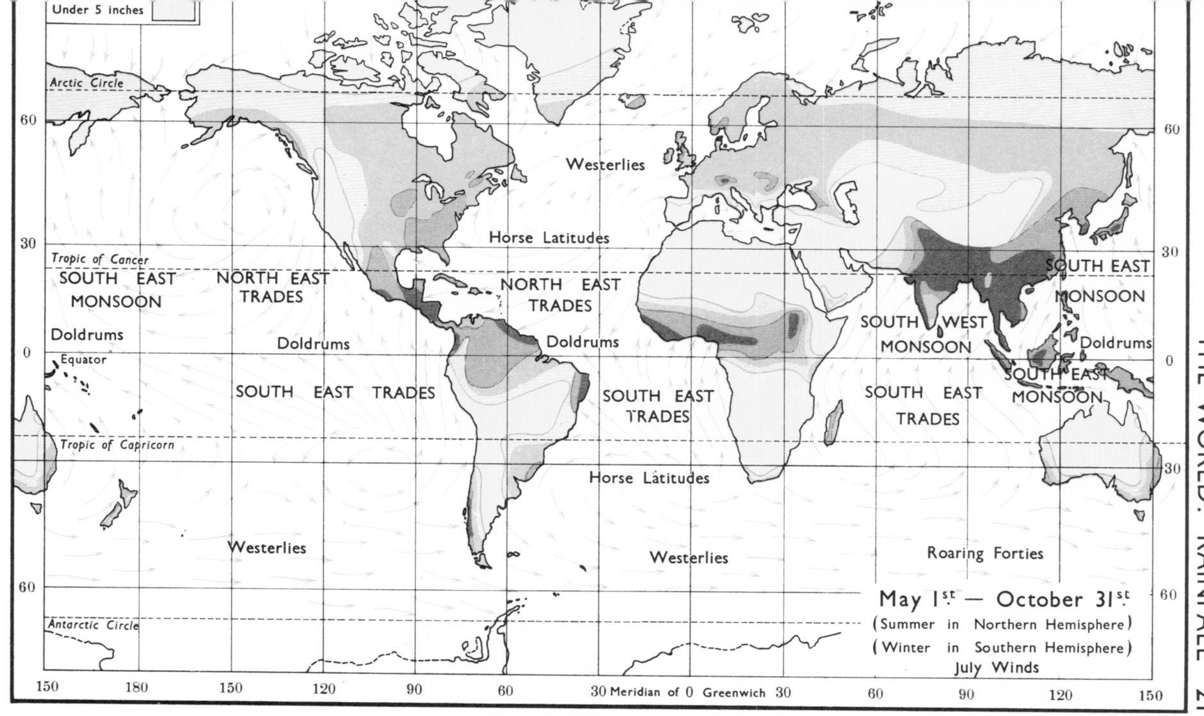
Under 5 inches
Arctic Circle
Tropic of Cancer
Equator
Tropic of Capricorn
Antarctic Circle
SOUTH EAST MONSOON
NORTH EAST TRADES
Doldrums
SOUTH EAST TRADES
Westerlies
Horse Latitudes
NORTH EAST TRADES
Doldrums
SOUTH EAST TRADES
Horse Latitudes
Westerlies
SOUTH WEST MONSOON
SOUTH EAST TRADES
SOUTH EAST MONSOON
Doldrums
SOUTH EAST MONSOON
Roaring Forties
May 1st. — October 31st.
(Summer in Northern Hemisphere)
(Winter in Southern Hemisphere)
July Winds
150 180 150 120 90 60 30 Meridian of 0 Greenwich 30 60 90 120 150

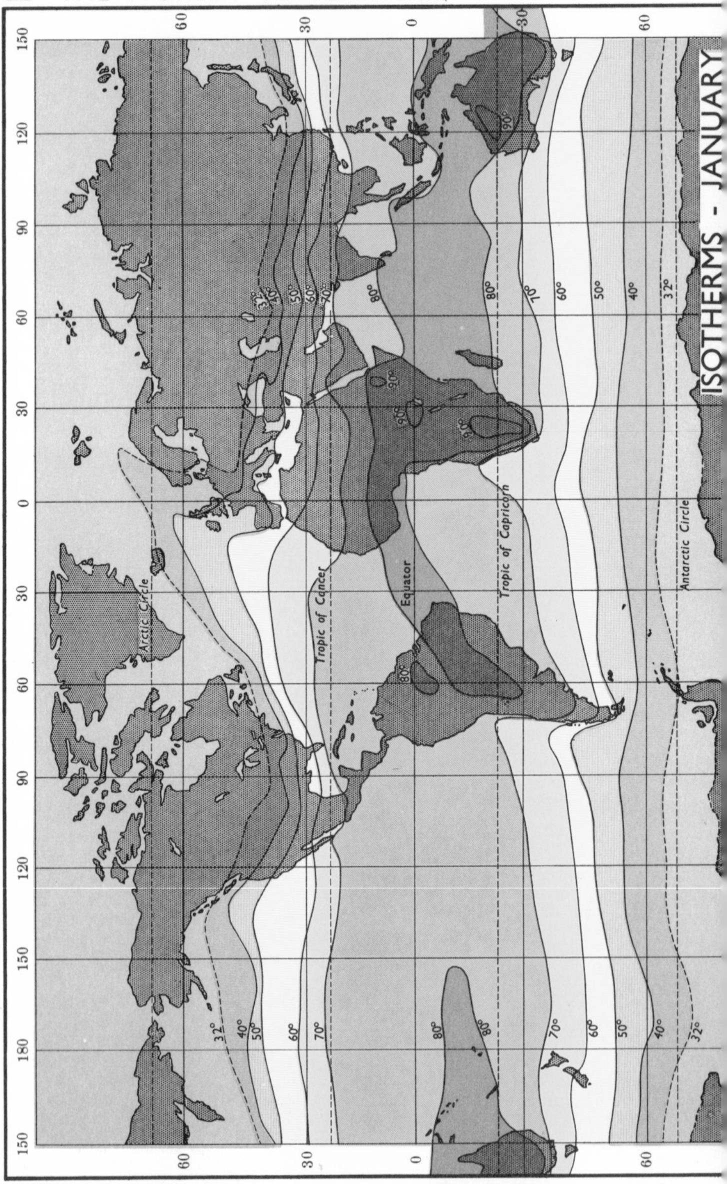

ISOTHERMS - JANUARY

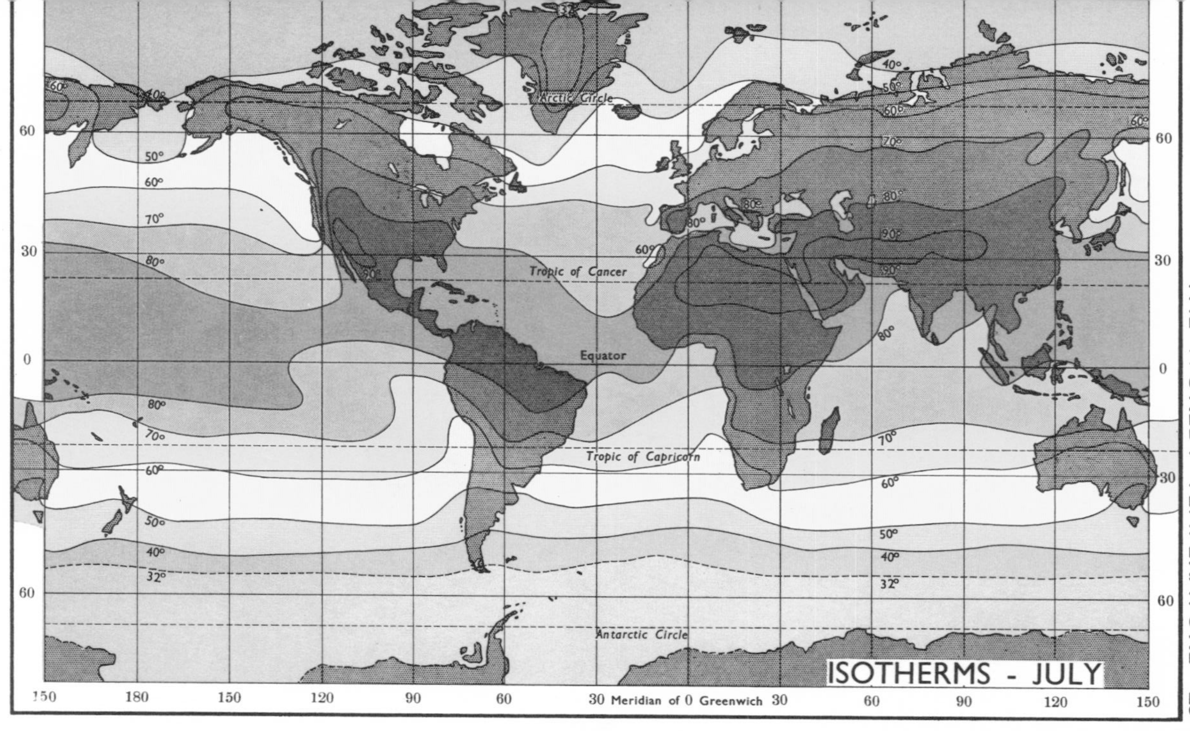
ISOTHERMS - JULY
Arctic Circle
Tropic of Cancer
Equator
Tropic of Capricorn
Antarctic Circle
50°
60°
70°
80°
90°
40°
32°
150
180
150
120
90
60
30 Meridian of 0 Greenwich 30
60
90
120
150
60
30
0
30
60

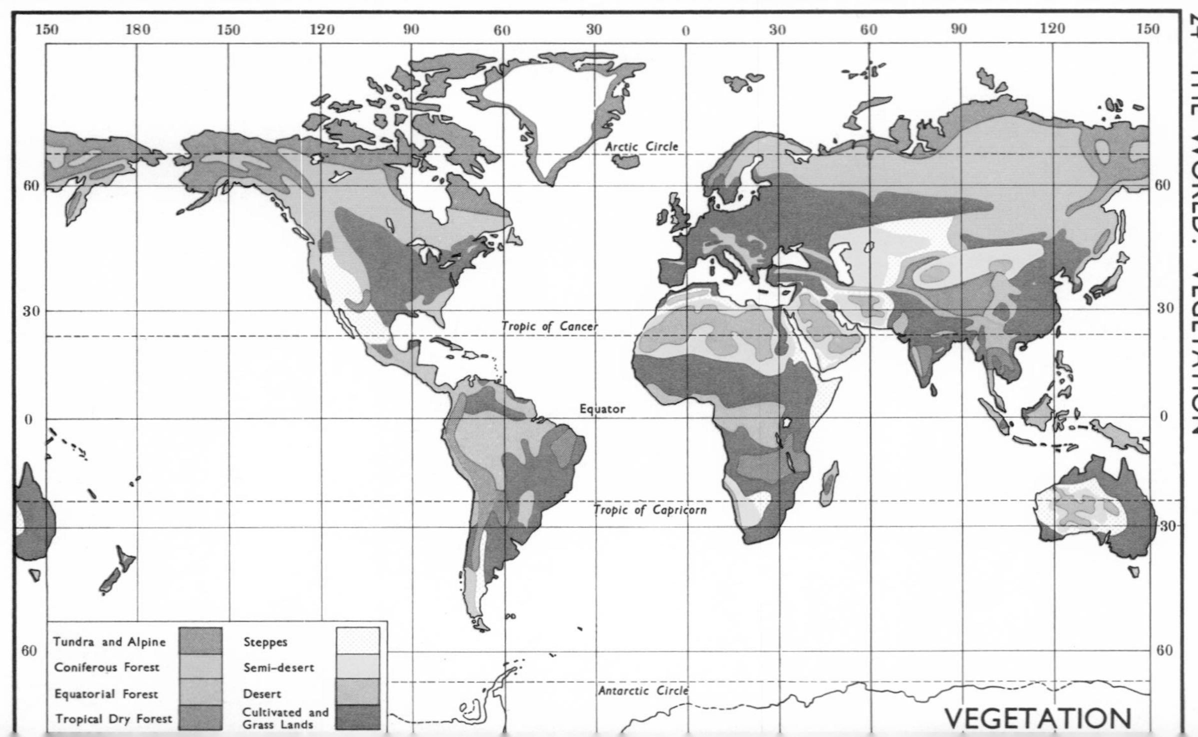
VEGETATION
Tundra and Alpine
Coniferous Forest
Equatorial Forest
Tropical Dry Forest
Steppes
Semi-desert
Desert
Cultivated and Grass Lands
Arctic Circle
Tropic of Cancer
Equator
Tropic of Capricorn
Antarctic Circle
150
180
150
120
90
60
30
0
30
60
90
120
150
60
30
0
30
60

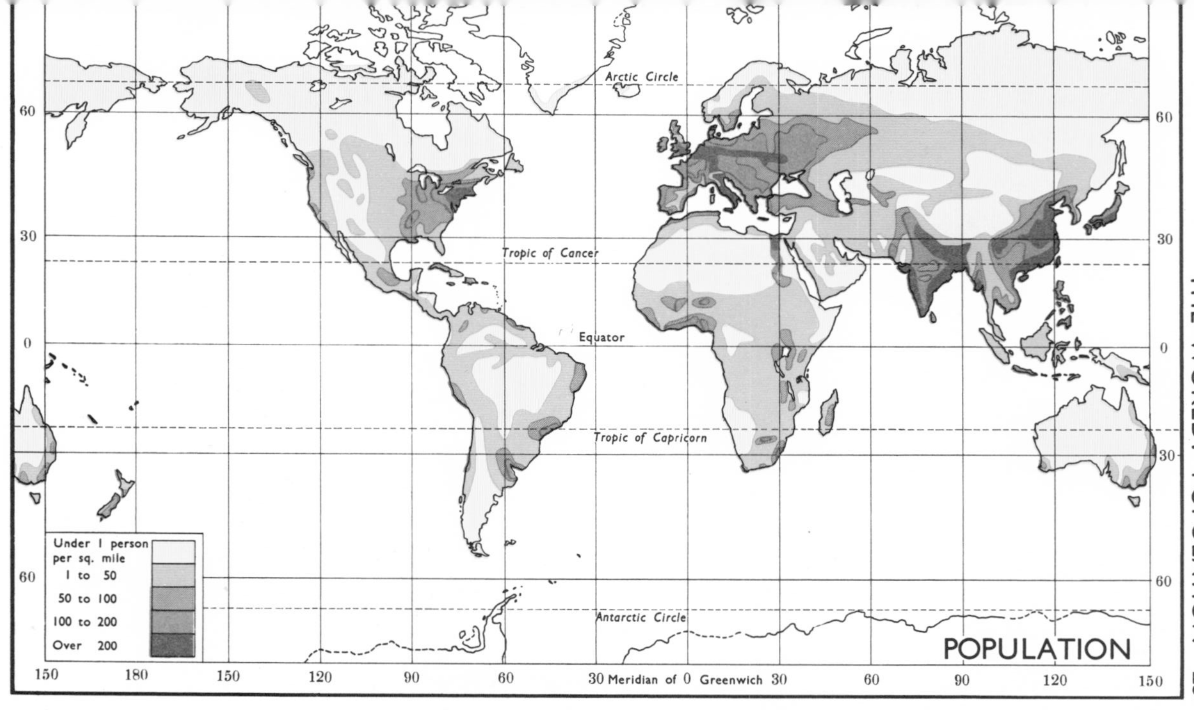
POPULATION
Under I person per sq. mile
I to 50
50 to 100
100 to 200
Over 200
Arctic Circle
Tropic of Cancer
Equator
Tropic of Capricorn
Antarctic Circle
Meridian of 0 Greenwich

CEREALS

Arctic Circle
NORTH
Prairies
AMERICA
EUROPE
Steppes
A S I A
Northern Tropic
AFRICA
Equator
SOUTH
AMERICA
Southern Tropic
Veld
AUSTRALIA
Downs
Pampas

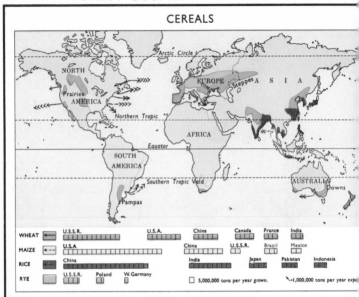

WHEAT — U.S.S.R., U.S.A., China, Canada, France, India

MAIZE — U.S.A, China, U.S.S.R., Brazil, Mexico

RICE — China, India, Japan, Pakistan, Indonesia

RYE — U.S.S.R., Poland, W. Germany

□ 5,000,000 tons per year grown.

↖ =1,000,000 tons per year exp

BEEF & MUTTON

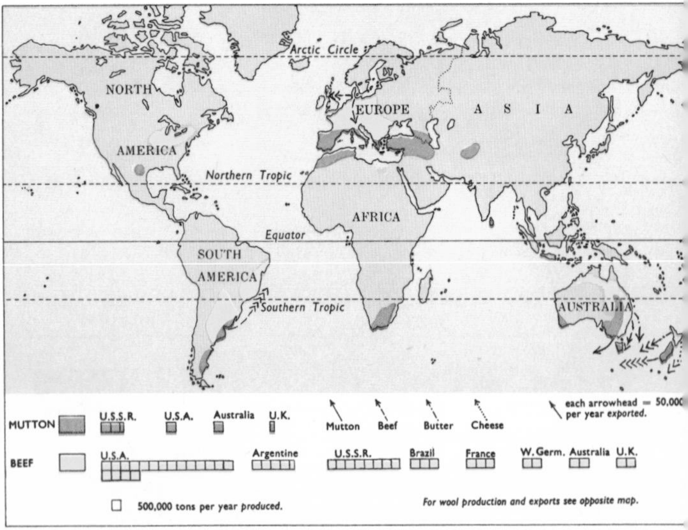

Arctic Circle
NORTH
AMERICA
EUROPE
A S I A
Northern Tropic
AFRICA
Equator
SOUTH
AMERICA
Southern Tropic
AUSTRALIA

MUTTON — U.S.S.R., U.S.A., Australia, U.K.

Mutton, Beef, Butter, Cheese

↖ each arrowhead = 50,00 per year *exported.*

BEEF — U.S.A., Argentine, U.S.S.R., Brazil, France, W. Germ., Australia, U.K.

□ 500,000 tons per year *produced.*

For wool production and exports see opposite map.

FUEL & POWER

Arctic Circle
Scandinavia
British
NORTH
Alberta
AMERICA
Illinois
St. Lawrence
California
Texas
Appalachian
Mexico
Northern Tropic
Venezuela
Franco-Belgian
Ruhr
Silesia
EUROPE
Alps
Romania
Don Basin
Caspian
Middle East
Sahara
A S I A
Kuznetsk
China
Japan
Kyushu
Bengal
AFRICA
Equator
SOUTH AMERICA
Borneo
East Indies
Southern Tropic
Natal
AUSTRALIA
New South Wales

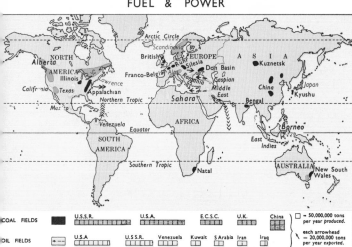

		Producers							Scale
COAL FIELDS		U.S.S.R.	U.S.A.	E.C.S.C.	U.K.	China			□ = 50,000,000 tons per year *produced*.
OIL FIELDS	← - -	U.S.A	U.S.S.R.	Venezuela	Kuwait	S Arabia	Iran	Iraq	each arrowhead = 20,000,000 tons per year *exported*.
HYDRO-ELECTRIC POWER		U.S.A.	Canada	U.S.S.R.	Japan, Sweden	Italy	France, Switzerland	Norway	= 20,000 million Kwh. p.a. *produced*.

FIBRES & RUBBER

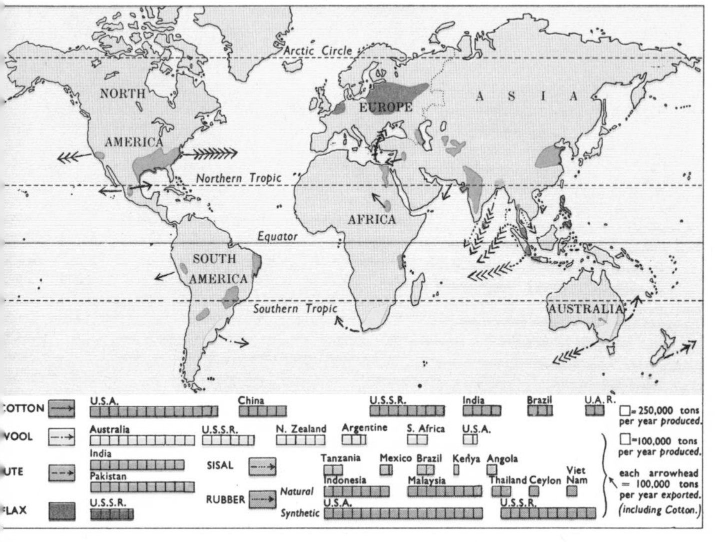

Key to Contours
Over 12000 feet
6000 - 12000 feet
3000 - 6000 feet
1500 - 3000 feet
600 - 1500 feet
0 - 600 feet
Sea level
Below sea level
0 - 100 fathoms
100 - 1000 fathoms
Below 1000 fathoms
ICELAND
Mt. Hekla 4910'
ARCTIC OCEAN
Arctic Circle
70 N.
Lofoten Is.
Vest Fiord
Faeroes
Trondheim Fiord
SCANDINAVIAN PEN
Galdhopiggen 8097'
Sogne Fd.
Hardanger Fd.
Shetland Is.
Orkney Is.
Rockall
St. Kilda
C. Wrath
Hebrides
Ben Nevis 4406'
Grampians
Malin Hd.
ATLANTIC OCEAN
Lindesnes
Skagerrak
Kattegat
Vaner
L. Vatter
Gotland
Oland
Dal
Gulf
NORTH SEA
Jutland Pena.
Zealand
Bornholm
Rugen
BALT
Central Plain
Shannon
Irish Sea
C. Clear
St. George's Chan.
Severn
Trent
Midland Plain
Thames
Land's End
Usselmeer
Frisian Is.
Str. of Dover
English Channel
Channel Is.
Ushant
GREAT
Weser
Elbe
Oder
Vist
Harz Mts.
Sudeten Mts.
Rhine
Meuse
Seine
Marne
PLAIN OF FRANCE
Loire
Main
Bohemian Forest
Vosges Mts.
Black Forest
Danube
Bay of Biscay
C. Ortegal
C. Finisterre
Jura Mts.
ALPS
Auvergne Mts.
Garonne
Mt. Blanc 15781'
Rhone
THE
Plain of Lombardy
Drava
Sava
Cantabrian Mts.
Cevennes
IBERIAN
Douro
Sierra de Guadarrama
PYRENEES
Mt. Maladetta 11168'
G. of Lions
G. of Genoa
Po
Dinaric Alps
Adriatic Sea
Tagus
PENINSULA
Corsica
Apennines
Mt. Corno 9583'
C. St. Vincent
Guadiana
Sierra Morena
Str. of Bonifacio
Tiber
Balearic Is.
Sardinia
Minorca
Majorca
Iviza
Mt. Vesuvius 3891'
Tyrrhenian Sea
Str. of Otranto
Guadalquivir
Sierra Nevada
Mt. Mulhacen 11420'
Str. of Gibraltar
MEDITERRANEA
Stromboli
G. of Taranto
Sicily
Str. of Messina
C. Bon
C. Passero
Malta
ATLAS MTS.
AFRICA
Gulf of Sidra
20
A
10
B
0
C
10
D
b
50
c
40
d
30
e
B
0
C
Long. 10 East
D

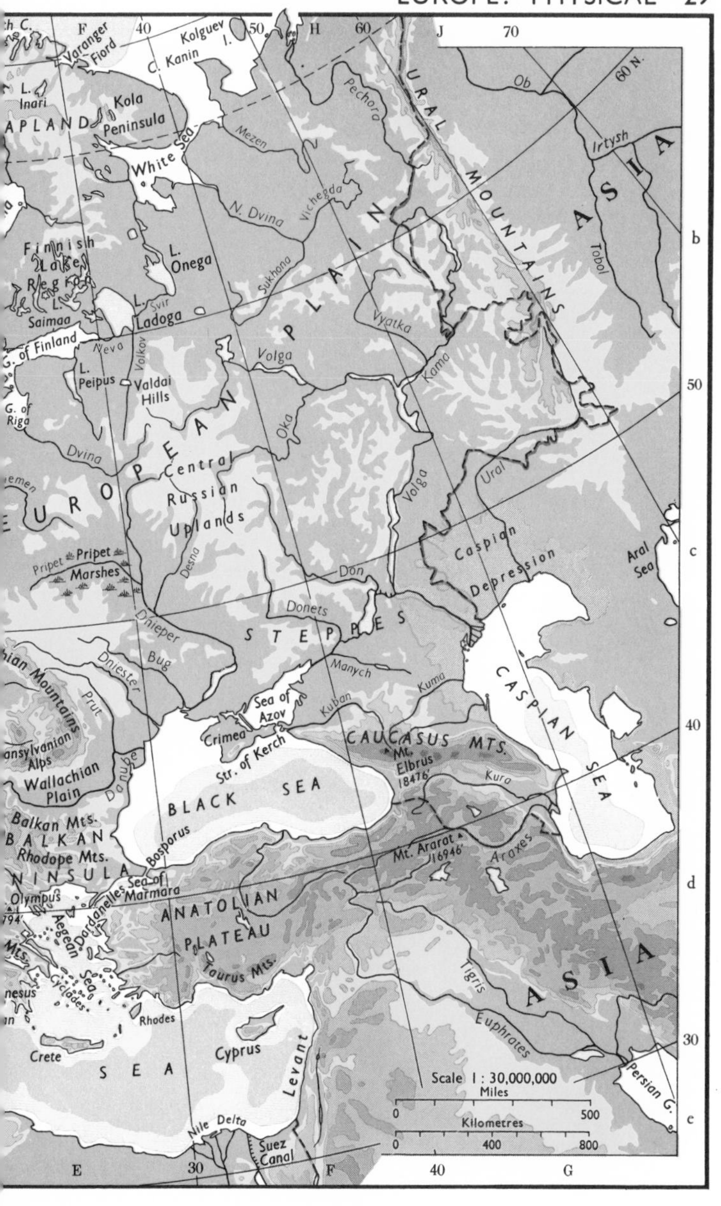
Varanger Fiord
Kolguev I.
C. Kanin
L. Inari
Kola Peninsula
LAPLAND
White Sea
Pechora
Mezen
URAL MOUNTAINS
Ob
Irtysh
ASIA
N. Dvina
Vichegda
Tobol
Finnish Lake Region
L. Onega
Sukhona
L. Saimaa
Svir
L. Ladoga
Vyatka
G. of Finland
Neva
Volkov
L. Peipus
Valdai Hills
Volga
Kama
G. of Riga
EUROPEAN PLAIN
Oka
Dvina
Central Russian Uplands
Ural
Volga
Pripet Marshes
Desna
Caspian Depression
Aral Sea
Don
Dnieper
Donets
STEPPES
Dniester
Bug
Manych
Kuma
Prut
Sea of Azov
Kuban
CASPIAN SEA
Crimea
Str. of Kerch
CAUCASUS MTS.
Mt. Elbrus 18476'
Transylvanian Alps
Wallachian Plain
Danube
BLACK SEA
Kura
Balkan Mts.
BALKAN PENINSULA
Rhodope Mts.
Bosporus
Mt. Ararat 16946'
Araxes
Sea of Marmara
Olympus
Dardanelles
ANATOLIAN PLATEAU
Aegean Sea
Taurus Mts.
Tigris
ASIA
Cyclades
Rhodes
Euphrates
Cyprus
Crete
SEA
Levant
Persian G.
Nile Delta
Suez Canal
Scale 1 : 30,000,000
Miles
0
500
Kilometres
0
400
800
60 N.
50
40
30
b
c
d
e
E
F
G
H
J
70

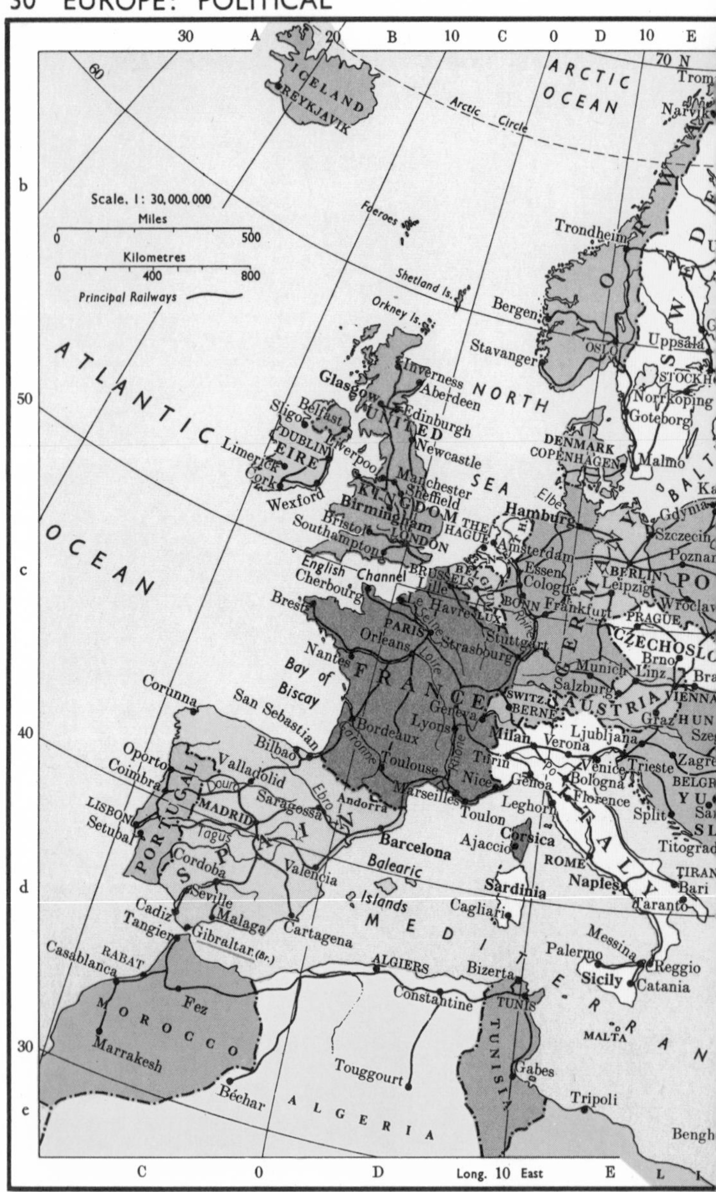
Scale. 1: 30,000,000
Miles
0 500
Kilometres
0 400 800
Principal Railways
ATLANTIC OCEAN
ICELAND
REYKJAVIK
ARCTIC OCEAN
Arctic Circle
Faeroes
Shetland Is.
Orkney Is.
NORTH SEA
UNITED KINGDOM
EIRE
Glasgow
Inverness
Aberdeen
Edinburgh
Newcastle
Belfast
Sligo
DUBLIN
Limerick
Cork
Wexford
Liverpool
Manchester
Sheffield
Birmingham
Bristol
Southampton
LONDON
English Channel
Cherbourg
Brest
Bay of Biscay
FRANCE
PARIS
Le Havre
Lille
Orleans
Nantes
Bordeaux
Toulouse
Lyons
Geneva
Nice
Marseilles
Toulon
Strasbourg
Seine
Loire
Garonne
Rhone
Andorra
SPAIN
PORTUGAL
Corunna
San Sebastian
Bilbao
Oporto
Coimbra
Valladolid
MADRID
Saragossa
Ebro
Douro
Tagus
LISBON
Setubal
Cordoba
Seville
Cadiz
Malaga
Gibraltar (Br.)
Valencia
Cartagena
Barcelona
Balearic Islands
MEDITERRANEAN
Tangier
RABAT
Casablanca
Fez
MOROCCO
Marrakesh
Béchar
ALGIERS
Constantine
Touggourt
ALGERIA
Bizerta
TUNIS
TUNISIA
Gabes
Tripoli
Benghazi
MALTA
Sicily
Palermo
Messina
Reggio
Catania
Sardinia
Cagliari
Corsica
Ajaccio
ITALY
ROME
Naples
Bari
Taranto
Leghorn
Genoa
Turin
Milan
Verona
Venice
Bologna
Florence
Po
SWITZ.
BERNE
AUSTRIA
VIENNA
Salzburg
Graz
Munich
Linz
Ljubljana
Trieste
Zagreb
Split
Titograd
BELGRADE
YUGOSLAVIA
TIRANA
HUNGARY
CZECHOSLOVAKIA
PRAGUE
Brno
Bratislava
GERMANY
Stuttgart
Frankfurt
BONN
Cologne
Essen
Leipzig
BERLIN
Hamburg
Elbe
Rhine
LUX.
BELGIUM
BRUSSELS
NETH.
THE HAGUE
Amsterdam
DENMARK
COPENHAGEN
POLAND
Szczecin
Poznan
Wroclaw
Gdynia
BALTIC
NORWAY
SWEDEN
Bergen
Stavanger
OSLO
Trondheim
Narvik
Tromsø
Uppsala
STOCKHOLM
Norrkoping
Goteborg
Malmo
70 N
60
50
40
30
b
c
d
e
A
B
C
D
E
Long. 10 East

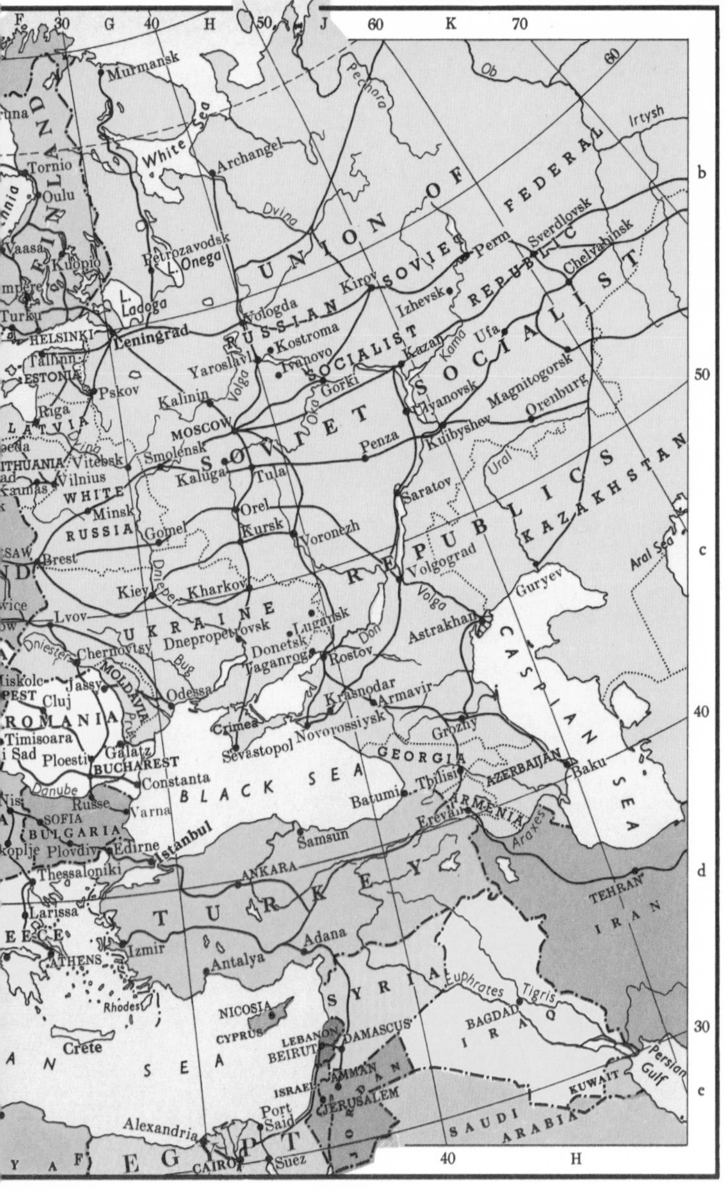
F
30
G
40
H
50
J
60
K
70
b
50
c
40
d
30
e
40
H
Murmansk
White Sea
Archangel
Pechora
Ob
Irtysh
60
Tornio
Oulu
Vaasa
Kuopio
Turku
FINLAND
Petrozavodsk
L. Onega
L. Ladoga
HELSINKI
Leningrad
Tallinn
ESTONIA
Pskov
Riga
LATVIA
Dvina
LITHUANIA
Vitebsk
Vilnius
WHITE RUSSIA
Minsk
Brest
Vologda
Kostroma
Yaroslavl
Ivanovo
Kalinin
MOSCOW
Smolensk
Kaluga
Tula
Orel
Kursk
Voronezh
Gomel
Kiev
Dnieper
Kharkov
Lvov
UKRAINE
Dnepropetrovsk
Lugansk
Donetsk
Taganrog
Rostov
Don
Chernovtsy
Dniester
MOLDAVIA
Bug
Odessa
Jassy
Prut
Cluj
ROMANIA
Timisoara
Ploesti
Galatz
BUCHAREST
Constanta
Danube
Russe
Varna
SOFIA
BULGARIA
Plovdiv
Edirne
Istanbul
Thessaloniki
Larissa
ATHENS
Rhodes
Crete
Izmir
Antalya
ANKARA
TURKEY
Samsun
Adana
Crimea
Sevastopol
Novorossiysk
Krasnodar
Armavir
BLACK SEA
Batumi
Tbilisi
GEORGIA
ARMENIA
Erevan
AZERBAIJAN
Baku
Grozny
Astrakhan
Volga
Volgograd
Saratov
Penza
Gorki
Oka
Kazan
Kama
Kirov
Izhevsk
Perm
Sverdlovsk
Chelyabinsk
Ufa
Magnitogorsk
Orenburg
Kuibyshev
Ulyanovsk
Ural
Guryev
KAZAKHSTAN
Aral Sea
CASPIAN SEA
UNION OF SOVIET SOCIALIST REPUBLICS
RUSSIAN SOVIET FEDERAL SOCIALIST REPUBLIC
Araxes
TEHRAN
IRAN
SYRIA
Euphrates
Tigris
BAGDAD
IRAQ
Persian Gulf
KUWAIT
SAUDI ARABIA
NICOSIA
CYPRUS
LEBANON
BEIRUT
DAMASCUS
AMMAN
JORDAN
ISRAEL
JERUSALEM
Port Said
Alexandria
CAIRO
Suez
EGYPT
SEA

GREAT BRITAIN: CLIMATE

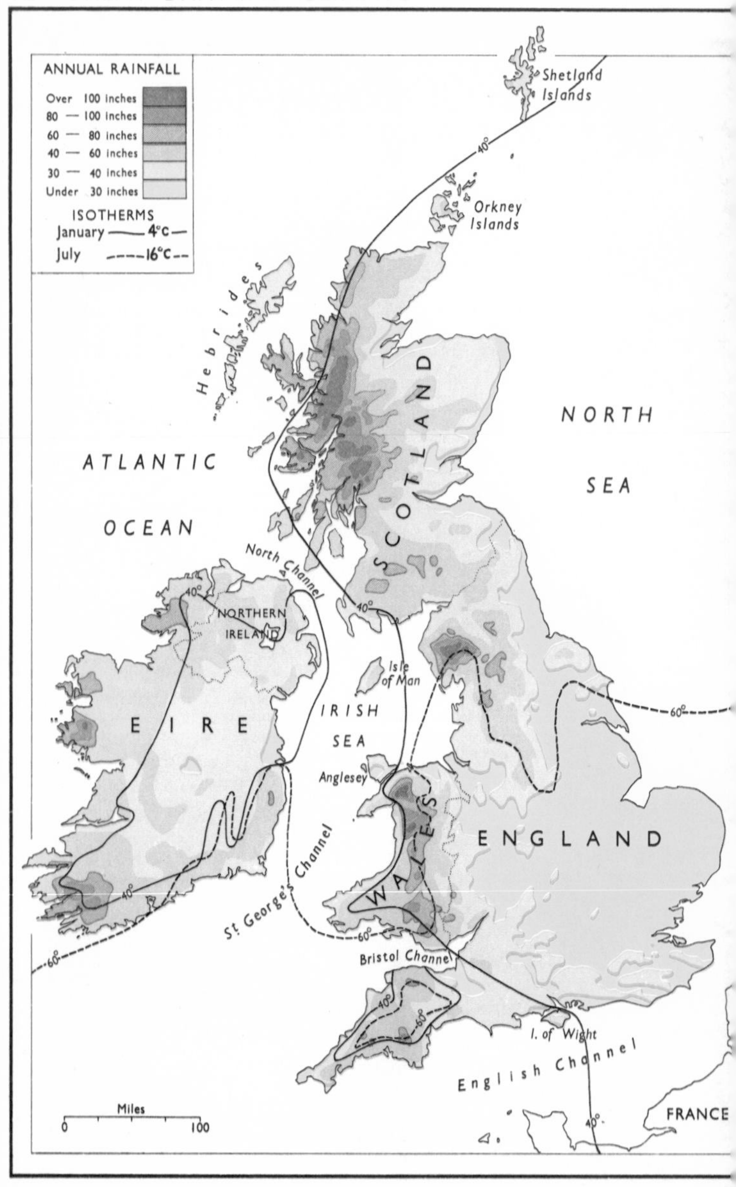

ANNUAL RAINFALL
Over 100 inches
80 — 100 inches
60 — 80 inches
40 — 60 inches
30 — 40 inches
Under 30 inches
ISOTHERMS
January —— 4°c —
July ---- 16°c --
Shetland Islands
Orkney Islands
Hebrides
ATLANTIC OCEAN
SCOTLAND
NORTH SEA
North Channel
NORTHERN IRELAND
Isle of Man
IRISH SEA
EIRE
Anglesey
WALES
ENGLAND
St George's Channel
Bristol Channel
I. of Wight
English Channel
FRANCE
Miles
0
100
40°
60°

Moorland
Woodland
Grassland
Arable Land
Shetland Islands
Orkney Islands
Hebrides
NORTH SEA
ATLANTIC OCEAN
SCOTLAND
North Channel
NORTHERN IRELAND
Isle of Man
IRISH SEA
EIRE
Anglesey
WALES
ENGLAND
St. George's Channel
Bristol Channel
I. of Wight
English Channel
FRANCE
Miles
0
100

GREAT BRITAIN: POPULATION

Persons per sq. mile
Over — 400
200 — 400
1 — 200
Very Sparse
Towns
Over 1,000,000
500,000 — 1,000,000
250,000 — 500,000
Shetland Islands
Orkney Islands
Hebrides
SCOTLAND
NORTH SEA
ATLANTIC OCEAN
Edinburgh
GLASGOW
Newcastle
NORTHERN IRELAND
Belfast
Isle of Man
IRISH SEA
EIRE
Dublin
ENGLAND
Leeds
Kingston-upon-Hull
Bradford
Manchester
Liverpool
Sheffield
Anglesey
Stoke-on-Trent
Nottingham
WALES
Leicester
BIRMINGHAM
Coventry
St. George's Channel
Bristol
LONDON
Cardiff
Croydon
I. of Wight
English Channel
FRANCE
Miles
0
100

oalfields
otton Goods
'oollen Goods
Shetland Islands
Orkney Islands
Hebrides
Woollens
SCOTLAND
Distilleries
NORTH SEA
Aluminium
Jute
Dundee
ATLANTIC OCEAN
Paisley
Glasgow
Cars
Shipbuilding
Iron
Steel
Edinburgh
NORTHERN IRELAND
Belfast
Shipbuilding
Linen
Shipbuilding
Sunderland
Iron
Chemicals
Salt
Steel
Middlesbrough
Iron
Steel
ENGLAND
Isle of Man
Leeds
EIRE
IRISH SEA
Liverpool
Cars
Glass
Manchester
St. Helens
Silk
Sheffield
Cutlery
Dublin
Brewing
Anglesey
Chemicals
Salt
Stoke
Pottery
Silk
Lace
Nottingham
Norwich
Leather
Leather
Brewing
Birmingham
Cars
Engineering
Coventry
WALES
Northampton
Leather
St. George's Channel
Oxford
Cars
Iron
Tin
Steel
Plate
Cardiff
LONDON
Miscellaneous Industries
Dagenham
Cars
Paper
China Clay
I. of Wight
English Channel
Miles
0
100
FRANCE

Scale 1 : 6,000,000
Miles
0 25 50 75 100
Kilometres
0 50 100 150
SHETLAND ISLANDS
on the same scale.
Unst
Yell
Mainland
Foula
Fair Isle
Orkney Islands
ORKNEY ISLANDS
Mainland
Hoy
Pentland Firth
Duncansby Hd.
C. Wrath
Butt of Lewis
North Minch
Lewis
Harris
N. Uist
S. Uist
Little Minch
OUTER HEBRIDES
INNER HEBRIDES
St. Kilda
Skye
Ardnamurchan Pt.
Tiree
Mull
Firth of Lorne
Jura
Islay
L. Shin
NORTH WEST HIGHLANDS
L. Maree
Beauly
L. Ness
Glen More
Ben Nevis 4406'
Rannoch Moor
GRAMPIAN
MOUNTAINS
Cairngorms
Ben Macdhui 4296'
Spey
Don
Dee
Tay
Moray Firth
Kinnairds Hd.
Buchan Ness
Sidlaw Hills
Ochil Hills
Firth of Tay
Firth of Forth
St. Abbs Hd.
L. Awe
L. Lomond
Campsie Fells
CENTRAL LOWLANDS
Pentland Hills
Lammermuir Hills
Tweed
Clyde
Firth of Clyde
Arran
Kintyre
Mull of Kintyre
North Channel
SOUTHERN UPLANDS
Nith
Cheviot Hills
Farne Is.
Tyne
Eden
Tees
Lake
Solway Firth
Antrim Plateau
Belfast
Bann
Lough Neagh
Sperrin Mts.
Foyle
L. Foyle
Malin Hd.
Donegal Mts.
Bloody Foreland
Donegal Bay
Dogger Bank
ATLANTIC OCEAN
NORTH SEA

IRISH SEA
Morecambe Bay
Liverpool Bay
Anglesey
Holy I.
Menai Strait
Snowdon 3560'
Cardigan Bay
Plynlimon 2468'
CAMBRIAN MOUNTAINS
Black Mts.
Brecon Beacons
Usk
Taff
Wye
Dee
Teifi
Towy
St. Davids Hd.
St. George's Channel
Worms Hd.
Bristol Channel
Exmoor
Exe
Taw
Yes Tor 2028'
Dartmoor
Bodmin Moor
Tamar
Eddystone Lighthouse
Hartland Pt.
Lizard Hd.
Lands End
Scilly Isles
Start Pt.
Lyme Bay
Portland Bill
ENGLISH CHANNEL
Alderney
CHANNEL
Guernsey
Sark
ISLANDS
Jersey
Pt. de Barfleur
FRANCE
Seine
Isle of Wight
St. Catherines Pt.
Solent
Salisbury Plain
Avon
Mendip Hills
White Horse Hills
Kennet
Cotswold Hills
Thames
Cherwell
Severn
Chiltern Hills
London Basin
North Downs
The Weald
South Downs
Wey
Lea
Beachy Head
Dungeness
Str. of Dover
N. Foreland
The Naze
The Broads
East Anglian Heights
The Fens
Great Ouse
Welland
Nene
Northampton Heights
Midland Plain
Midland Gap
Trent
Cheshire Plain
Ribble
The Peak 2088'
Derwent
Dove
CHAIN
Vale of York
Aire
Don
Ouse
Lincoln Edge
Witham
Lincoln Wolds
Humber
Spurn Hd.
The Wash
Yorkshire Wolds
Dundalk Bay
Howth Hd.
Wicklow Hd.
Wicklow Mts.
Liffey
Boyne
Slaney
Barrow
Nore
Suir
Carnsore Pt.
CENTRAL PLAIN
Bog of Allen
Slieve Bloom
L. Ree
Shannon
L. Derg
Silvermine Mts.
Golden Vale
Knockmealdown Mts.
Blackwater
Lee
Cork Harbour
Old Head of Kinsale
Slieve Aughty
Mayo
L. Mask
L. Corrib
Mts. of Connemara
Galway Bay
Aran Is.
Slyne Hd.
Achill Hd.
Carrantuohill 3414'
Mts. of Kerry
Brandon Hd.
Dingle Bay
Valentia I.
Kenmare Bay
Bantry Bay
C. Clear
Key to Contours
Over 3000 feet
1500 - 3000 feet
600 - 1500 feet
200 - 600 feet
0 - 200 feet
Sea level
0 - 100 fathoms
100 - 1000 fathoms
Below 1000 fathoms
10
B
8
6
D
4
Long. 2 West
F
0
G
d
c
f
52
50

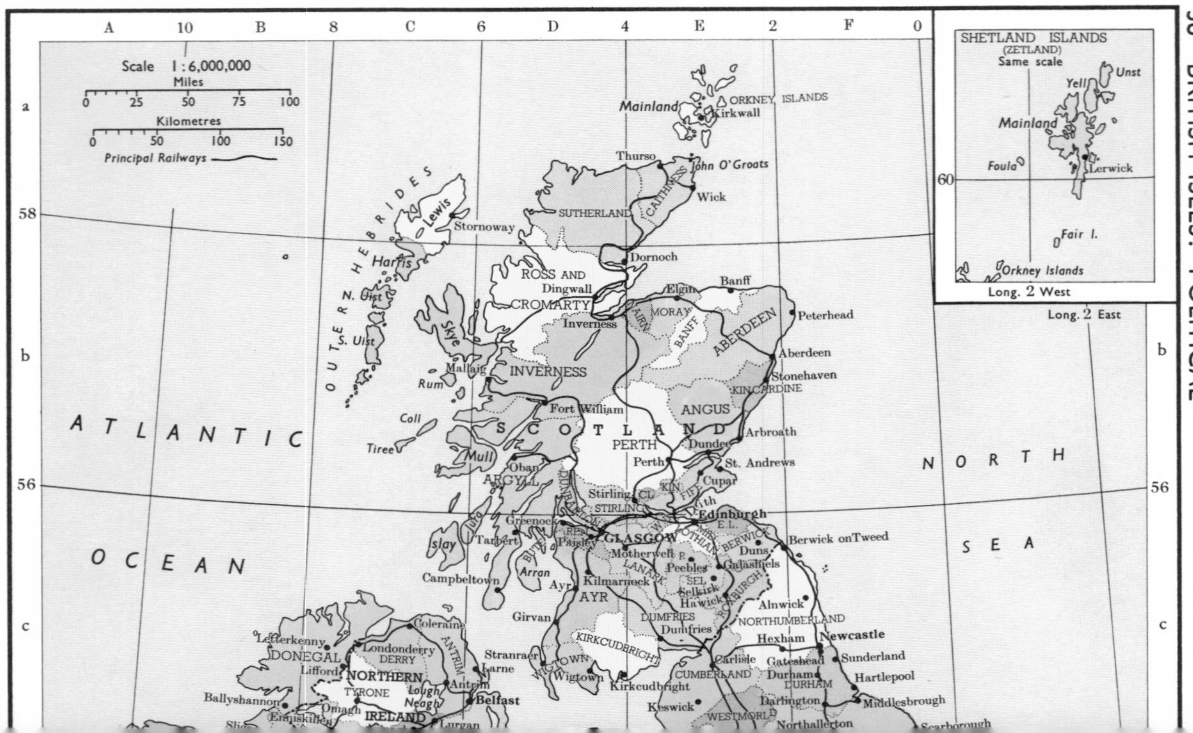
A 10 B 8 C 6 D 4 E 2 F 0
a b c
58
56
Scale 1:6,000,000
Miles
0 25 50 75 100
Kilometres
0 50 100 150
Principal Railways
SHETLAND ISLANDS
(ZETLAND)
Same scale
Unst
Yell
Mainland
Foula
Lerwick
60
Fair I.
Orkney Islands
Long. 2 West
Long. 2 East
ORKNEY ISLANDS
Mainland
Kirkwall
Thurso
John O' Groats
Wick
CAITHNESS
SUTHERLAND
Dornoch
OUTER HEBRIDES
Lewis
Stornoway
Harris
N. Uist
S. Uist
ROSS AND CROMARTY
Dingwall
Inverness
NAIRN
MORAY
Elgin
Banff
BANFF
ABERDEEN
Peterhead
Aberdeen
Stonehaven
KINCARDINE
Skye
Mallaig
Rum
INVERNESS
Fort William
ANGUS
Arbroath
ATLANTIC
OCEAN
Coll
Tiree
SCOTLAND
PERTH
Dundee
Perth
St. Andrews
Mull
Oban
ARGYLL
DUNBARTON
KIN.
FIFE
Cupar
Stirling
CL.
STIRLING
Leith
Edinburgh
E.L.
NORTH
SEA
Jura
Islay
Greenock
REN.
GLASGOW
Paisley
Tarbert
W.L.
MID.
LOTHIAN
BERWICK
Duns
Berwick on Tweed
BUTE
Arran
Motherwell
P.
Peebles
Galashiels
LANARK
SEL.
Selkirk
Campbeltown
Ayr
Kilmarnock
AYR
Hawick
ROXBURGH
Alnwick
Girvan
DUMFRIES
Dumfries
NORTHUMBERLAND
KIRKCUDBRIGHT
Hexham
Newcastle
Letterkenny
DONEGAL
Lifford
Coleraine
Londonderry
DERRY
ANTRIM
Stranraer
Larne
WIGTOWN
Wigtown
Kirkcudbright
Carlisle
CUMBERLAND
Gateshead
Sunderland
Durham
DURHAM
Hartlepool
NORTHERN
TYRONE
Lough Neagh
Antrim
Belfast
Ballyshannon
Omagh
Enniskillen
IRELAND
Lurgan
Keswick
Darlington
Middlesbrough
WESTMORLD
Northallerton
Scarborough

IRISH SEA
ENGLISH CHANNEL
FRANCE
CHANNEL ISLANDS
(Br.)
Alderney
Guernsey
Sark
Jersey
St. Peter Port
St. Helier
Scilly Is.
Lands End
Long. 4 West
ENGLAND
WALES
EIRE
LONDON
BIRMINGHAM
Manchester
Liverpool
Birkenhead
Leeds
Bradford
Sheffield
Hull
Nottingham
Leicester
Coventry
Stoke
Bristol
Cardiff
Swansea
Plymouth
Exeter
Southampton
Portsmouth
Brighton
Dover
Folkestone
Canterbury
Chatham
Maidstone
Croydon
Norwich
Gt. Yarmouth
Ipswich
Harwich
Colchester
Chelmsford
Cambridge
Peterborough
Northampton
Bedford
Buckingham
Aylesbury
Hertford
Oxford
Reading
Windsor
Guildford
Aldershot
Winchester
Salisbury
Bournemouth
Poole
Dorchester
Weymouth
Taunton
Bath
Wells
Swindon
Gloucester
Cheltenham
Worcester
Hereford
Monmouth
Newport
Merthyr
Brecon
Carmarthen
Haverfordwest
Pembroke
Fishguard
Cardigan
Aberystwyth
Dolgelley
Montgomery
Bangor
Holyhead
Conway
Wrexham
Chester
Crewe
Shrewsbury
Wolverhampton
Kidderminster
Warwick
Rugby
Stafford
Derby
Lincoln
Grantham
Boston
Kings Lynn
Wisbech
Cromer
Grimsby
Doncaster
Huddersfield
Halifax
Oldham
Stockport
Macclesfield
Warrington
Bolton
Blackburn
Preston
Burnley
Penzance
Falmouth
Truro
Launceston
Barnstaple
Torquay
Hastings
Lewes
Newhaven
Chichester
Isle of Wight
Calais
Boulogne
Dieppe
le Havre
Cherbourg
Dublin
Dun Laoghaire
Drogheda
Dundalk
Wicklow
Arklow
Wexford
Rosslare
Enniscorthy
Waterford
Kilkenny
Carlow
Naas
Navan
Kells
Athlone
Tullamore
Longford
Carrick on Shannon
Roscommon
Galway
Castlebar
Westport
Clifden
Athenry
Ballinasloe
Portumna
Maryborough
Ennis
Kilrush
Limerick
Tipperary
Clonmel
Cashel
Fermoy
Mallow
Cork
Cobh
Kinsale
Youghal
Lismore
Bandon
Bantry
Kenmare
Killarney
Tralee
Dingle
NORFOLK
West SUFFOLK East
ESSEX
KENT
SUSSEX
West
East
SURREY
HANTS.
BERKS
WILTS
DORSET
SOMERSET
DEVON
CORNWALL
GLOUCS.
OXFORD
BUCKS
BEDS.
HERTS
WORCS
HEREFORD
SALOP
STAFFS.
CHESHIRE
DERBY
NOTTS
LEICS
RUT.
WARWICK
LINCOLN
Lindsey
Kestn
Holld
NORTHANTS
CAM & ELY
MON
GLAMORGAN
BRECKNOCK
RADNOR
CARDIGAN
CARMARTHEN
PEMBROKE
MONT-GOMERY
MERIONETH
CAERNARVON
ANGLESEY
DENBIGH
FLINT
W. Riding
York
E. Riding
LOUTH
MEATH
WEST MEATH
LONG
ROSCOMMON
GALWAY
CLARE
LIMERICK
TIPPERARY
KILKENNY
CARLOW
WICKLOW
WEXFORD
WATERFORD
CORK
KERRY
LAOIGHIS
OFFALY
KILDARE
DUBLIN
d
e
f
52
50
10
B
8
C
6
D
E
2
F
0
G

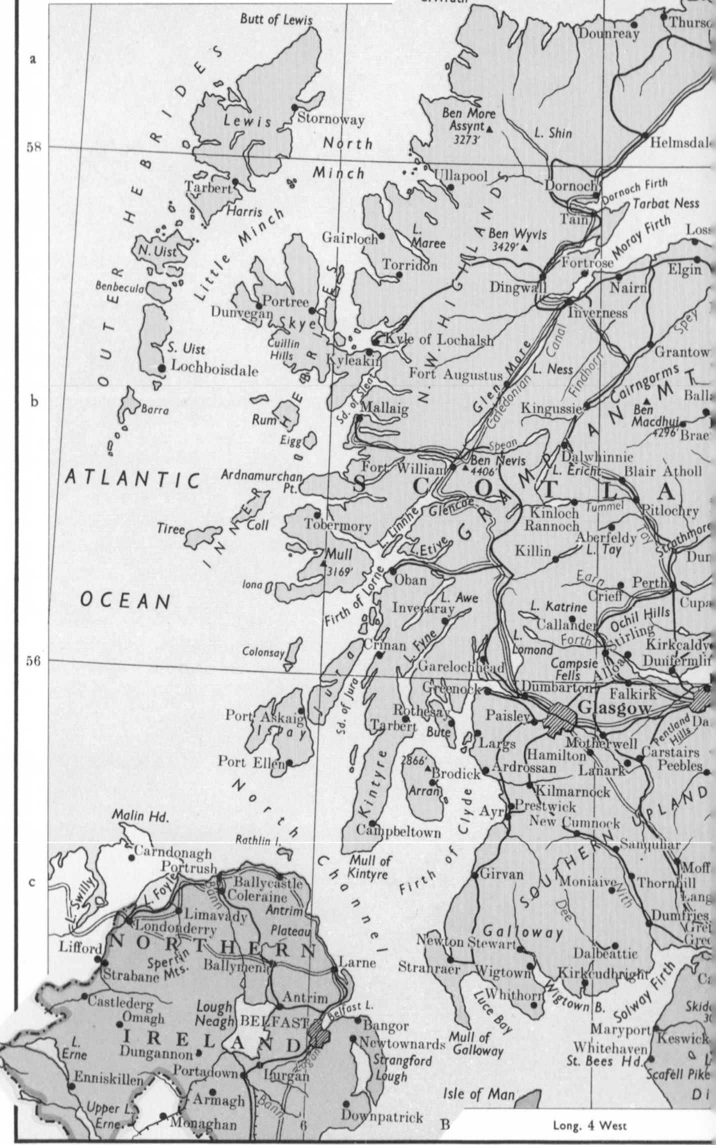
C. Wrath
Butt of Lewis
Pentland
Thurso
Dounreay
Lewis
Stornoway
North
Minch
Ben More
Assynt
3273'
L. Shin
Helmsdale
OUTER HEBRIDES
Tarbert
Harris
Little Minch
Ullapool
Dornoch
Dornoch Firth
Tarbat Ness
Tain
N. Uist
Gairloch
L. Maree
Ben Wyvis
3429'
Moray Firth
Torridon
Fortrose
Elgin
Benbecula
Dingwall
Nairn
Portree
Dunvegan
Skye
Inverness
Cuillin
Hills
Kyle of Lochalsh
Kyleakin
S. Uist
Lochboisdale
Fort Augustus
L. Ness
Caledonian Canal
Glen More
Findhorn
Grantown
Spey
Cairngorms
Barra
Rum
Eigg
Mallaig
Sd. of Sleat
N.W. HIGHLANDS
Kingussie
Ben
Macdhui
4296'
Spean
Ben Nevis
4406'
Dalwhinnie
L. Ericht
Blair Atholl
Fort William
ATLANTIC
Ardnamurchan
Pt.
SCOTLAND
GRAMPIAN MTS.
Glencoe
Kinloch
Rannoch
Tummel
Pitlochry
Tiree
Coll
Tobermory
INNER HEBRIDES
L. Linnhe
L. Etive
Aberfeldy
L. Tay
Tay
Strathmore
Killin
Mull
3169'
Oban
Iona
OCEAN
Earn
Perth
Crieff
Firth of Lorne
L. Awe
Inveraray
L. Katrine
Callander
Ochil Hills
Cupar
Forth
Stirling
Kirkcaldy
L. Lomond
Colonsay
Crinan
L. Fyne
Jura
Garelochhead
Campsie
Fells
Alloa
Dunfermline
Dumbarton
Falkirk
Greenock
Glasgow
Port Askaig
Islay
Sd. of Jura
Rothesay
Tarbert
Bute
Paisley
Largs
Motherwell
Pentland Hills
Hamilton
Carstairs
Peebles
Port Ellen
Kintyre
2866'
Brodick
Arran
Ardrossan
Lanark
Kilmarnock
North Channel
Malin Hd.
Ayr
Prestwick
New Cumnock
Campbeltown
Firth of Clyde
SOUTHERN UPLANDS
Rathlin I.
Carndonagh
Portrush
Sanquhar
Moffat
Mull of
Kintyre
Girvan
Moniaive
Thornhill
Ballycastle
Coleraine
Bann
L. Foyle
L. Swilly
Antrim
Plateau
Limavady
Londonderry
Dee
Nith
Dumfries
Galloway
Newton Stewart
Lifford
NORTHERN
Sperrin Mts.
Ballymena
Larne
Stranraer
Wigtown
Dalbeattie
Kirkcudbright
Strabane
Solway Firth
Castlederg
Antrim
Wigtown B.
Whithorn
Luce Bay
Omagh
Lough
Neagh
BELFAST
Belfast L.
Bangor
Maryport
Keswick
IRELAND
L.
Erne
Dungannon
Newtownards
Mull of
Galloway
Whitehaven
St. Bees Hd.
Lagan
Strangford
Lough
Portadown
Lurgan
Scafell Pike
Enniskillen
Armagh
Isle of Man
Upper L.
Erne
Monaghan
Downpatrick
Long. 4 West
8
A
6
4
B
a
b
c
58
56

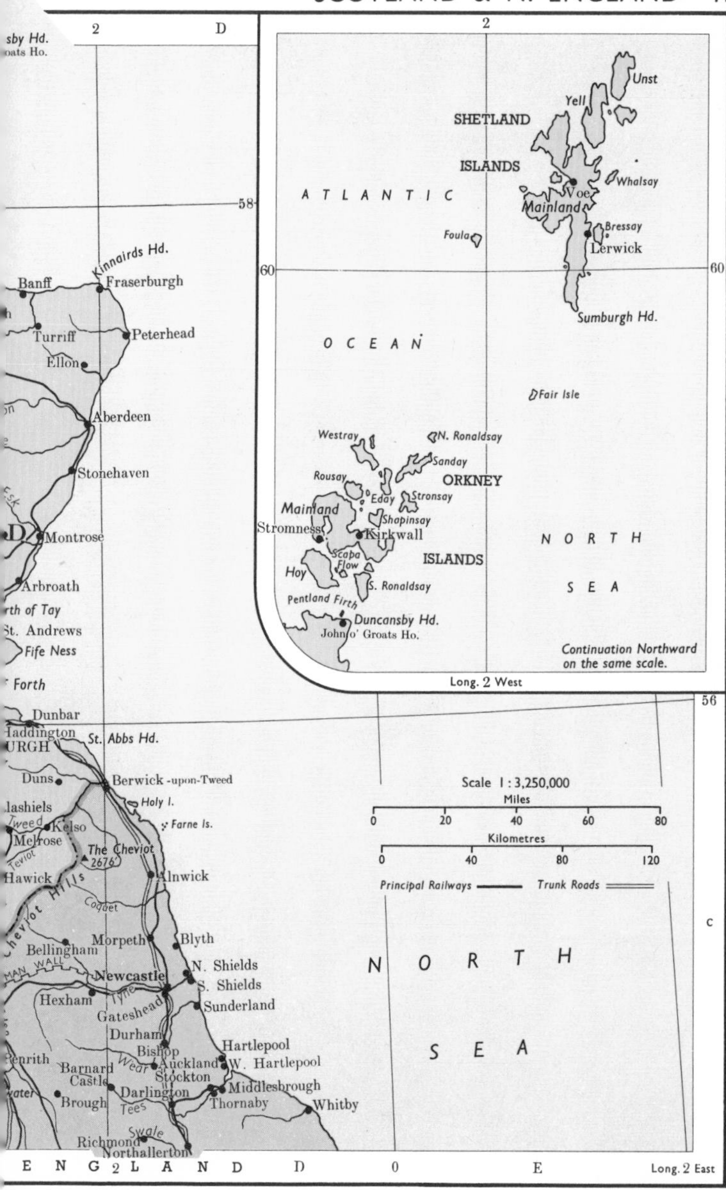
SHETLAND
ISLANDS
Unst
Yell
Whalsay
Voe
Mainland
Bressay
Lerwick
Foula
Sumburgh Hd.
A T L A N T I C
O C E A N
Fair Isle
Westray
N. Ronaldsay
Sanday
Rousay
ORKNEY
Eday
Stronsay
Mainland
Shapinsay
Stromness
Kirkwall
Scapa Flow
ISLANDS
Hoy
S. Ronaldsay
Pentland Firth
Duncansby Hd.
John o' Groats Ho.
N O R T H
S E A
Continuation Northward on the same scale.
Long. 2 West
Kinnairds Hd.
Banff
Fraserburgh
Turriff
Peterhead
Ellon
Aberdeen
Stonehaven
Montrose
Arbroath
St. Andrews
Fife Ness
Dunbar
St. Abbs Hd.
Duns
Berwick -upon-Tweed
Holy I.
Farne Is.
Kelso
Melrose
The Cheviot 2676
Hawick
Alnwick
Cheviot Hills
Coquet
Morpeth
Blyth
Bellingham
Newcastle
N. Shields
S. Shields
Hexham
Tyne
Sunderland
Gateshead
Durham
Hartlepool
Bishop Auckland
W. Hartlepool
Wear
Barnard Castle
Stockton
Middlesbrough
Brough
Darlington
Thornaby
Whitby
Tees
Swale
Richmond
Northallerton
Scale 1 : 3,250,000
Miles
0 20 40 60 80
Kilometres
0 40 80 120
Principal Railways
Trunk Roads
N O R T H
S E A
E N G L A N D
Long. 2 East

A NORTHERN IRELAND
B
4
C
a
54
b
52
c
50
Monaghan
Mourne Mts.
Newry
Dundalk
Cavan
Ardee
Drogheda
Dundalk B.
Carlingford L.
Navan
Trim
Boyne
Balbriggan
EIRE
Howth Hd.
Dun Laoghaire
Naas
Kildare
Wicklow Mts.
Athy
Wicklow
Carlow
Arklow
Gorey
Slaney
Barrow
Enniscorthy
Wexford
Rosslare
Carnsore Pt.
St. George's Channel
Snaefell 2034'
Peel
Ramsey
Isle of Man
Douglas
Calf of Man
IRISH SEA
Ulverston
Barrow -in-Furness
Walney
Morecambe Bay
Blackpool
Lytham
Southport
Preston
Wigan
St. Helens
Liverpool Bay
Liverpool
Birkenhead
Wirral
Cheshire Plain
Chester
Amlwch
Holyhead
Holy I.
Anglesey
Llandudno
Rhyl
Conway
Denbigh
Bangor
Menai Str.
Mold
Caernarvon
Wrexham
Dee
Whitchurch
Portmadoc
L. Bala
Llangollen
Lleyn
Oswestry
Dolgelley
Vyrnwy
Shrewsbury
CAMBRIAN MOUNTAINS
Welshpool
Dyfi
Montgomery
Cardigan Bay
Machynlleth
Severn
Aberystwyth
WALES
Rhayader
Llandrindod Wells
Kington
Wye
Cardigan
Teifi
Lampeter
Fishguard
Brecon
Black Mts.
St. David's Hd.
Carmarthen
Brecon Beacons
Usk
Haverfordwest
Towy
Milford
Merthyr Tydfil
Aber-gavenny
Monmouth
Pembroke
Llanelly
Milford Haven
Rhondda
Taff
Carmarthen Bay
Gower
Port Talbot
Newport
Worms Hd.
Swansea
Swansea B.
CARDIFF
Barry
Bristol Channel
Bristol
Weston -super-Mare
Wells
Lundy I.
Ilfracombe
Minehead
Barnstaple Bay
Bridgwater
Hartland Pt.
Barnstaple
Bideford
Parrett
Taunton
Taw
Exe
Tiverton
Bude
Crediton
Okehampton
Axminster
Exeter
Launceston
Tamar
Bodmin Moor
Lyme Bay
Padstow
Weymouth
Bodmin
Newquay
Tavistock
Torquay
Liskeard
Truro
St. Austell
Dartmouth
St. Ives
Plymouth
Penzance
Start Pt.
Falmouth
Land's End
Lizard Hd.
6
Scale 1 : 3,250,000
Miles
0 20 40 60 80
Kilometres
0 40 80 120
Principal Railways
Trunk Roads

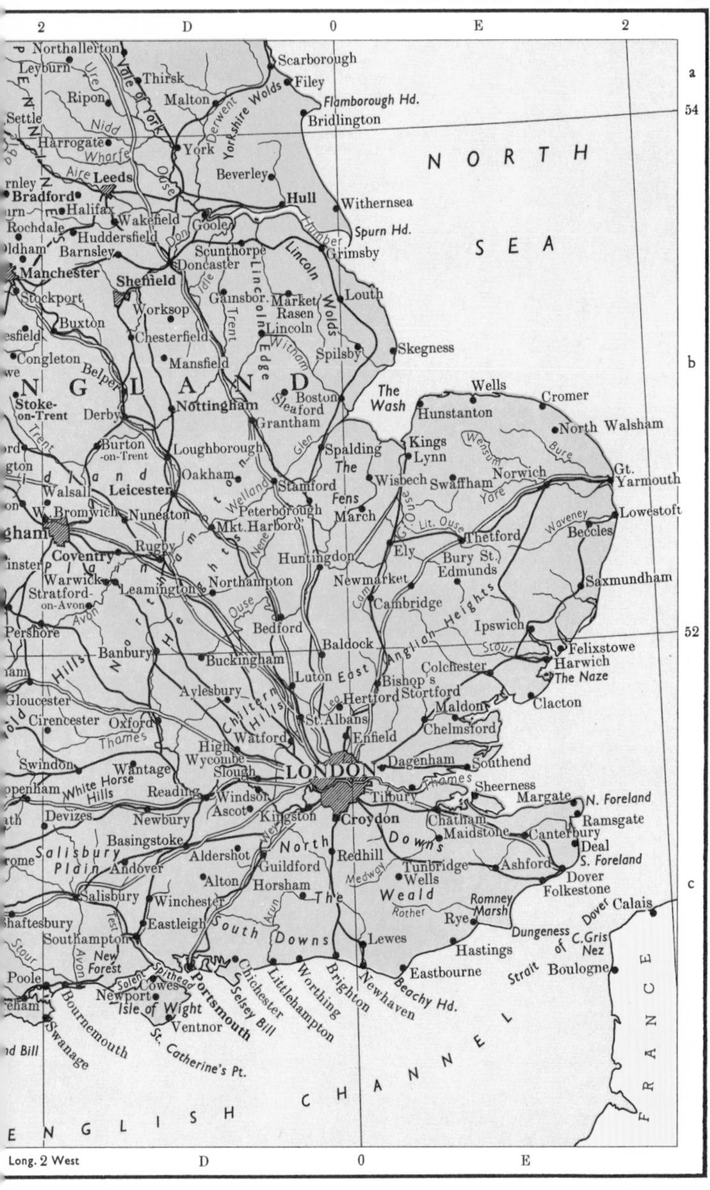
2
D
0
E
2
a
54
b
52
c
Northallerton
Leyburn
Ure
Thirsk
Vale of York
Scarborough
Filey
Ripon
Malton
Derwent
Yorkshire Wolds
Flamborough Hd.
Settle
Nidd
Bridlington
Harrogate
York
Wharfe
NORTH
Aire
Leeds
Ouse
Beverley
Bradford
Halifax
Hull
Withernsea
Wakefield
Goole
Humber
Spurn Hd.
Rochdale
Huddersfield
Don
SEA
Barnsley
Scunthorpe
Lincoln
Grimsby
Manchester
Doncaster
Sheffield
Idle
Stockport
Gainsbor.
Market Rasen
Louth
Worksop
Trent
Lincoln Edge
Wolds
Buxton
Lincoln
Chesterfield
Witham
Skegness
Spilsby
Congleton
Mansfield
Belper
ENGLAND
Boston
The Wash
Wells
Cromer
Stoke-on-Trent
Derby
Nottingham
Sleaford
Hunstanton
Grantham
North Walsham
Trent
Burton -on-Trent
Loughborough
Glen
Spalding
Kings Lynn
Wensum
Bure
Midland
Oakham
The Fens
Wisbech
Swaffham
Norwich
Gt. Yarmouth
Walsall
Leicester
Stamford
Welland
Yare
W. Bromwich
Nuneaton
Peterborough
Fens
March
Gt. Ouse
Lit. Ouse
Waveney
Lowestoft
Mkt. Harboro'
Nene
Thetford
Beccles
Coventry
Rugby
Huntingdon
Ely
Bury St. Edmunds
Warwick
Leamington
Northampton
Newmarket
Saxmundham
Stratford-on-Avon
Cam
Cambridge
Avon
Ouse
Northampton Heights
East Anglian Heights
Bedford
Ipswich
Pershore
Baldock
Stour
Felixstowe
Banbury
Buckingham
Colchester
Harwich
Hills
Luton
Bishop's Stortford
The Naze
Aylesbury
Hertford
Gloucester
Lea
Maldon
Clacton
Chiltern Hills
St. Albans
Cirencester
Oxford
Chelmsford
Thames
Watford
Enfield
High Wycombe
Swindon
Wantage
Slough
LONDON
Dagenham
Southend
Thames
White Horse Hills
Reading
Sheerness
Windsor
Tilbury
Margate
N. Foreland
Ascot
Kingston
Devizes
Newbury
Croydon
Chatham
Ramsgate
Wey
Maidstone
Canterbury
Basingstoke
North Downs
Deal
Salisbury Plain
Aldershot
Redhill
Tunbridge Wells
Andover
Guildford
Ashford
S. Foreland
Medway
Dover
Alton
Horsham
Folkestone
Weald
Salisbury
The
Winchester
Romney Marsh
Rother
Dover
Calais
Rye
Test
Arun
Eastleigh
South Downs
Dungeness
Shaftesbury
Strait of
C. Gris Nez
Southampton
Lewes
Hastings
Stour
Avon
New Forest
Chichester
Boulogne
Solent
Spithead
Littlehampton
Worthing
Brighton
Newhaven
Eastbourne
Poole
Cowes
Portsmouth
Selsey Bill
Beachy Hd.
Newport
Isle of Wight
Bournemouth
Ventnor
FRANCE
Swanage
St. Catherine's Pt.
ENGLISH CHANNEL
Long. 2 West
D
0
E

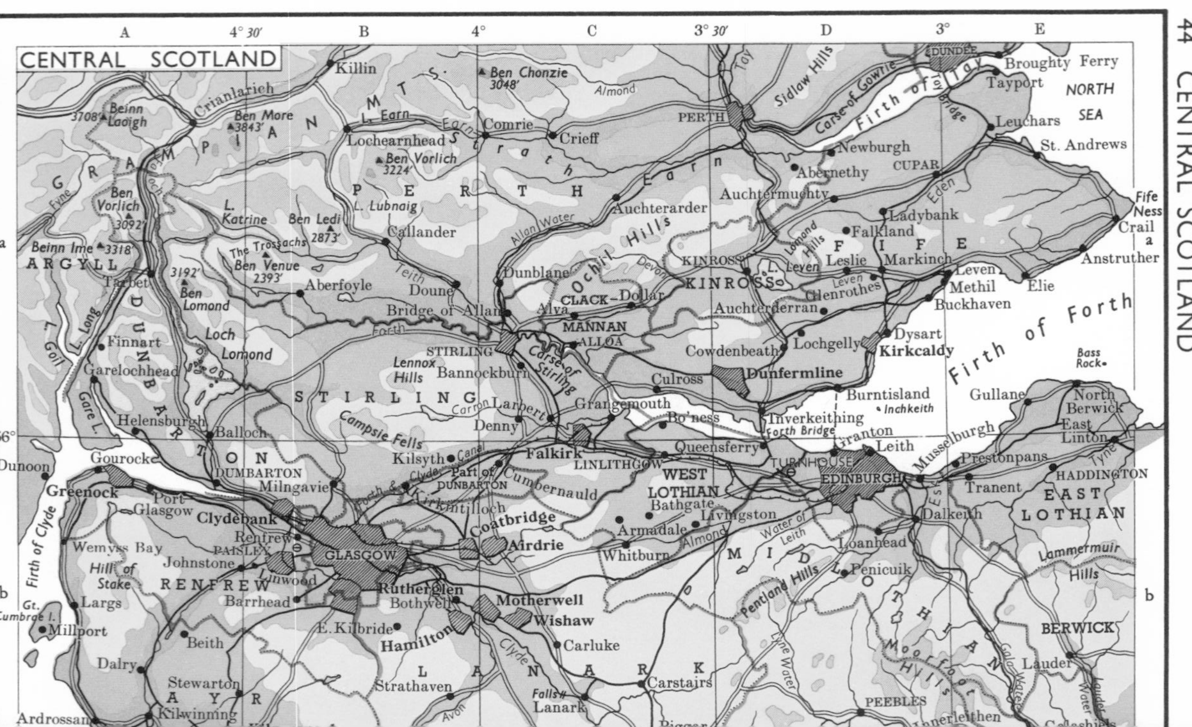

CENTRAL SCOTLAND
A
4° 30'
B
4°
C
3° 30'
D
3°
E
a
b
56°
Killin
Ben Chonzie 3048'
Almond
Crianlarich
Beinn Laoigh 3708'
Ben More 3843'
L. Earn
Comrie
Crieff
PERTH
Tay
Sidlaw Hills
Carse of Gowrie
Firth of Tay
Tay Bridge
DUNDEE
Broughty Ferry
Tayport
NORTH SEA
Leuchars
St. Andrews
Lochearnhead
Ben Vorlich 3224'
Strath Earn
Newburgh
Abernethy
CUPAR
Eden
Auchtermuchty
Auchterarder
Ben Vorlich 3092'
L. Katrine
Ben Ledi 2873'
L. Lubnaig
Callander
Allan Water
Ochil Hills
Ladybank
Falkland
Lomond Hills
Fife Ness
Crail
Beinn Ime 3318'
ARGYLL
Tarbet
The Trossachs
Ben Venue 2393'
Ben Lomond 3192'
Aberfoyle
Teith
Doune
Dunblane
Devon
KINROSS
L. Leven
Leslie
Markinch
FIFE
Anstruther
Leven
Methil
Elie
Glenrothes
Buckhaven
Bridge of Allan
Alva
CLACKMANNAN
Dollar
Auchterderran
Firth of Forth
Loch Lomond
Finnart
L. Long
L. Goil
Forth
STIRLING
ALLOA
Cowdenbeath
Lochgelly
Dysart
Kirkcaldy
Bass Rock
Garelochhead
Gare L.
Lennox Hills
Bannockburn
Carse of Stirling
Culross
Dunfermline
STIRLING
Carron
Larbert
Grangemouth
Burntisland
Inchkeith
Gullane
North Berwick
East Linton
Helensburgh
Balloch
Campsie Fells
Denny
Bo'ness
Inverkeithing
Forth Bridge
Granton
Leith
Musselburgh
DUNBARTON
Dunoon
Gourock
Kilsyth
Forth & Clyde Canal
Falkirk
LINLITHGOW
Queensferry
TURNHOUSE
EDINBURGH
Prestonpans
Tyne
HADDINGTON
Greenock
Port Glasgow
Milngavie
Part of DUNBARTON
Cumbernauld
Kirkintilloch
WEST LOTHIAN
Bathgate
Livingston
Tranent
EAST LOTHIAN
Esk
Dalkeith
Clydebank
Coatbridge
Armadale
Almond
Water of Leith
Renfrew
PAISLEY
GLASGOW
Airdrie
Whitburn
Loanhead
Lammermuir Hills
Firth of Clyde
Wemyss Bay
Johnstone
Linwood
Hill of Stake
RENFREW
Rutherglen
MIDLOTHIAN
Pentland Hills
Penicuik
Largs
Barrhead
Bothwell
Motherwell
Wishaw
Gt. Cumbrae I.
Millport
E. Kilbride
Hamilton
BERWICK
Beith
Clyde
Carluke
Moorfoot Hills
Lauder
Dalry
LANARK
Gala Water
Lauder Water
Stewarton
AYR
Strathaven
Falls
Lanark
Carstairs
Lyne Water
PEEBLES
Ardrossan
Kilwinning
Avon

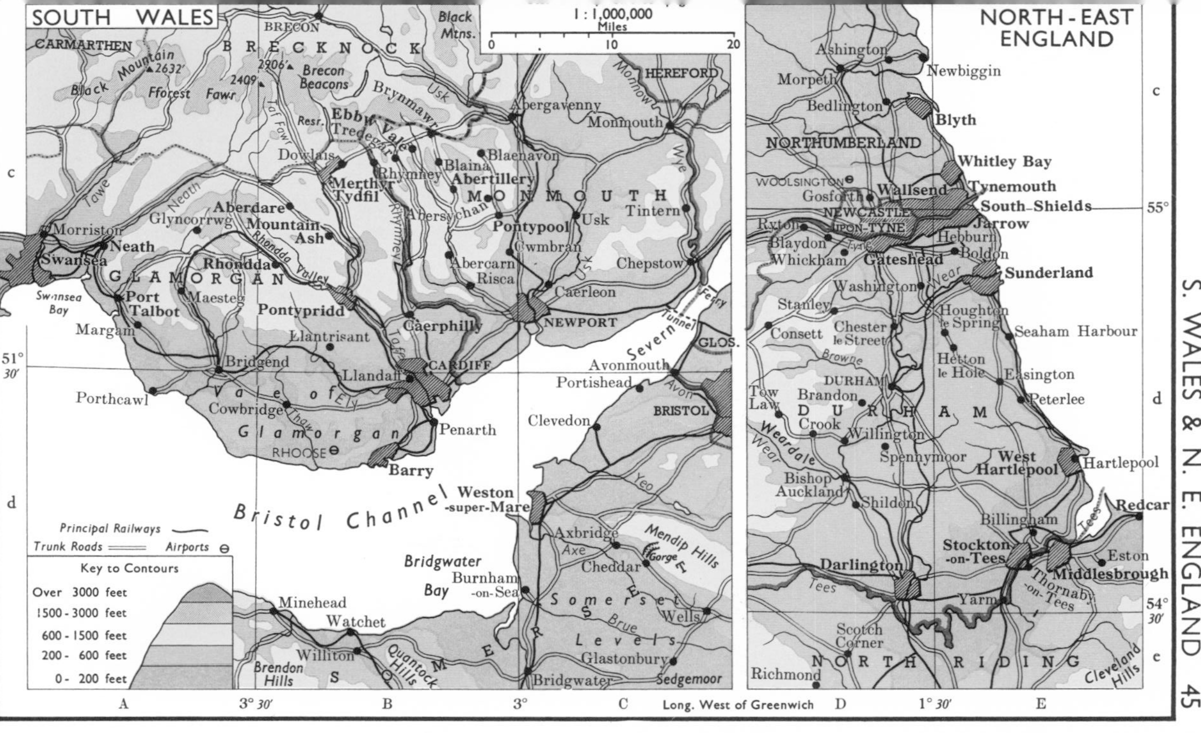
SOUTH WALES
NORTH-EAST ENGLAND
1 : 1,000,000
Miles
0
10
20
Key to Contours
Over 3000 feet
1500 - 3000 feet
600 - 1500 feet
200 - 600 feet
0 - 200 feet
Principal Railways
Trunk Roads
Airports
Long. West of Greenwich
A
B
C
D
E
c
d
e
51° 30'
55°
54° 30'
3° 30'
3°
1° 30'
CARMARTHEN
BRECON
HEREFORD
GLOS.
BRISTOL
NEWPORT
CARDIFF
Swansea
Swansea Bay
Morriston
Neath
Port Talbot
Margam
Porthcawl
Glyncorrwg
Maesteg
Aberdare
Mountain Ash
Rhondda
Pontypridd
Llantrisant
Bridgend
Cowbridge
Llandaff
Caerphilly
Penarth
Barry
Merthyr Tydfil
Dowlais
Tredegar
Ebbw Vale
Rhymney
Brynmawr
Blaina
Abertillery
Abersychan
Blaenavon
Abergavenny
Pontypool
Abercarn
Risca
Cwmbran
Caerleon
Usk
Monmouth
Tintern
Chepstow
Avonmouth
Portishead
Clevedon
Weston -super-Mare
Burnham -on-Sea
Bridgwater
Bridgwater Bay
Axbridge
Cheddar
Wells
Glastonbury
Sedgemoor
Watchet
Williton
Minehead
Brendon Hills
Quantock Hills
Mendip Hills
Gorge
Bristol Channel
Severn
Tunnel
Ferry
Wye
Monnow
Usk
Taff
Rhymney
Ely
Thaw
Neath
Tawe
Taf Fawr
Rhondda Valley
Avon
Yeo
Axe
Brue
Black Mtns.
Brecon Beacons
Black Mountain
Fforest Fawr
2906'
2632'
2409'
Resr.
RHOOSE
B R E C K N O C K
G L A M O R G A N
M O N M O U T H
Vale of Ely
Glamorgan
S o m e r s e t
L e v e l s
S O M E R S E T
Ashington
Newbiggin
Morpeth
Bedlington
Blyth
Whitley Bay
Tynemouth
South Shields
Jarrow
Wallsend
NEWCASTLE UPON-TYNE
Gosforth
WOOLSINGTON
Ryton
Blaydon
Whickham
Gateshead
Hebburn
Boldon
Sunderland
Washington
Houghton le Spring
Seaham Harbour
Hetton le Hole
Easington
Peterlee
Chester le Street
Stanley
Consett
DURHAM
Brandon
Crook
Willington
Spennymoor
Tow Law
Bishop Auckland
Shildon
West Hartlepool
Hartlepool
Billingham
Stockton -on-Tees
Thornaby -on-Tees
Middlesbrough
Eston
Redcar
Yarm
Darlington
Scotch Corner
Richmond
NORTHUMBERLAND
D U R H A M
N O R T H   R I D I N G
Weardale
Cleveland Hills
Tyne
Wear
Browne
Tees

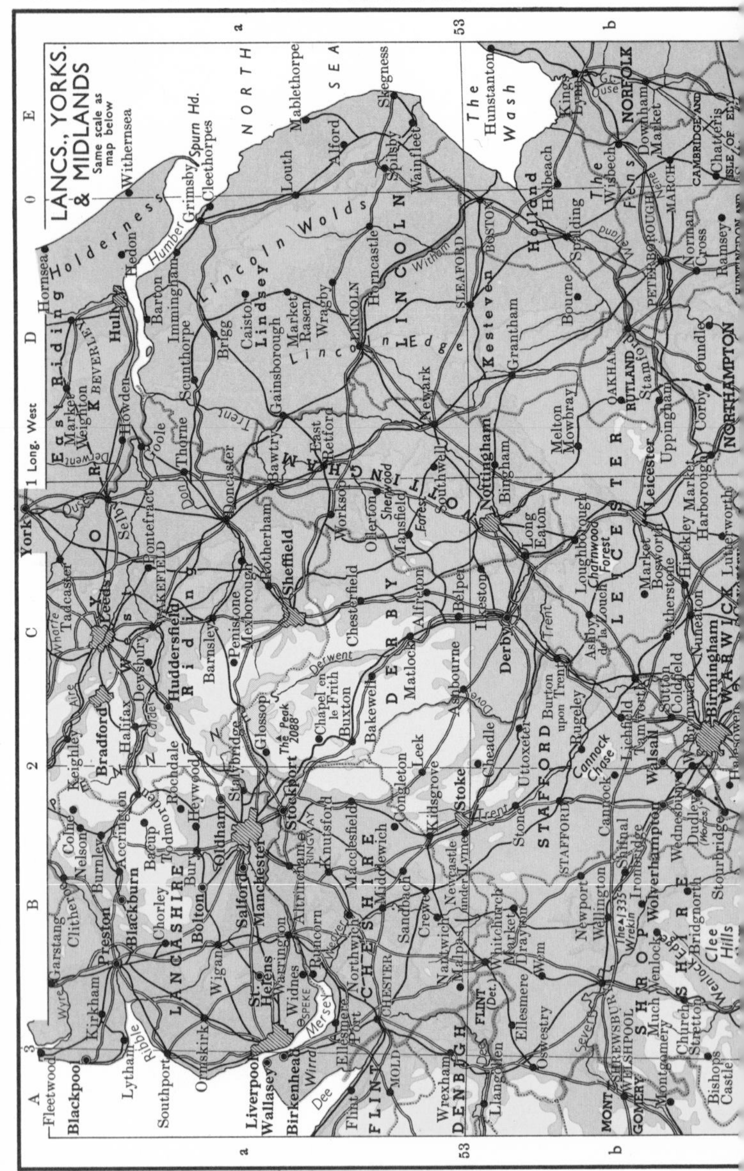
LANCS., YORKS. & MIDLANDS
Same scale as map below
NORTH SEA
Holderness
East Riding
West Riding
Lincoln Wolds
Lindsey
Lincoln Edge
Kesteven
Holland
The Fens
The Wash
LANCASHIRE
CHESHIRE
DERBY
NOTTINGHAM
LINCOLN
LEICESTER
RUTLAND
NORTHAMPTON
NORFOLK
STAFFORD
SHROPSHIRE
WARWICK
FLINT
DENBIGH
MONTGOMERY
Sherwood Forest
Charnwood Forest
Cannock Chase
The Peak 2088'
The Wrekin 1335
Clee Hills
York
Leeds
Bradford
Hull
Sheffield
Manchester
Liverpool
Birmingham
Nottingham
Leicester
Derby
Stoke
Preston
Blackpool
Fleetwood
Grimsby
Cleethorpes
Spurn Hd.
Humber
Trent
Ouse
Mersey
Dee
1 Long. West
53

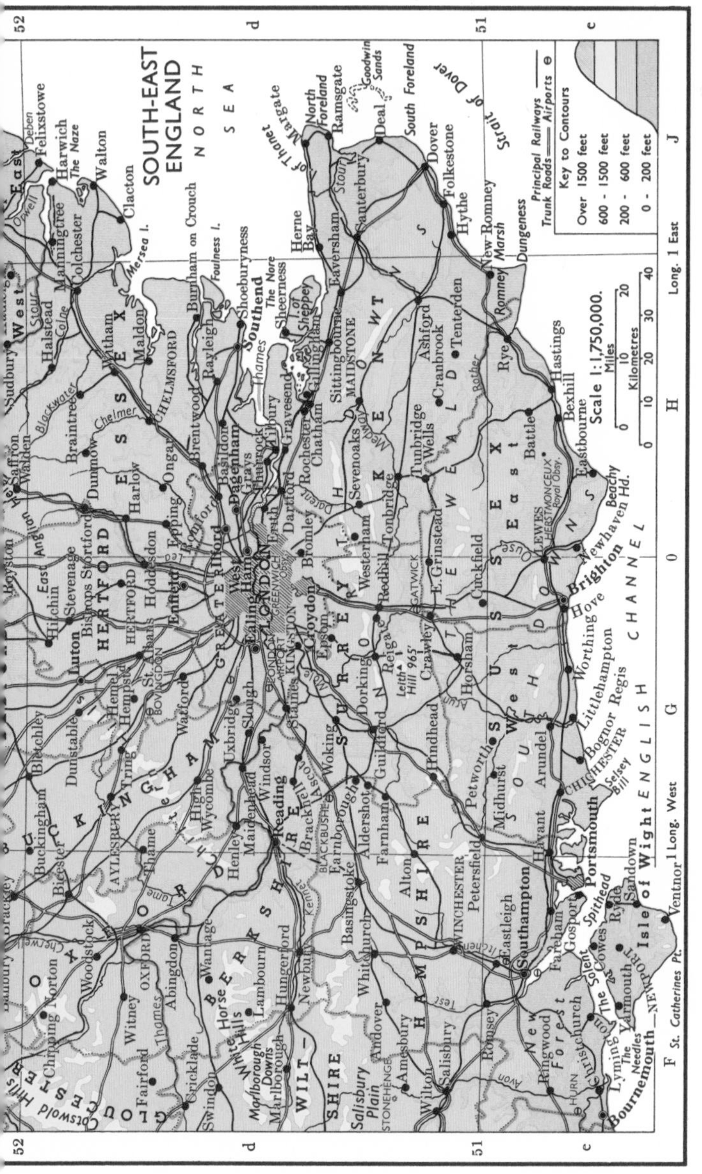
SOUTH-EAST ENGLAND
NORTH SEA
ENGLISH CHANNEL
Strait of Dover
Scale 1:1,750,000.
Miles
Kilometres
Key to Contours
Over 1500 feet
600 - 1500 feet
200 - 600 feet
0 - 200 feet
Principal Railways
Trunk Roads
Airports
Long. 1 West
Long. 1 East
LONDON
Isle of Wight

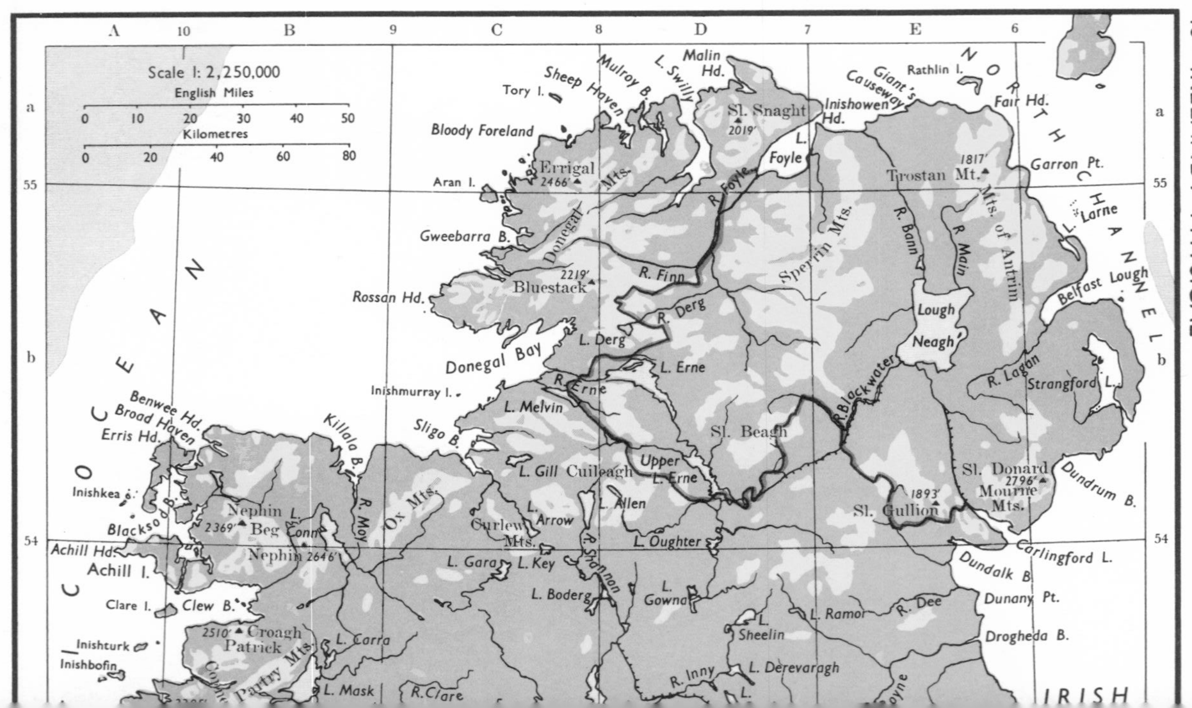
NORTH CHANNEL
OCEAN
IRISH
Scale 1: 2,250,000
English Miles
0 10 20 30 40 50
Kilometres
0 20 40 60 80
Tory I.
Sheep Haven
Mulroy B.
L. Swilly
Malin Hd.
Sl. Snaght
2019'
Inishowen Hd.
Giant's Causeway
Rathlin I.
Fair Hd.
Garron Pt.
Trostan Mt.
1817'
Mts. of Antrim
Larne
Belfast Lough
Bloody Foreland
Errigal
2466'
Mts.
Aran I.
L. Foyle
R. Foyle
Donegal
Gweebarra B.
Sperrin Mts.
R. Bann
R. Main
2219'
Bluestack
R. Finn
Rossan Hd.
R. Derg
Lough Neagh
L. Derg
Donegal Bay
L. Erne
R. Blackwater
R. Lagan
Strangford L.
Inishmurray I.
R. Erne
Benwee Hd.
Broad Haven
Erris Hd.
L. Melvin
Killala B.
Sligo B.
Sl. Beagh
Upper L. Erne
L. Gill
Cuilcagh
Sl. Donard
2796'
Mourne Mts.
Dundrum B.
Inishkea
Ox Mts.
R. Moy
L. Allen
1893'
Sl. Gullion
Nephin Beg
2369'
L. Conn
Curlew Mts.
L. Arrow
Blacksod B.
Nephin 2646'
R. Shannon
L. Oughter
Achill Hd.
Achill I.
L. Gara
L. Key
Carlingford L.
Dundalk B.
Clare I.
Clew B.
L. Boderg
L. Gowna
L. Ramor
R. Dee
Dunany Pt.
2510'
Croagh Patrick
L. Carra
L. Sheelin
Drogheda B.
Inishturk
Inishbofin
Partry Mts.
R. Inny
L. Derevaragh
L. Mask
R. Clare
A
10
B
9
C
8
D
7
E
6
a
b
55
54

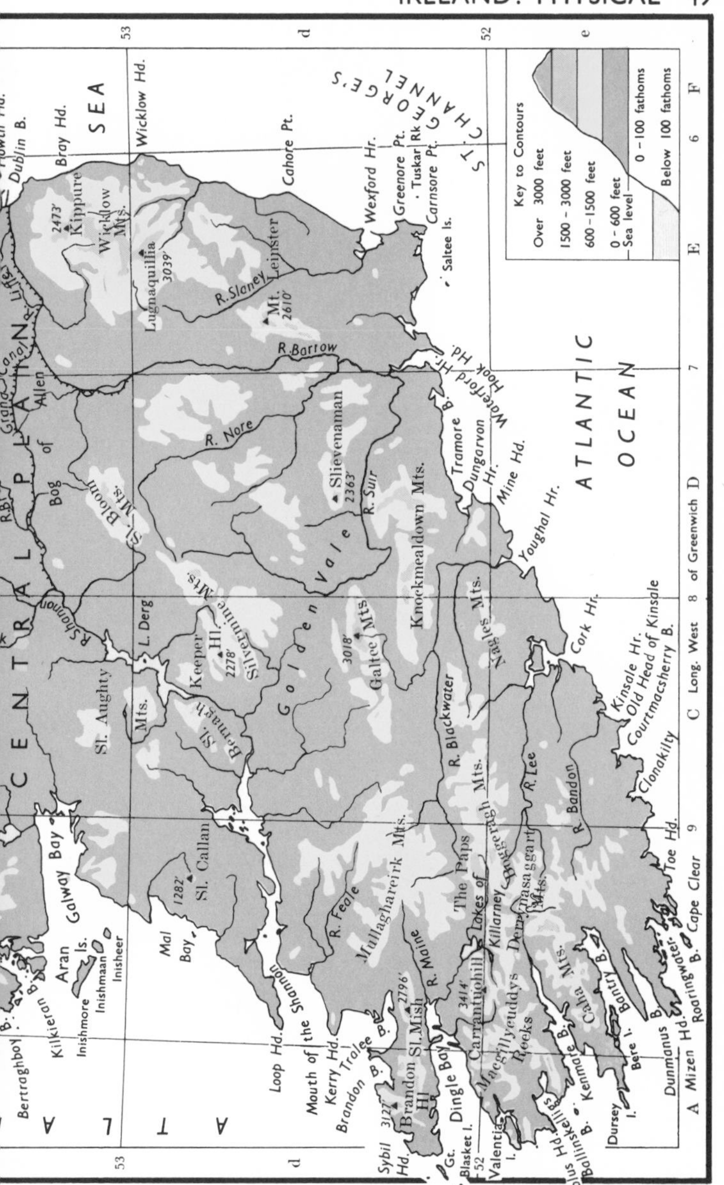

CENTRAL PLAIN
ATLANTIC OCEAN
SEA
ST. GEORGE'S CHANNEL
Dublin B.
Bray Hd.
Wicklow Hd.
Kippure 2473'
Wicklow Mts.
Lugnaquillia 3039'
Mt. Leinster 2610'
R. Slaney
R. Barrow
Grand Canal
Bog of Allen
Sl. Bloom Mts.
R. Nore
Slievenaman 2363'
R. Suir
Golden Vale
Galtee Mts. 3018'
Knockmealdown Mts.
Cahore Pt.
Wexford Hr.
Greenore Pt.
Tuskar Rk
Carnsore Pt.
Saltee Is.
Hook Hd.
Waterford Hr.
Tramore B.
Dungarvan Hr.
Mine Hd.
Youghal Hr.
Cork Hr.
Kinsale Hr.
Old Head of Kinsale
Courtmacsherry B.
Clonakilty
Toe Hd.
Cape Clear
Roaringwater B.
Mizen Hd.
Dunmanus B.
Bantry B.
Bere I.
Dursey I.
Kenmare B.
Ballinskelligs B.
Bolus Hd.
Valentia I.
Gt. Blasket I.
Sybil Hd.
Dingle Bay
Brandon Hd. 3127'
Brandon B.
Tralee B.
Kerry Hd.
Mouth of the Shannon
Loop Hd.
Sl. Mish 2796'
Carrantuohill 3414'
Macgillycuddys Reeks
Caha Mts.
Derrynasaggart Mts.
Boggeragh Mts.
Lakes of Killarney
The Paps
R. Maine
R. Feale
Mullaghareirk Mts.
R. Blackwater
Nagles Mts.
R. Lee
R. Bandon
Shannon
Mal Bay
Sl. Callan 1282'
Galway Bay
Aran Is.
Inishmore
Inishmaan
Inisheer
Kilkieran B.
Bertraghboy B.
Sl. Aughty Mts.
L. Derg
R. Shannon
Keeper Hl. 2278'
Silvermine Mts.
Sl. Bernagh
Key to Contours
Over 3000 feet
1500 - 3000 feet
600 - 1500 feet
0 - 600 feet
Sea level
0 - 100 fathoms
Below 100 fathoms
Long. West 8 of Greenwich

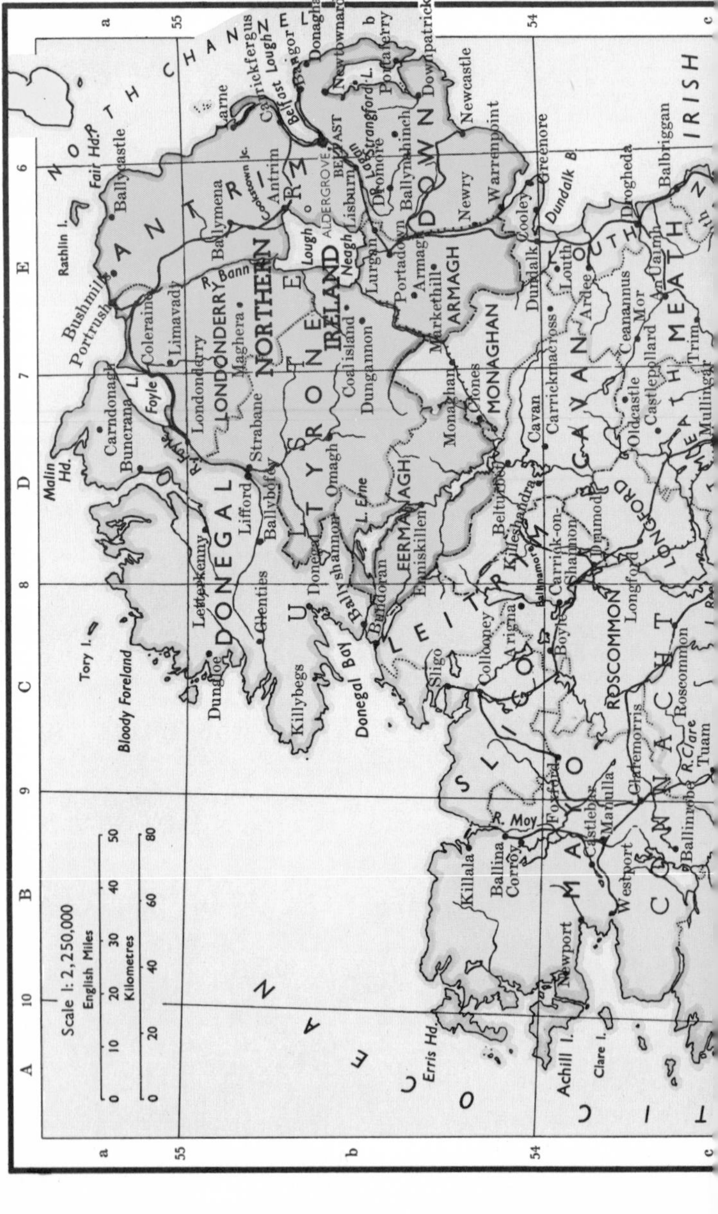

NORTH CHANNEL
IRISH
Scale 1: 2,250,000
English Miles
0 10 20 30 40 50
Kilometres
0 20 40 60 80
NORTHERN IRELAND
ANTRIM
LONDONDERRY
TYRONE
FERMANAGH
ARMAGH
DOWN
DONEGAL
MONAGHAN
CAVAN
LEITRIM
SLIGO
MAYO
ROSCOMMON
LONGFORD
LOUTH
MEATH
CONNACHT
ULSTER
Rathlin I.
Fair Hd.
Ballycastle
Bushmills
Portrush
Coleraine
Limavady
Ballymena
Larne
Carrickfergus
Belfast Lough
Bangor
Donaghadee
Newtownards
Strangford L.
Portaferry
Downpatrick
Newcastle
Warrenpoint
Newry
Ballynahinch
Dromore
Lisburn
BELFAST
ALDERGROVE
Antrim
Cookstown Jc.
Lough Neagh
R. Bann
Maghera
Londonderry
Strabane
L. Foyle
Carndonagh
Buncrana
Malin Hd.
Letterkenny
Lifford
Ballybofey
Omagh
Coalisland
Dungannon
Portadown
Lurgan
Armagh
Markethill
Monaghan
Clones
Cooley
Greenore
Dundalk B.
Dundalk
Louth
Ardee
Drogheda
Balbriggan
Carrickmacross
Cavan
Belturbet
Killeshandra
Ballinamore
Carrick-on-Shannon
Drumod
Longford
Ceanannus Mor
Oldcastle
Castlepollard
Trim
Mullingar
An Uaimh
L. Erne
Enniskillen
Ballyshannon
Bundoran
Donegal
Donegal Bay
Killybegs
Glenties
Dungloe
Tory I.
Bloody Foreland
Sligo
Collooney
Arigna
Boyle
Roscommon
Castlerea
Claremorris
Tuam
R. Clare
Ballinrobe
Castlebar
Manulla
Foxford
R. Moy
Ballina
Corroy
Killala
Westport
Newport
Achill I.
Clare I.
Erris Hd.

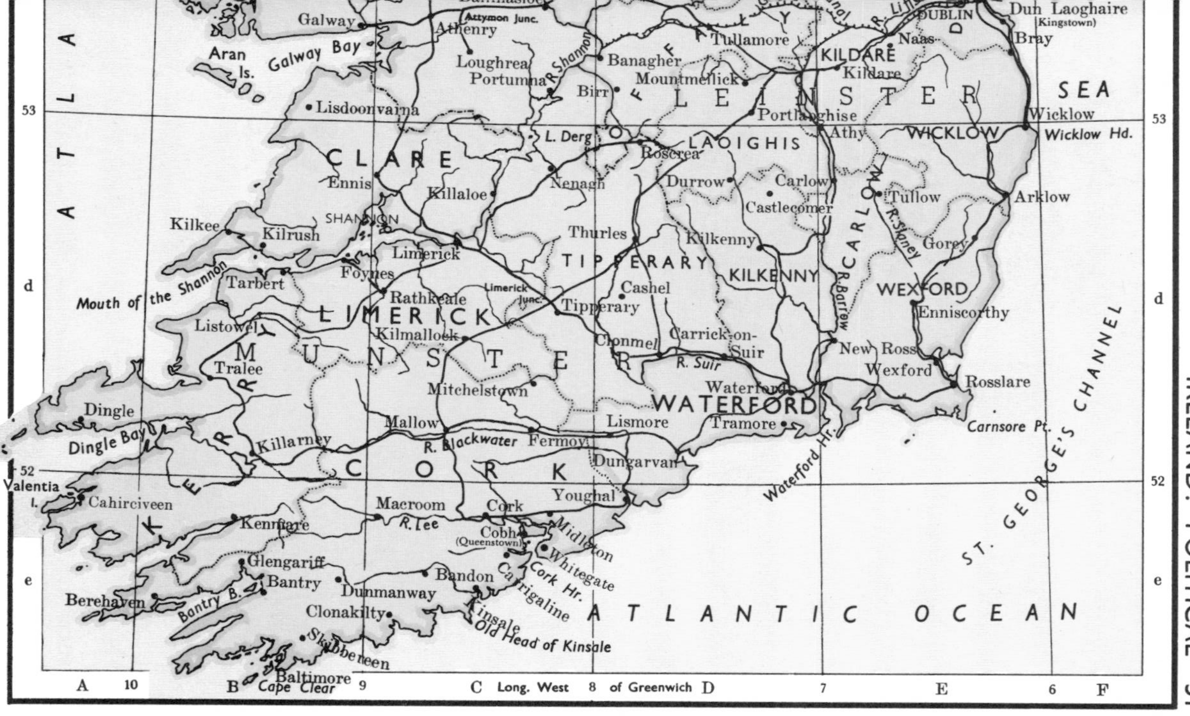

Galway
Attymon Junc.
Athenry
Aran Is.
Galway Bay
Loughrea
Portumna
R. Shannon
Banagher
Birr
Tullamore
Mountmellick
KILDARE
Kildare
Naas
DUBLIN
Dun Laoghaire
(Kingstown)
Bray
LEINSTER
SEA
Lisdoonvarna
Portlaoighise
Wicklow
Wicklow Hd.
Athy
WICKLOW
L. Derg
Roscrea
LAOIGHIS
CLARE
Ennis
Nenagh
Killaloe
Durrow
Carlow
Castlecomer
CARLOW
Tullow
R. Slaney
Arklow
SHANNON
Kilkee
Kilrush
Thurles
Kilkenny
Gorey
Limerick
TIPPERARY
KILKENNY
WEXFORD
R. Barrow
Mouth of the Shannon
Tarbert
Foynes
Rathkeale
Limerick Junc.
Tipperary
Cashel
Enniscorthy
LIMERICK
Listowel
Kilmalloch
Clonmel
Carrick-on-Suir
New Ross
MUNSTER
Tralee
R. Suir
Wexford
Rosslare
Mitchelstown
Waterford
WATERFORD
ST. GEORGE'S CHANNEL
Dingle
Mallow
Lismore
Tramore
Carnsore Pt.
Dingle Bay
Killarney
R. Blackwater
Fermoy
KERRY
Dungarvan
CORK
Waterford Hr.
Valentia I.
Cahirciveen
Macroom
Cork
Youghal
Kenmare
R. Lee
Cobh
(Queenstown)
Midleton
Whitegate
Glengariff
Bantry
Bandon
Cork Hr.
Berehaven
Bantry B.
Dunmanway
Carrigaline
Clonakilty
Kinsale
ATLANTIC OCEAN
Old Head of Kinsale
Skibbereen
Baltimore
Cape Clear
A 10 B 9 C Long. West 8 of Greenwich D 7 E 6 F
53 d 52 e

SHIPPING FORECAST CHART
Scale 1 : 45,000,000
SOUTH-EAST ICELAND
FAEROES
FAIR ISLE
VIKING
BAILEY
HEBRIDES
CROMARTY
FORTIES
FORTH
FISHER
ROCKALL
MALIN
TYNE
DOGGER
GERMAN BIGHT
IRISH SEA
HUMBER
THAMES
SHANNON
LUNDY
FASTNET
DOVER
WIGHT
SOLE
PLYMOUTH
PORTLAND
FINISTERRE
BISCAY
Long. 5 West
SCOTLAND
NORTHERN IRELAND
EIRE
WALES
ATLANTIC
OCEAN
IRISH SEA
Orkney Islands
Kirkwall
Thurso
Wick
Outer Hebrides
The Minch
Stornoway
Benbecula
Skye
Barra
Tiree
Mull
Islay
Moray Firth
Dingwall
DALCROSS
Inverness
Mallaig
Tobermory
Oban
DYCE
Dundee
Perth
Stirling
Firth of Forth
Greenock
TURNHOUSE
Leith
Edinburgh
RENFREW
Glasgow
PRESTWICK
Ayr
PORT ELLEN
MACHRIHANISH
Malin Hd.
to Greenock 248
Londonderry
Larne
ALDERGROVE
Belfast
North Channel
Dumfries
Stranraer
Newcastle
Carlisle
Solway Firth
Donegal Bay
Sligo
Newry
Dundalk
Isle of Man
Douglas
RONALDSWAY
Heysham
Barrow
Lancaster
Preston
Blackpool
Bradford
Bolton
Liverpool
Birkenhead
SPEKE
RINGWAY
Athlone
COLLINSTOWN
DUBLIN
Galway
Shannon
Holyhead
Anglesey
Chester
Crewe
Stoke
Dun Laoghaire
SHANNON
Limerick
Stafford
Shrewsbury
Wolverhampton
Birmingham
Dingle
Wexford
Waterford
Rosslare
St. George's Channel
Cork
Cobh
Bantry
Fishguard
St. David's Hd.
Hereford
Newport
Swansea
Cardiff
Bristol
Bristol Channel
WHITCHURCH
Salisbury
Southampton
HURN
Fastnet Rock
Liverpool to Quebec 3228, New York 3512
Lundy I.
Barnstaple
Exeter
Weymouth
Plymouth
ST. JUST
Lands End
Scilly Is.
Falmouth
Penzance
ENGLISH
Southampton to Quebec 3320, New York 3560
to Cape Town 6195
Guernsey
Channel Islands (Br.)
Jersey
Key to Contours
Over 3000 feet
1500 - 3000 feet
600 - 1500 feet
0 - 600 feet
Sea level
Below sea level
0 - 100 fathoms
100 - 1000 fathoms
Below 1000 fathoms
Long. 4 West

Scale 1 : 7,500,000
Miles
Kilometres
Principal Railways
Airports
Canals
Steamship Routes
(Distances in Statute Miles)
NORTH SEA
NORWAY
Stavanger
Arendal
Kristiansand
Lindesnes
Skagerrak
The Skaw
To Baltic Ports
Frederikshavn
Aalborg
Lim Fiord
DENMARK
Aarhus
Horsens
Esbjerg
Odense
Funen
Flensburg
North Frisian Is.
Heligoland
Kiel
Kiel Canal
Cuxhaven
Elbe
FUHLSBUTTEL
Hamburg
Wilhelmshaven
Emden
East Frisian Is.
West Frisian Is.
Dogger Bank
to Oslo 551
to Oslo 616
to Oslo 615
to Bergen 451
to Hamburg 552
to Hamburg 470
Flamborough Hd.
Grimsby
Humber
The Wash
Gt. Yarmouth
Norwich
Cambridge
Bedford
Luton
Northampton
Ipswich
Harwich
Southend
LONDON
Thames
ROCHESTER
Tilbury
Dover
GATWICK
Folkestone
LYDD
Strait of Dover
Newhaven
Brighton
Dieppe
Le Havre
Rouen
Seine
PARIS
LE BOURGET
Amiens
Reims
FRANCE
Boulogne
LE TOUQUET
Calais
Dunkirk
Lille
Ostend
Flushing
Ghent
Antwerp
BRUSSELS
MELSBROECK
BELGIUM
Meuse
Namur
Charleroi
Liege
LUX.
LUXEMBOURG
Saarbrucken
IJmuiden
Amsterdam
SCHIPHOL
THE HAGUE
Hook of Holland
Rotterdam
Utrecht
Arnhem
Leeuwarden
Groningen
IJsselmeer
NETHERLANDS
Tilburg
Eindhoven
Munchen Gladbach
Aachen
Maas
Duisburg
Hamborn
Essen
Wuppertal
Dusseldorf
Cologne
BONN
Koblenz
Moselle
Rhine
Frankfurt
Mannheim
GERMANY
WESTERN
Munster
Dortmund
Dortmund Ems Canal
Ems
Mittelland Canal
Osnabruck
Bielefeld
Hanover
Bremen
Weser
Long. 4 East

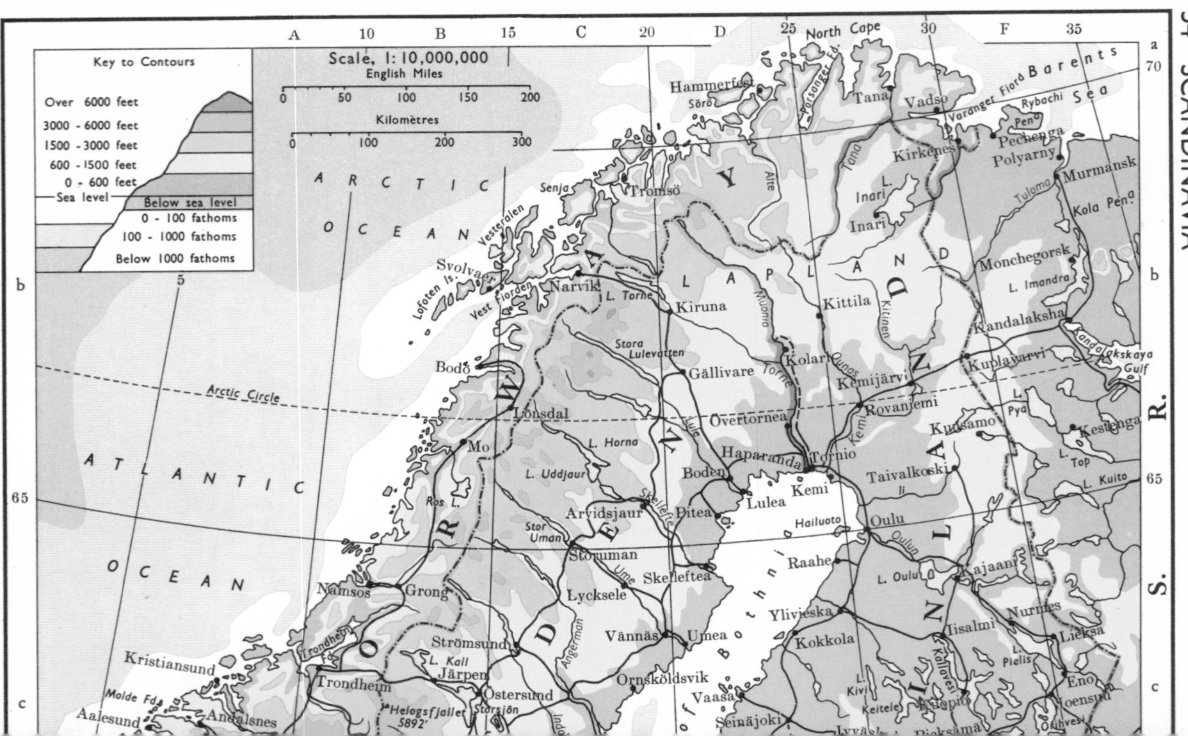

Key to Contours
Over 6000 feet
3000 - 6000 feet
1500 - 3000 feet
600 - 1500 feet
0 - 600 feet
Sea level
Below sea level
0 - 100 fathoms
100 - 1000 fathoms
Below 1000 fathoms
Scale, 1: 10,000,000
English Miles
0 50 100 150 200
Kilomètres
0 100 200 300
ARCTIC OCEAN
ATLANTIC OCEAN
Barents Sea
Arctic Circle
North Cape
Porsanger Fd.
Varanger Fiord
Rybachi Pen.
Kola Pen.
Kandalakskaya Gulf
Lofoten Is.
Vesteraalen
Vest Fiorden
Senja
Sörö
Hammerfest
Tromsö
Tana
Vadsö
Kirkenes
Pechenga
Polyarny
Murmansk
Tuloma
Monchegorsk
L. Imandra
Kandalaksha
Kuplayarvi
Kestenga
L. Top
L. Kuito
L. Pya
Kuusamo
L. Inari
Inari
Kitinen
Kittila
Ounas
Kolari
Kemijärvi
Rovaniemi
Kemi
Taivalkoski
Ii
Oulu
Oulun
L. Oulu
Kajaani
Nurmes
Lieksa
L. Pielis
Eno
Joensuu
Orihvesi
Iisalmi
Kallavesi
Kuopio
Keitele
L. Kivi
Kokkola
Ylivieska
Raahe
Hailuoto
Seinäjoki
Vaasa
Gulf of Bothnia
Tornio
Haparanda
Overtornea
Torne
Muonio
Alte
Kiruna
Gällivare
Stora Lulevatten
L. Torne
Narvik
Lule
Boden
Lulea
Pitea
Skellefte
Skelleftea
Umea
Ume
Vännäs
Örnsköldsvik
Lycksele
Storuman
Stor Uman
Arvidsjaur
L. Horna
L. Uddjaur
Angerman
Lönsdal
Bodö
Svolvaer
Mo
Ros L.
Grong
Namsos
Strömsund
Östersund
Storsjön
Järpen
L. Kall
Helogsfjallet 5892'
Trondheim
Trondheim Fd.
Kristiansund
Andalsnes
Molde Fd.
Aalesund
LAPLAND
FINLAND
NORWAY
SWEDEN
U.S.S.R.

Galdhopiggen
8097'
Sogne Fiord
Hardanger Fiord
Hardanger Field
Fagernes
Bergen
Haugesund
Stavanger
Egersund
Dalen
Otra
Lindesnes
Kristiansand
Arendal
Skagerrak
The Skaw
Glomma
Lillehammer
Hamar
Kongsvinger
OSLO
Oslo Fiord
Drammen
Tonsberg
Skien
Larvik
Moss
Frederikstad
Strömstad
Vänersborg
Uddevalla
Särna
Sveg
Ljusdal
Oster Dal
Vaster Dal
Siljan
Malung
Klar
Leksand
Falun
Dal
Ludvika
Avesta
Filipstad
Karlstad
Kristinehamn
Västerås
Örebro
Amal
L. Väner
Lidköping
Skövde
Trollhättan
Alingsås
Borås
Gota
Göteborg
Jönköping
L. Vätter
Motala
Norrköping
Eskilstuna
Katrineholm
Nykoping
Linköping
Vimmerby
Tranås
Nässjö
Vetlanda
Oskarshamn
Värnamo
Växjö
Nybro
Kalmar
Öland
Karlskrona
Kristianstad
Atran
L. Bolmen
Lagan
Falkenberg
Kattegat
Halmstad
Angelholm
Hälsingborg
Helsingör
Landskrona
Malmö
Ystad
Bornholm
(Den.)
Hudiksvall
Söderhamn
Gävle
Öregrund
Sala
Uppsala
Molaren
STOCKHOLM
Norrtälje
Södertälje
Gulf of Bothnia
Baltic Sea
Visby
Larbro
Gotland
Burgsvik
Frederikshavn
Lim Fiord
Aalborg
Nykobing
Viborg
Randers
Aarhus
Horsens
North Sea
Ringkobing
DENMARK
Fredericia
Esbjerg
Kolding
Odense
Fünen
Zealand
COPENHAGEN
Korsor
Möen
Tonder
Sylt
Flensburg
Lolland
Falster
Heligoland
Schleswig
Canal
Kiel
Lübeck
Lübeck B.
Cuxhaven
Weser
Elbe
Wilhelmshaven
Hamburg
GERMANY
Stralsund
Rostock
Sassnitz
Rügen
Usedom I.
Swinoujscie
Szczecin
Kolobrzeg
Slupsk
Gdynia
G. of Danzig
Gdansk
POLAND
Tampere
Pori
Rauma
Akaa
Hämeenlinna
Uusikaupunki
Loimaa
Turku
Riihimäki
Salo
HELSINKI
Aland Is.
(Fin.)
Mariehamn
Hango
Porkkala
Lahti
Mikkeli
L. Saimaa
Kouvola
Borga
Kotka
Vyborg
Lake Ladoga
Gulf of Finland
Kronstadt
Leningrad
Gatchina
TALLINN
Paldiski
Tapa
Narva
Luga
Lake Chudskoe
(L. Peipus)
ESTONIA
Parnu
Tartu
Valga
Pskov
Hiiu I.
Saare I.
Gulf of Riga
Ventspils
Venta
Riga
LATVIA
Rezekne
Jelgava
Krustpils
Dvina
Daugavpils
Liepaja
Siauliai
Polotsk
Klaipeda
LITHUANIA
Sovetsk
Niemen
Kaunas
VILNIUS
WHITE RUSSIA
Kaliningrad
Chernyakhovsk
Suwalki
Grodno
MINSK
A
B
C
D
E
d
e
60
55
15
25
Long. East 20 of Greenwich

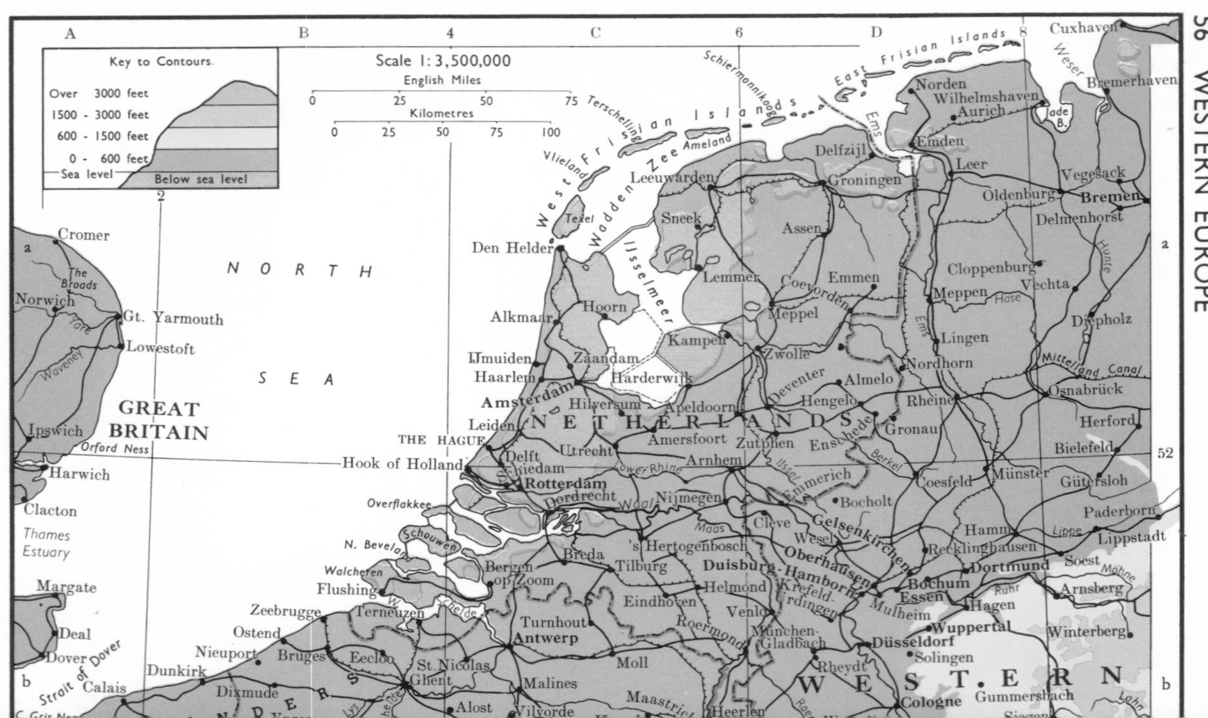
Key to Contours.
Over 3000 feet
1500 - 3000 feet
600 - 1500 feet
0 - 600 feet
Sea level
Below sea level
Scale 1: 3,500,000
English Miles
0 25 50 75
Kilometres
0 25 50 75 100
NORTH SEA
GREAT BRITAIN
NETHERLANDS
WESTERN
West Frisian Islands
East Frisian Islands
Wadden Zee
IJsselmeer
Texel
Vlieland
Terschelling
Ameland
Schiermonnikoog
Cuxhaven
Bremerhaven
Weser
Jade B.
Norden
Wilhelmshaven
Aurich
Emden
Ems
Delfzijl
Leer
Vegesack
Bremen
Oldenburg
Delmenhorst
Groningen
Leeuwarden
Sneek
Assen
Den Helder
Lemmer
Coevorden
Emmen
Cloppenburg
Vechta
Meppen
Hase
Diepholz
Hunte
Alkmaar
Hoorn
Meppel
Lingen
Kampen
Zwolle
IJmuiden
Zaandam
Harderwijk
Nordhorn
Mittelland Canal
Haarlem
Amsterdam
Deventer
Almelo
Osnabrück
Hilversum
Apeldoorn
Hengelo
Rheine
Herford
Leiden
Gronau
THE HAGUE
Amersfoort
Zutphen
Enschede
Bielefeld
Utrecht
Berkel
52
Hook of Holland
Delft
Schiedam
Arnhem
Lower Rhine
IJssel
Emmerich
Coesfeld
Münster
Gütersloh
Rotterdam
Dordrecht
Waal
Nijmegen
Bocholt
Paderborn
Overflakkee
Cleve
Gelsenkirchen
Hamm
Lippe
Lippstadt
Schouwen
Maas
Wesel
Recklinghausen
Soest
N. Beveland
's Hertogenbosch
Oberhausen
Möhne
Breda
Tilburg
Duisburg-Hamborn
Dortmund
Walcheren
Bergen op Zoom
Bochum
Arnsberg
Flushing
Helmond
Krefeld-Uerdingen
Essen
Ruhr
Zeebrugge
Terneuzen
W. Schelde
Eindhoven
Mulheim
Hagen
Venlo
Wuppertal
Turnhout
Roermond
Winterberg
Ostend
Antwerp
München-Gladbach
Düsseldorf
Nieuport
Bruges
Eecloo
Solingen
St. Nicolas
Moll
Rheydt
Dunkirk
Ghent
Malines
Cologne
Gummersbach
Dixmude
Lys
Maastricht
Heerlen
Alost
Vilvorde
Lahn
Cromer
The Broads
Norwich
Yare
Gt. Yarmouth
Lowestoft
Waveney
Ipswich
Orford Ness
Harwich
Clacton
Thames Estuary
Margate
Deal
Dover
Strait of Dover
Calais

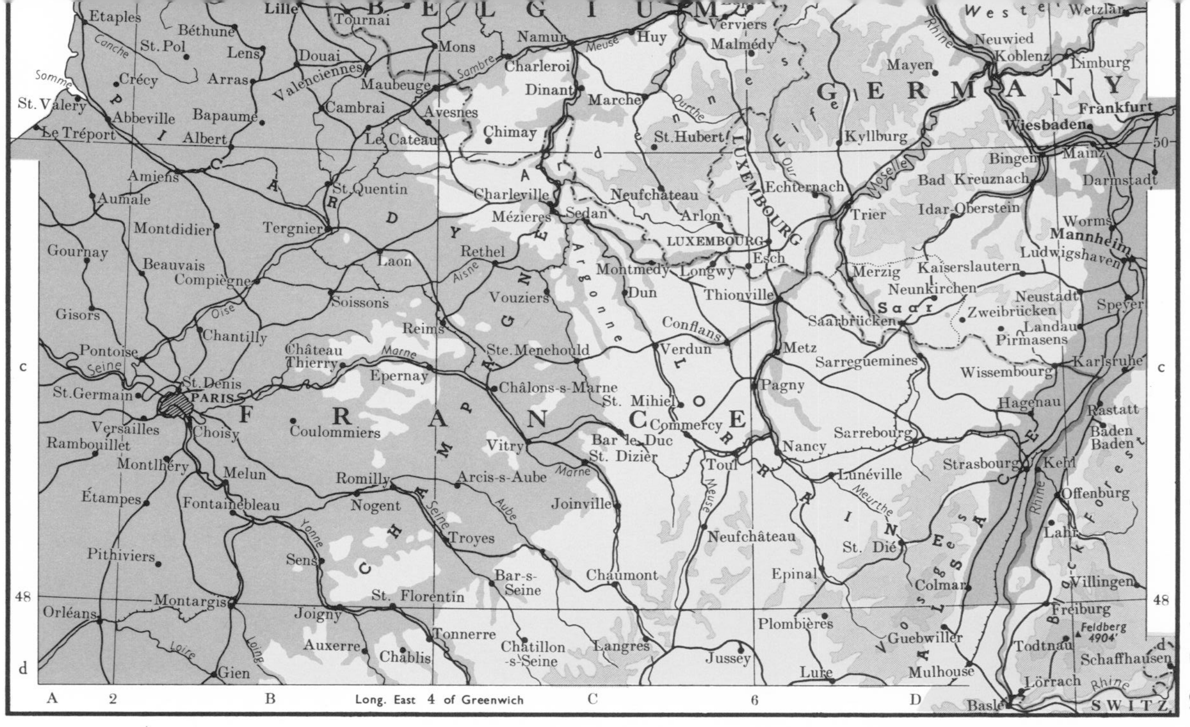
BELGIUM
GERMANY
FRANCE
LUXEMBOURG
SAAR
SWITZ.
ARDENNES
EIFEL
LORRAINE
ALSACE
VOSGES
CHAMPAGNE
PICARDY
Argonne
Black Forest
Westerwald
Long. East 4 of Greenwich
Lille
Tournai
Mons
Namur
Huy
Verviers
Malmédy
Charleroi
Dinant
Marche
St. Hubert
Neufchateau
Arlon
Chimay
Maubeuge
Avesnes
Valenciennes
Douai
Cambrai
Le Cateau
St. Quentin
Etaples
Béthune
Lens
Arras
Bapaume
Albert
St. Pol
Crécy
Abbeville
St. Valery
Le Tréport
Amiens
Aumale
Montdidier
Beauvais
Compiègne
Tergnier
Laon
Soissons
Reims
Rethel
Charleville
Mézieres
Sedan
Montmedy
Longwy
Esch
Thionville
Metz
Verdun
Conflans
Dun
Vouziers
Ste. Menehould
Châlons-s-Marne
St. Mihiel
Commercy
Toul
Nancy
Pagny
Lunéville
Sarrebourg
Sarreguemines
Saarbrücken
Merzig
Trier
Echternach
Kyllburg
Mayen
Neuwied
Koblenz
Limburg
Wetzlar
Wiesbaden
Frankfurt
Mainz
Darmstadt
Bingen
Bad Kreuznach
Idar-Oberstein
Kaiserslautern
Neunkirchen
Zweibrücken
Pirmasens
Landau
Neustadt
Ludwigshaven
Mannheim
Worms
Speyer
Karlsruhe
Rastatt
Baden Baden
Offenburg
Kehl
Lahr
Villingen
Freiburg
Feldberg 4904'
Todtnau
Schaffhausen
Lörrach
Basle
Mulhouse
Guebwiller
Colmar
Strasbourg
Hagenau
Wissembourg
St. Dié
Epinal
Plombières
Lure
Neufchâteau
Jussey
Langres
Chaumont
Joinville
St. Dizier
Bar le Duc
Vitry
Arcis-s-Aube
Troyes
Bar-s-Seine
Châtillon -s-Seine
Tonnerre
Chablis
Auxerre
St. Florentin
Joigny
Sens
Nogent
Romilly
Epernay
Château Thierry
Coulommiers
Chantilly
St. Denis
PARIS
Choisy
Melun
Fontainebleau
Montargis
Gien
Orléans
Pithiviers
Étampes
Montlhéry
Versailles
St. Germain
Rambouillet
Pontoise
Gisors
Gournay
Rhine
Moselle
Meuse
Sambre
Somme
Oise
Marne
Aisne
Aube
Seine
Yonne
Loing
Loire
Ourthe
Our
Meurthe
Canche

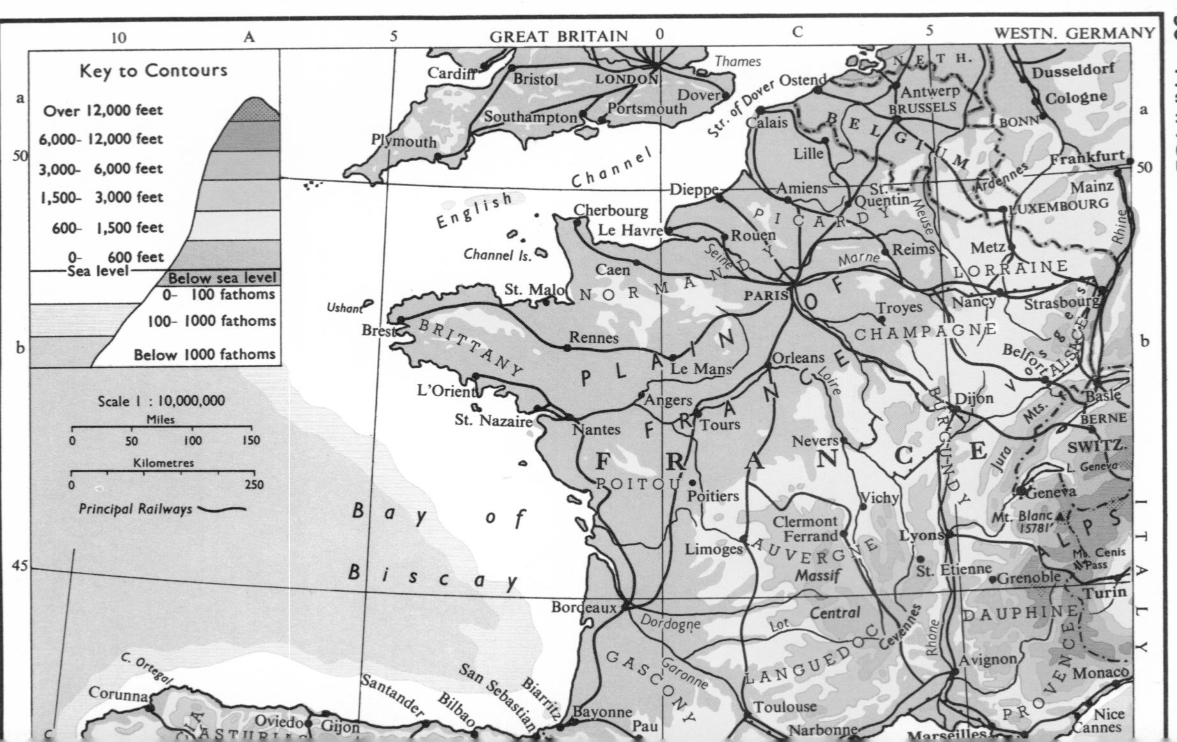
Key to Contours
Over 12,000 feet
6,000– 12,000 feet
3,000– 6,000 feet
1,500– 3,000 feet
600– 1,500 feet
0– 600 feet
Sea level
Below sea level
0– 100 fathoms
100– 1000 fathoms
Below 1000 fathoms
Scale 1 : 10,000,000
Miles
0 50 100 150
Kilometres
0 250
Principal Railways
GREAT BRITAIN
WESTN. GERMANY
ITALY
SWITZ.
BELGIUM
NETH.
LUXEMBOURG
FRANCE
English Channel
Str. of Dover
Bay of Biscay
Channel Is.
Ushant
LONDON
Bristol
Cardiff
Plymouth
Southampton
Portsmouth
Dover
Thames
BRUSSELS
Antwerp
Ostend
Dusseldorf
Cologne
BONN
Frankfurt
Mainz
Rhine
Ardennes
Meuse
Calais
Lille
Amiens
St. Quentin
Dieppe
Rouen
Le Havre
Cherbourg
Caen
PARIS
Reims
Metz
Nancy
Strasbourg
Troyes
Seine
Marne
St. Malo
Rennes
Le Mans
Orleans
Loire
Angers
Tours
Nantes
St. Nazaire
L'Orient
Brest
Belfort
Basle
BERNE
Dijon
Geneva
L. Geneva
Jura
Mt. Blanc 15781'
Mt. Cenis Pass
Turin
Grenoble
Lyons
St. Etienne
Rhone
Vichy
Nevers
Clermont Ferrand
Poitiers
Limoges
Massif Central
Cevennes
Avignon
Monaco
Nice
Cannes
Marseilles
Narbonne
Toulouse
Lot
Dordogne
Garonne
Bordeaux
Bayonne
Pau
Biarritz
San Sebastian
Bilbao
Santander
Gijon
Oviedo
Corunna
C. Ortegal
ASTURIAS
NORMANDY
BRITTANY
PICARDY
CHAMPAGNE
LORRAINE
ALSACE
BURGUNDY
AUVERGNE
LANGUEDOC
GASCONY
POITOU
DAUPHINE
PROVENCE
ALPS
Vosges Mts.
PLAIN OF FRANCE
10
A
5
0
C
5
a
b
50
45

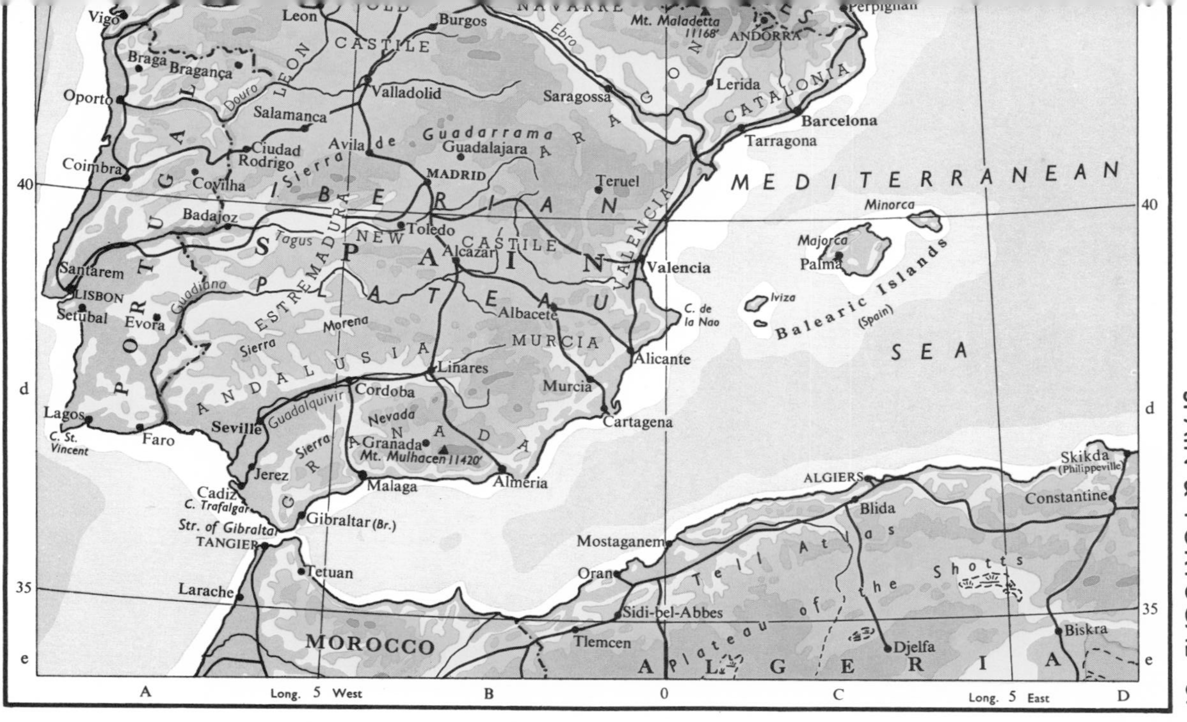
MEDITERRANEAN
SEA
Balearic Islands
(Spain)
Minorca
Majorca
Palma
Iviza
C. de la Nao
Perpignan
ANDORRA
Mt. Maladetta 11168'
CATALONIA
Barcelona
Tarragona
Lerida
Ebro
ARAGON
Saragossa
Teruel
Valencia
VALENCIA
Alicante
Cartagena
Murcia
MURCIA
Albacete
Alcazar
NEW CASTILE
Toledo
MADRID
Guadalajara
Sierra de Guadarrama
Burgos
Valladolid
CASTILE
Leon
LEON
Salamanca
Avila
Ciudad Rodrigo
Douro
Bragança
Braga
Vigo
Oporto
Coimbra
Covilha
PORTUGAL
Badajoz
Tagus
ESTREMADURA
Santarem
LISBON
Setubal
Evora
Guadiana
Sierra Morena
Faro
Lagos
C. St. Vincent
ANDALUSIA
Guadalquivir
Cordoba
Linares
Seville
Jerez
Cadiz
C. Trafalgar
Sierra Nevada
GRANADA
Granada
Mt. Mulhacen 11420'
Malaga
Almeria
Gibraltar (Br.)
Str. of Gibraltar
TANGIER
Tetuan
Larache
MOROCCO
IBERIAN PENINSULA
SPAIN
Oran
Mostaganem
Sidi-bel-Abbes
Tlemcen
ALGIERS
Blida
Djelfa
Constantine
Skikda (Philippeville)
Biskra
Tell Atlas
Plateau of the Shotts
ALGERIA
40
35
d
e
A
B
C
D
0
Long. 5 West
Long. 5 East

WESTERN GERMANY
FRANCE
ALGERIA
TUNISIA
Munich
Linz
VIENNA
Salzburg
L. Constance
Basle
Zurich
BERNE
Luzern
Innsbruck
AUSTRIA
Szombath
Graz
SWITZERLAND
Lausanne
L. Geneva
Jura Mts.
Geneva
Simplon Pass
St. Gotthard Pass
TRENT-ALTO ADIGE
Brenner Pass
Klagenfurt
Bolzano
Mt. Blanc 15781'
V. D'AOSTA
THE ALPS
L. Como
L. Garda
Trento
VENETO
FRIULI-VEN. GIULIA
Ljubljana
SLOVENIA
Zagreb
Milan
Brescia
Trieste
Mt. Cenis Pass
PIEDMONT
LOMBARDY
Verona
Plain of Lombardy
Turin
Venice
Rijeka
CROATIA
Parma
Po
EMILIA-ROMAGNA
Bologna
BOSNIA
LIGURIA
Genoa
Spezia
Riviera
Gulf of Genoa
Forli
Rimini
SAN MARINO
Zadar
Monaco
Nice
Pisa
Leghorn
Florence
TUSCANY
MARCHES
Ancona
ADRIATIC
APENNINES
Split
Toulon
C. Corse
Bastia
Perugia
UMBRIA
Elba
Corsica (Fr.)
Ajaccio
9583'
Mt. Corno
ABRUZZI
Tiber
LATIUM
MOLISE
ROME
Str. of Bonifacio
Cassino
Anzio
Foggia
CAMPANIA
APULIA
Vesuvius
Sassari
Olbia
Naples
Potenza
Taran
Sardinia (Italy)
Capri
Salerno
BASILICATA
Oristano
TYRRHENIAN SEA
Cosenza
Cagliari
C. Spartivento
Str. of Messina
CALABRIA
Stromboli
MEDITERRANEAN SEA
Messina
Trapani
Palermo
Reggio
C. Spartive
Mt. Etna 10741'
Skikda (Philippeville)
Annaba
Bizerta
Sicily
Catania
C. Bon
Ragusa
Syracuse
TUNIS
Pantelleria (It.)
C. Passero
Susa
Qairwan
MALTA

Key to Contours
Over 12000 feet
6000 - 12000 feet
3000 - 6000 feet
1500 - 3000 feet
600 - 1500 feet
0 - 600 feet
Sea level
Below sea level
0 - 100 fathoms
100 - 1000 fathoms
Below 1000 fathoms
Miskolc
Debrecen
Satu Mare
Hungarian Plain
Szolnok
Oradea
Cluj
TRANSYLVANIA
Carpathian Mts.
Muresul
Tisa
Kecskemet
Szeged
Arad
Subotica
ROMANIA
Sibiu
Timisoara
BANAT
VOJVODINA
Transylvanian Alps
Novi Sad
Sava
BELGRADE
Iron Gates
Ploesti
WALLACHIA
BUCHAREST
Wallachian Plain
DOBRUJA
Constanta
Craiova
Svishtov
Russe
Danube
Pleven
Kolarovgrad
Varna
Kragujevac
SERBIA
Balkan Mts.
Nis
Trnovo
BULGARIA
BLACK SEA
Burgas
MONTENEGRO
SOFIA
Yambol
KOSMET
Plovdiv
Stara Zagora
Maritsa
Titograd
Rhodope Mts.
Edirne
Midye
Scutari
Skoplje
THRACE
Istanbul
Bosporus
Durazzo
TIRANA
MACEDONIA
Drama
Kavalla
Tekirdag
Sea of Marmara
Bitolj
ALBANIA
Brindisi
Thessaloniki
Gelibolu
Valona
Str. of Otranto
Mt. Olympus
9794'
Lemnos
Dardanelles
Balikesir
TURKEY
Corfu
Yannina
Pindus Mts.
Larissa
THESSALY
Volos
AEGEAN SEA
Mytilene
Giresun
Manisa
Ionian Is.
Lamia
Euboea
Chios
Izmir
IONIAN SEA
Agrinion
GREECE
Patras
ATHENS
Andros
Menderez
Corinth
Piraeus
Argos
Nauplia
Pyrgos
Cyclades
Dodecanese
Filiatra
PELOPONNESUS
Kalamata
Yithion
C. Matapan
Rhodes
Scale 1 : 10,000,000
Miles
0
50
100
150
Kilometres
0
250
Principal Railways
Canea
Candia
Crete
Long. 20 East
20
25
E
D
E
45
40
35
b
c

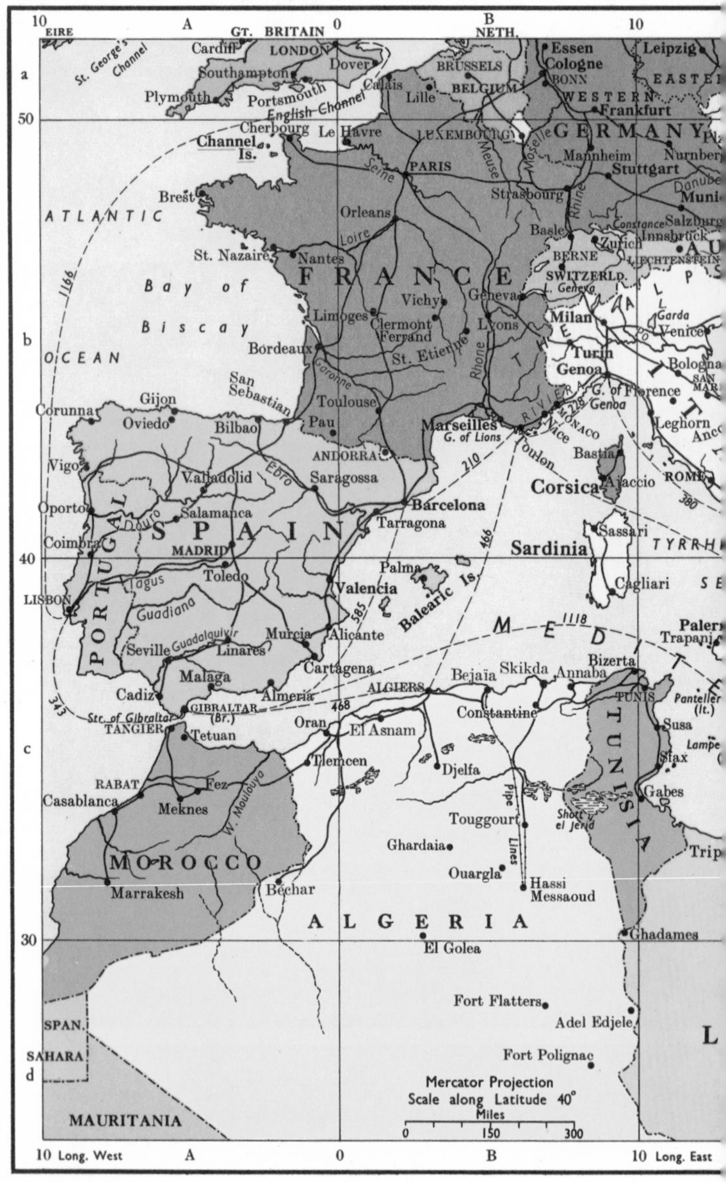
EIRE
GT. BRITAIN
NETH.
St. George's Channel
Cardiff
LONDON
Dover
Southampton
Plymouth
Portsmouth
Calais
English Channel
Lille
BRUSSELS
BELGIUM
Essen
Cologne
BONN
Leipzig
EASTERN
WESTERN
Frankfurt
GERMANY
Cherbourg
Le Havre
Channel Is.
LUXEMBOURG
Moselle
Meuse
Mannheim
Nurnberg
Stuttgart
Seine
PARIS
Danube
Brest
Strasbourg
Rhine
ATLANTIC
Orleans
Basle
Constance
Salzburg
Loire
Zurich
Innsbruck
St. Nazaire
Nantes
BERNE
LIECHTENSTEIN
FRANCE
SWITZERLD.
Bay of Biscay
L. Geneva
Geneva
Vichy
Limoges
Clermont Ferrand
Lyons
Milan
L. Garda
Venice
ALPS
Po
OCEAN
Bordeaux
St. Etienne
Rhone
Turin
Bologna
Genoa
SAN MARINO
Garonne
San Sebastian
RIVIERA
G. of Genoa
Florence
Gijon
Toulouse
MONACO
Corunna
Oviedo
Bilbao
Pau
Nice
Leghorn
Marseilles
G. of Lions
Toulon
Bastia
ANDORRA
Vigo
Ebro
Valladolid
Saragossa
Corsica
Ajaccio
ROME
Oporto
Douro
Salamanca
Barcelona
Tarragona
SPAIN
Coimbra
MADRID
Sardinia
Sassari
TYRRH
Toledo
Palma
Tagus
Valencia
Cagliari
LISBON
PORTUGAL
Guadiana
Balearic Is.
MEDITERRANEAN
Palermo
Trapani
Murcia
Alicante
Seville
Guadalquivir
Linares
Cartagena
Bizerta
Malaga
Bejaïa
Skikda
Annaba
Cadiz
Almeria
ALGIERS
TUNIS
Pantelleria (It.)
Str. of Gibraltar
GIBRALTAR (Br.)
Constantine
TANGIER
Oran
El Asnam
Susa
Tetuan
Lampedusa
Tlemcen
Sfax
TUNISIA
RABAT
Fez
Djelfa
Moulouya
Casablanca
Meknes
Gabes
Pipe Lines
Touggourt
Shott el Jerid
Ghardaia
Tripoli
MOROCCO
Ouargla
Marrakesh
Bechar
Hassi Messaoud
ALGERIA
Ghadames
El Golea
Fort Flatters
Adel Edjele
SPAN. SAHARA
Fort Polignac
Mercator Projection
Scale along Latitude 40°
Miles
0 150 300
MAURITANIA
1166
343
228
210
380
466
585
1118
468
a
b
c
d
50
40
30
10
A
0
B
10 Long. West
10 Long. East

C
20
D
30
E
a
50
b
40
c
30
d
POLAND
Wroclaw
Katowice
Lublin
Kiev
Dnieper
U. S. S. R.
Kharkov
Ostrava
Cracow
Przemysl
Lvov
Tarnopol
Brno
Kosice
UKRAINE
Dniester
Mogilev
Bratislava
Dnepropetrovsk
Miskolc
Tisza
Chernovtsy
MOLDAVIA
Prut
Zaporozhye
BUDAPEST
Debrecen
Satu Mare
HUNGARY
Jassy
Kishinev
Nikolaev
Berdyansk
Balaton
Cluj
Szeged
Arad
Sea of Azov
Pecs
ROMANIA
Odessa
Drava
Timisoara
Brasov
Galatz
Kerch
Zagreb
Novi Sad
Sava
Danube
Ploesti
Mouths of the Danube
Crimea
YUGO-
BELGRADE
BUCHAREST
Sevastopol
Yalta
Zadar
Craiova
Constanta
Sarajevo
DALMATIA
Russe
SLAVIA
Split
Nis
BLACK SEA
388
Varna
BULGARIA
Dubrovnik
SOFIA
Burgas
Inebolu
Sinope
ALBANIA
Plovdiv
Skoplje
Bosporus
Foggia
Durazzo
Edirne
Eregli
Bari
TIRANA
Kavalla
Istanbul
Uskudar
Samsun
Brindisi
GREECE
Sea of Marmara
Taranto
Thessaloniki
Valona
Dardanelles
ANKARA
G. of Taranto
Larissa
Balikesir
Yannina
Volos
AEGEAN SEA
TURKEY
IONIAN SEA
Euboea
Afyon
Tuz Golu
Reggio
Izmir
Patras
Pyrgos
ATHENS
Konya
Catania
Piraeus
Menderez
Adana
Syracuse
412
Kalamata
Dodecanese
Antalya
Mersin
MALTA
Cyclades
G. of Antalya
Iskenderon
Rhodes
1778
Aleppo
Canea
Candia
CYPRUS
Homs
Crete
NICOSIA
LEVANT
Limassol
Tripoli
SYRIA
674
893
LEBANON
BEIRUT
934
1065
260
DAMASCUS
236
MEDITERRANEAN SEA
Misurata
Derna
Haifa
Benghazi
BEIDA
Tel Aviv
Jaffa
AMMAN
Gulf of Sidra
Tobruk
Alexandria
Nile Delta
Port Said
JERUSALEM
Sirte
Agedabia
Matruh
Tanta
Suez Canal
JORDAN
El Ageila
ISRAEL
Maan
CAIRO
Suez
Eilat
Aqaba
Hun
El Faiyum
G. of Suez
G. of Aqaba
El Minya
SAUDI ARABIA
LIBYA
EGYPT
Asyut
RED SEA
Sebha
Nile
Qena
El Kharga
Principal Railways
Steamship Routes 466
(Distances in Statute Miles)

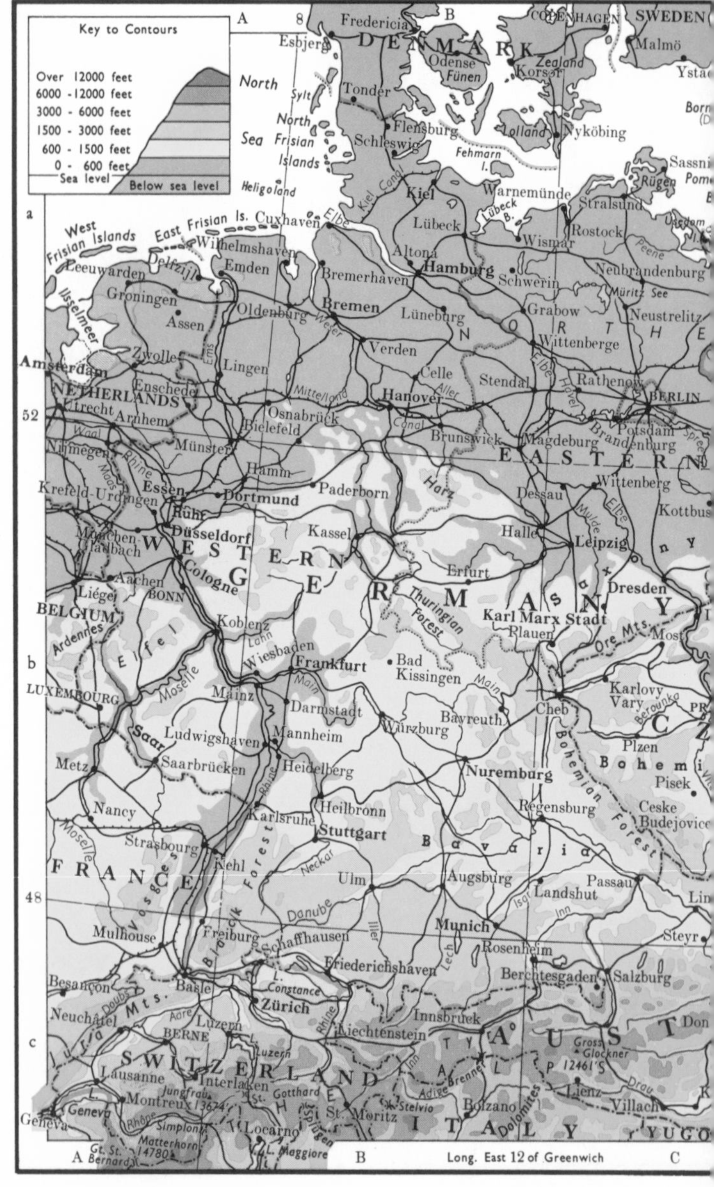
Key to Contours
Over 12000 feet
6000 - 12000 feet
3000 - 6000 feet
1500 - 3000 feet
600 - 1500 feet
0 - 600 feet
Sea level
Below sea level
DENMARK
COPENHAGEN
SWEDEN
Malmö
Fredericia
Esbjerg
Odense
Fünen
Zealand
Korsör
Tonder
Sylt
North Sea
North Frisian Islands
Flensburg
Schleswig
Lolland
Nyköbing
Fehmarn I.
Heligoland
Kiel Canal
Kiel
Warnemünde
Stralsund
Rügen
Lübeck
Lübeck B.
Rostock
Wismar
West Frisian Islands
East Frisian Is.
Cuxhaven
Elbe
Wilhelmshaven
Delfzijl
Emden
Leeuwarden
Groningen
Assen
Ijsselmeer
Altona
Hamburg
Schwerin
Neubrandenburg
Müritz See
Bremerhaven
Oldenburg
Bremen
Weser
Lüneburg
Grabow
Neustrelitz
Wittenberge
Verden
Zwolle
Amsterdam
Ems
Lingen
Celle
Stendal
Rathenow
BERLIN
Havel
NETHERLANDS
Enschede
Utrecht
Arnhem
Mittelland Canal
Hanover
Aller
Osnabrück
Bielefeld
Brunswick
Magdeburg
Potsdam
Brandenburg
Spree
Waal
Nijmegen
Münster
Maas
Rhine
Hamm
Paderborn
Harz
EASTERN
Wittenberg
Essen
Dortmund
Dessau
Krefeld-Urdingen
Ruhr
Düsseldorf
Kassel
Halle
Mulde
Leipzig
Kottbus
Mönchen-Gladbach
WESTERN GERMANY
Cologne
Erfurt
Aachen
Liége
BONN
Thuringian Forest
Dresden
BELGIUM
Karl Marx Stadt
Koblenz
Plauen
Ore Mts.
Most
Ardennes
Eifel
Lahn
Wiesbaden
Frankfurt
Bad Kissingen
Main
Moselle
LUXEMBOURG
Mainz
Darmstadt
Karlovy Vary
Berounka
Cheb
Bayreuth
Würzburg
Saar
Ludwigshaven
Mannheim
Plzen
Bohemia
Metz
Saarbrücken
Heidelberg
Nuremburg
Pisek
Nancy
Regensburg
Bohemian Forest
Heilbronn
Ceske Budejovice
Karlsruhe
Stuttgart
Strasbourg
Bavaria
Black Forest
Neckar
FRANCE
Vosges
Kehl
Ulm
Augsburg
Passau
Landshut
Isar
Inn
Danube
Iller
Lech
Munich
Mulhouse
Freiburg
Schaffhausen
Rosenheim
Steyr
Friederichshaven
Berchtesgaden
Salzburg
Besançon
Basle
L. Constance
Doubs
Jura Mts.
Zürich
Neuchâtel
Aare
Luzern
Innsbruck
BERNE
Liechtenstein
TYROL
AUSTRIA
Gross Glockner 12461'
L. Luzern
SWITZERLAND
Lausanne
Interlaken
Jungfrau 13674'
St. Gotthard
Brenner
Adige
Drau
Lienz
Villach
L. Geneva
Montreux
Stelvio
Bolzano
Dolomites
Rhône
Simplon
St. Moritz
Splügen
Locarno
ITALY
Geneva
Matterhorn 14780'
Gt. St. Bernard
L. Maggiore
YUGO
52
48
Long. East 12 of Greenwich

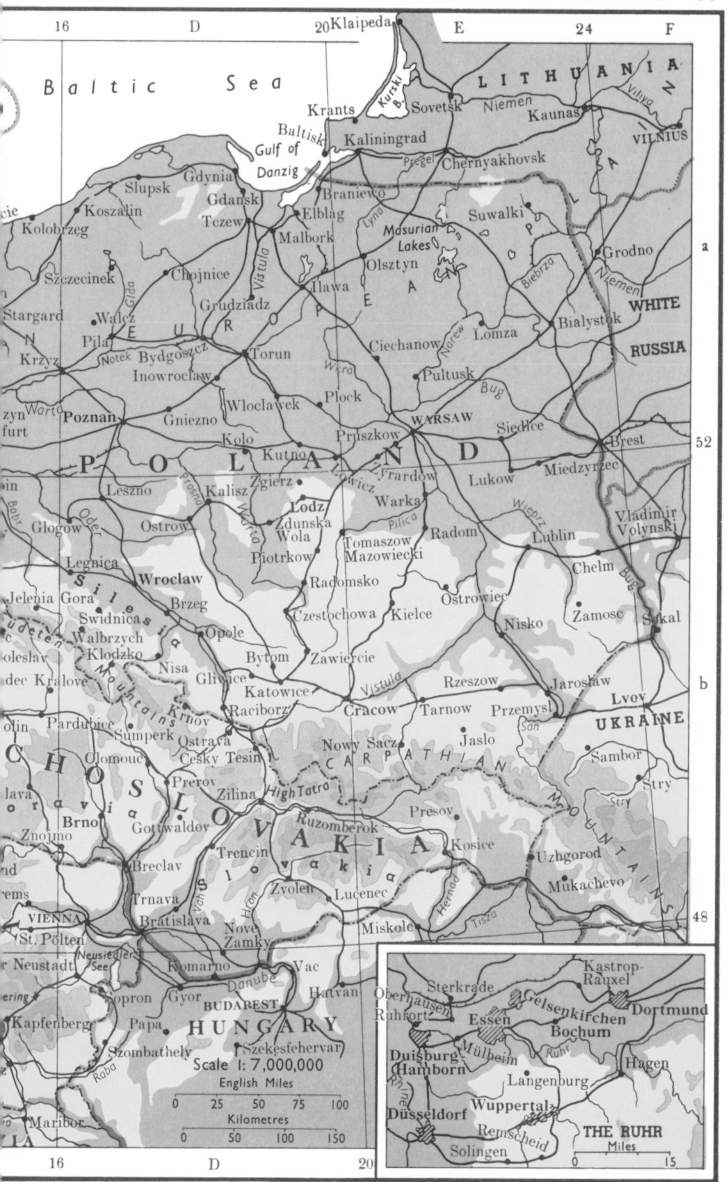
Baltic Sea
LITHUANIA
POLAND
CZECHOSLOVAKIA
HUNGARY
WHITE RUSSIA
UKRAINE
Klaipeda
Sovetsk
Kaunas
Vilnius
Kaliningrad
Chernyakhovsk
Gulf of Danzig
Gdynia
Gdansk
Slupsk
Koszalin
Kolobrzeg
Elblag
Malbork
Olsztyn
Masurian Lakes
Suwalki
Grodno
Bialystok
Torun
Bydgoszcz
Poznan
WARSAW
Brest
Lodz
Lublin
Wroclaw
Katowice
Cracow
Lvov
Brno
Bratislava
VIENNA
BUDAPEST
Carpathian Mountains
Scale 1: 7,000,000
English Miles
0 25 50 75 100
Kilometres
0 50 100 150
THE RUHR
Essen
Dortmund
Duisburg
Düsseldorf
Wuppertal
Miles
0 15

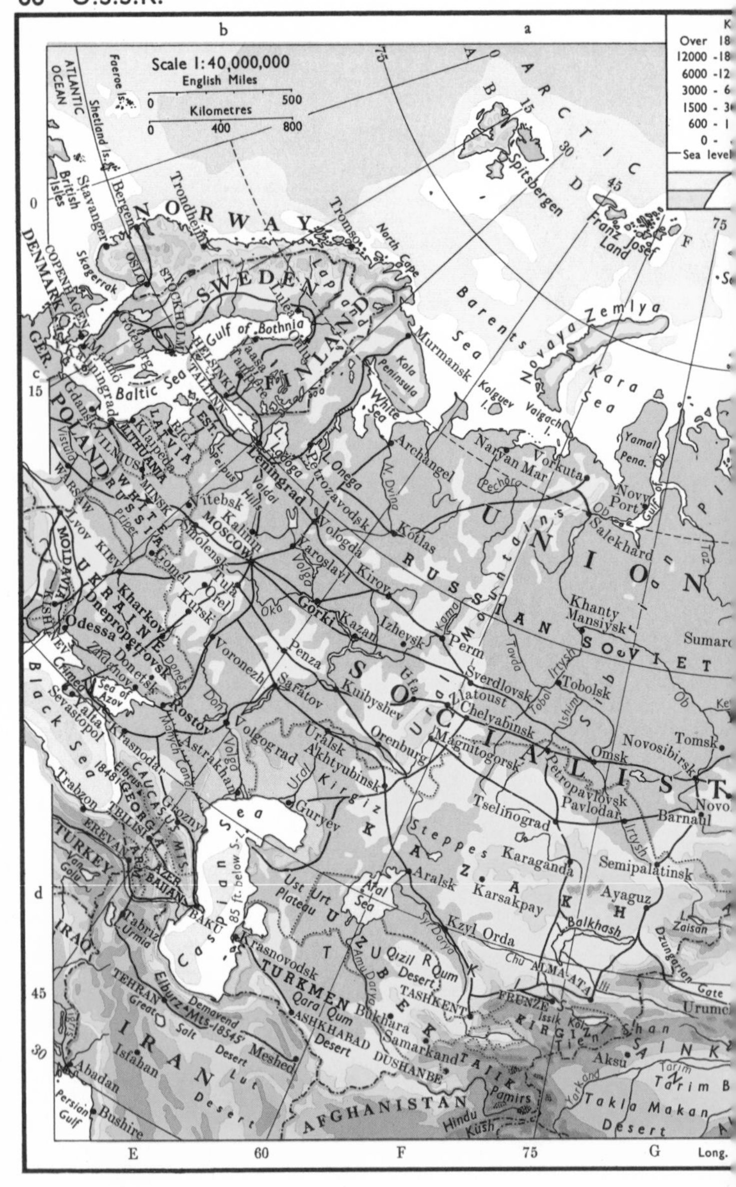
Scale 1:40,000,000
English Miles
0
500
Kilometres
0
400
800
ARCTIC OCEAN
ATLANTIC OCEAN
Faeroe Is.
Shetland Is.
British Isles
Spitsbergen
Franz Josef Land
Novaya Zemlya
Barents Sea
Kara Sea
North Cape
Tromso
NORWAY
SWEDEN
FINLAND
DENMARK
COPENHAGEN
OSLO
STOCKHOLM
HELSINKI
TALLINN
Bergen
Stavanger
Trondheim
Skagerrak
Goteborg
Malmö
Gulf of Bothnia
Baltic Sea
Lapland
Lulea
Oulu
Vaasa
Tampere
Kola Peninsula
Murmansk
White Sea
Archangel
Kolguev I.
Vaigach I.
Naryan Mar
Vorkuta
Yamal Pena.
Novy Port
Gulf of Ob
Salekhard
Pechora
N. Dvina
Kotlas
L. Onega
L. Ladoga
Petrozavodsk
Leningrad
L. Peipus
EST.
LATVIA
RIGA
LITHUANIA
Klaipeda
VILNIUS
Kaliningrad
Gdansk
POLAND
WARSAW
Vistula
GER.
WHITE RUSSIA
MINSK
Vitebsk
Valdai Hills
Kalinin
MOSCOW
Smolensk
Vologda
Yaroslavl
Kirov
Gomel
Pripet
Lvov
KIEV
MOLDAVIA
KISHINEV
UKRAINE
Kharkov
Dnepropetrovsk
Odessa
Zhdanov
Donetsk
Donets
Crimea
Sea of Azov
Yalta
Sevastopol
Black Sea
Tula
Orel
Kursk
Voronezh
Oka
Gorki
Volga
Kazan
Izhevsk
Kama
Perm
Penza
Saratov
Kuibyshev
Ufa
Sverdlovsk
Zlatoust
Chelyabinsk
Magnitogorsk
Orenburg
Ural Mountains
Rostov
Don
Manych Canal
Volgograd
Astrakhan
Krasnodar
Elbrus 18481
CAUCASUS MTS.
GEORGIA
TBILISI
Grozny
Trabzon
TURKEY
EREVAN
ARM.
AZER-BAIJAN
BAKU
Van Golu
Tabriz
L. Urmia
IRAQ
Caspian Sea
85 ft. below S.L.
Uralsk
Aktyubinsk
Ural
Guryev
Kirgiz Steppes
KAZAKH
Ust Urt Plateau
Aral Sea
Aralsk
Karsakpay
Karaganda
Tselinograd
Pavlodar
Petropavlovsk
Omsk
Novosibirsk
Tomsk
Barnaul
Irtysh
Semipalatinsk
Ayaguz
Balkhash
L. Zaisan
Dzungarian Gate
Urumchi
Kzyl Orda
Syr Darya
Chu
ALMA-ATA
Ili
FRUNZE
Issik Kol
KIRGIZ
Tien Shan
Aksu
SINKIANG
Tarim
Tarim Basin
Yarkand
Takla Makan Desert
Krasnovodsk
TURKMEN
UZBEK
Amu Darya
Qizil Qum Desert
TASHKENT
Qara Qum Desert
ASHKHABAD
Bukhara
Samarkand
DUSHANBE
TAJIK
Pamirs
Hindu Kush
AFGHANISTAN
Meshed
IRAN
TEHRAN
Elburz Mts.
Demavend 18545'
Great Salt Desert
Lut Desert
Isfahan
Abadan
Persian Gulf
Bushire
Tigris
UNION
SOVIET
SOCIALIST
RUSSIAN S.F.S.R.
Khanty Mansiysk
Tavda
Tobol
Tobolsk
Ishim
Ob
Taz
Sumaro
Siberia
Over 18
12000 - 18
6000 - 12
3000 - 6
1500 - 3
600 - 1
0 -
Sea level
a
b
c
d
0
15
30
45
60
75
E
F
G
Long.

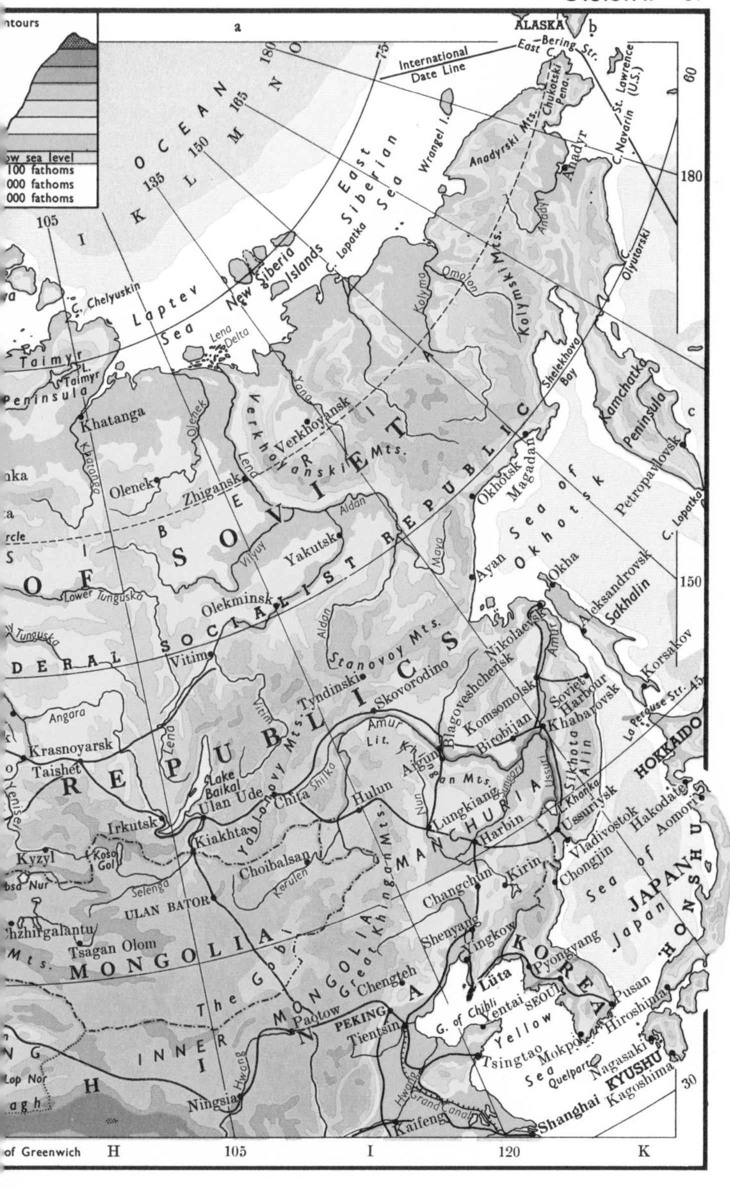

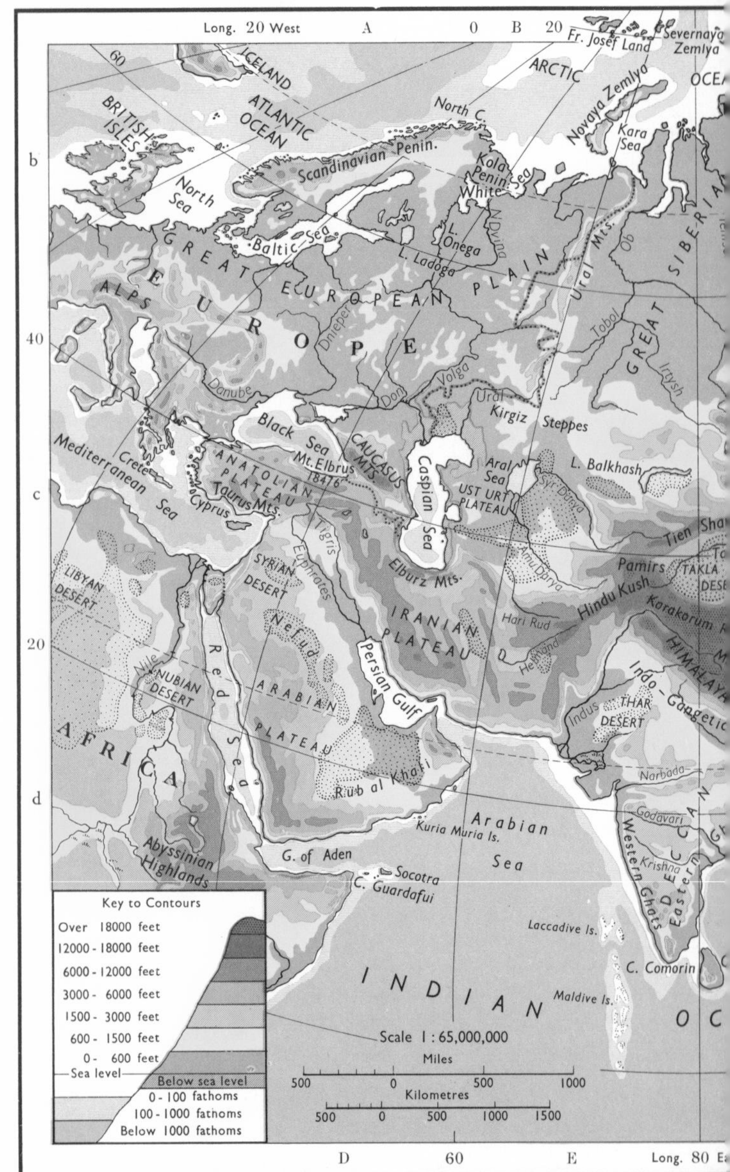

Long. 20 West
A
0
B
20
60
Fr. Josef Land
Severnaya Zemlya
ICELAND
ARCTIC
OCEAN
ATLANTIC OCEAN
BRITISH ISLES
North C.
Novaya Zemlya
Kara Sea
Scandinavian Penin.
Kola Penin.
White Sea
North Sea
L. Onega
N. Dvina
Baltic Sea
L. Ladoga
GREAT EUROPEAN PLAIN
Ural Mts.
Ob
SIBERIA
ALPS
EUROPE
Dnieper
Tobol
GREAT
40
Irtysh
Danube
Don
Volga
Ural
Kirgiz Steppes
Black Sea
CAUCASUS MTS.
Mt. Elbrus 18476
Caspian Sea
Aral Sea
L. Balkhash
Mediterranean Sea
Crete
ANATOLIAN PLATEAU
Taurus Mts.
UST URT PLATEAU
Syr Darya
c
Cyprus
Tigris
Euphrates
Tien Shan
SYRIAN DESERT
Elburz Mts.
Amu Darya
Pamirs
TAKLA
LIBYAN DESERT
Hindu Kush
Karakorum
IRANIAN PLATEAU
Hari Rud
Nefud
20
Helmand
HIMALAYA
Persian Gulf
Nile
NUBIAN DESERT
Red Sea
ARABIAN PLATEAU
Indo-Gangetic
Indus
THAR DESERT
AFRICA
Rub al Khali
Narbada
d
Arabian Sea
Godavari
Kuria Muria Is.
Western Ghats
Abyssinian Highlands
G. of Aden
Krishna
DECCAN
Socotra
C. Guardafui
Eastern Ghats
Laccadive Is.
C. Comorin
INDIAN OCEAN
Maldive Is.
Key to Contours
Over 18000 feet
12000 - 18000 feet
6000 - 12000 feet
3000 - 6000 feet
1500 - 3000 feet
600 - 1500 feet
0 - 600 feet
Sea level
Below sea level
0 - 100 fathoms
100 - 1000 fathoms
Below 1000 fathoms
Scale 1 : 65,000,000
Miles
500 0 500 1000
Kilometres
500 0 500 1000 1500
D
60
E
Long. 80 E

Laptev Sea
New Siberia Is.
Arctic Circle
Anadyr
Bering Str.
Bering Sea
Aleutian Is.
Kolyma
Kolymski Mts.
Cherskogo Mts.
Verkhoyanski Mts.
Kamchatka Penin.
Lena
Aldan
Tunguska
Sea of Okhotsk
Sakhalin
Kuril Is.
Stanovoy Mts.
Amur
Angara
L. Baikal
Yablonovy Mts.
Sikhote Alin
Hokkaido
Khingan Mts.
Sungari
Sayan Mts.
Sea of Japan
Honshu
Mountains
The Gobi
Korean Penin.
Shikoku
Kyushu
Yellow Sea
Hwang
Great Plain of China
Nan Shan
Tsaidam Basin
Tsinling Shan
Lun Mts.
TIBETAN PLATEAU
Red Basin
Yangtze
Ryukyu Is.
PACIFIC
Tropic of Cancer
OCEAN
Formosa (Taiwan)
Nan Ling
29030
Brahmaputra
Salween
Mekong
Si
Red
Irrawaddy
Luzon
Hainan
INDO-CHINA PENINSULA
Menam
Philippine Islands
Bay of Bengal
South China Sea
Palawan
Mindanao
Andaman Is.
Isthmus of Kra
C. Camau
Celebes Sea
Halmahera
Nicobar Is.
Natuna Is.
New Guinea
Malay Penin.
Serang
Borneo
Celebes
Buru
Sumatra
Arafura Sea
Java
Flores
Timor
AUSTRALIA
120
140
J
160
K
180
60
b
40
c
20
d
0
e
F
100
G
120
H
140

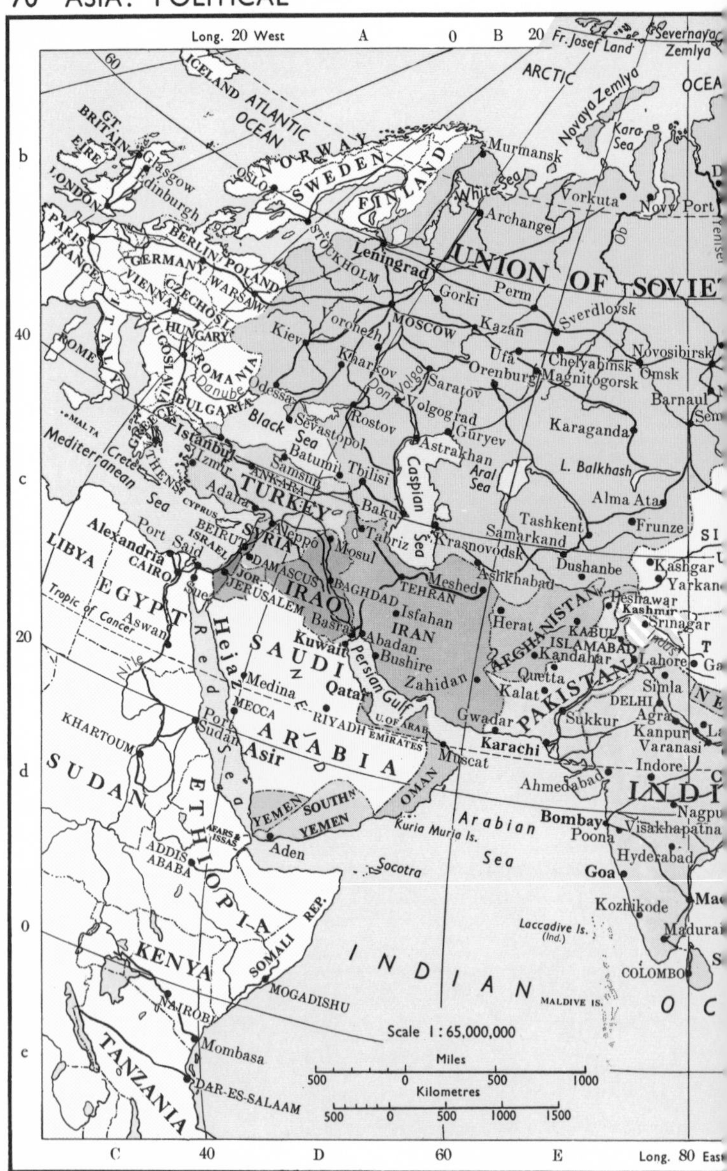

Long. 20 West
Long. 80 East
ARCTIC
OCEAN
ATLANTIC
OCEAN
ICELAND
GT. BRITAIN
EIRE
LONDON
Glasgow
Edinburgh
PARIS
FRANCE
NORWAY
OSLO
SWEDEN
STOCKHOLM
FINLAND
Fr. Josef Land
Severnaya Zemlya
Novaya Zemlya
Kara Sea
Murmansk
White Sea
Vorkuta
Novy Port
Archangel
Leningrad
UNION OF SOVIET
BERLIN
GERMANY
POLAND
WARSAW
CZECHOSL.
VIENNA
HUNGARY
ROMANIA
Danube
ITALY
ROME
YUGOSLAVIA
BULGARIA
GREECE
ATHENS
MALTA
Mediterranean Sea
Crete
CYPRUS
Istanbul
Izmir
ANKARA
TURKEY
Adana
Samsun
Black Sea
Odessa
Sevastopol
Batumi
Tbilisi
Kiev
Voronezh
Kharkov
MOSCOW
Gorki
Kazan
Perm
Sverdlovsk
Ufa
Chelyabinsk
Magnitogorsk
Orenburg
Novosibirsk
Omsk
Barnaul
Saratov
Volga
Don
Volgograd
Rostov
Guryev
Astrakhan
Karaganda
Caspian Sea
Aral Sea
L. Balkhash
Alma Ata
Frunze
Tashkent
Samarkand
Dushanbe
Krasnovodsk
Ashkhabad
Baku
Tabriz
Meshed
TEHRAN
Isfahan
IRAN
Abadan
Bushire
Zahidan
BEIRUT
SYRIA
Aleppo
Mosul
ISRAEL
DAMASCUS
JOR.
JERUSALEM
IRAQ
BAGHDAD
Basra
Kuwait
Port Said
Alexandria
CAIRO
Suez
LIBYA
EGYPT
Aswan
Nile
Tropic of Cancer
Red Sea
Hejaz
SAUDI ARABIA
NEUTRAL ZONE
Medina
MECCA
RIYADH
Qatar
Persian Gulf
U. OF ARAB EMIRATES
Muscat
OMAN
Asir
YEMEN
SOUTHN YEMEN
Aden
Port Sudan
KHARTOUM
SUDAN
ETHIOPIA
AFARS & ISSAS
ADDIS ABABA
SOMALI REP.
Socotra
Kuria Muria Is.
Arabian Sea
Herat
AFGHANISTAN
KABUL
ISLAMABAD
Peshawar
Kashmir
Srinagar
Indus
Lahore
Kandahar
Quetta
Kalat
PAKISTAN
Gwadar
Karachi
Sukkur
Simla
DELHI
Agra
Kanpur
Varanasi
Indore
Ahmedabad
INDIA
Nagpur
Bombay
Poona
Visakhapatnam
Hyderabad
Goa
Kozhikode
Madurai
COLOMBO
Laccadive Is. (Ind.)
MALDIVE IS.
Kashgar
Yarkand
KENYA
NAIROBI
Mombasa
MOGADISHU
TANZANIA
DAR-ES-SALAAM
INDIAN OCEAN
Scale 1 : 65,000,000
Miles
500 0 500 1000
Kilometres
500 0 500 1000 1500

SOCIALIST REPUBLICS
MONGOLIA
CHINA
JAPAN
KOREA
BURMA
LAOS
THAI.
CAM.
PHILIPPINES
MALAYSIA
INDONESIA
AUSTRALIA
PACIFIC OCEAN
Sea of Okhotsk
Sea of Japan
South China Sea
Bering Sea
Celebes Sea
Arafura Sea
Laptev Sea
Arctic Circle
Tropic of Cancer
International Date Line
Aleutian Is. (U.S.)
Kuril Is.
Ryukyu Is.
Sakhalin
Kamchatka Penin.
Hokkaido
Honshu
Shikoku
Kyushu
Formosa (Taiwan)
Hainan
Luzon
Mindanao
Palawan
Halmahera
Sumatra
Java
Kalimantan
Sulawesi
Timor (Port.)
Flores
West Irian
New Siberia Is.
Tiksi
Verkhoyansk
Yakutsk
Magadan
Okhotsk
Ayan
Nikolaevsk
Petropavlovsk
Khabarovsk
Soviet Harbour
Krasnoyarsk
L. Baikal
Irkutsk
Ulan Ude
Chita
Kyzyl
Kiakhta
ULAN BATOR
Choibalsan
Hailar
Changchun
Shenyang
Lüta
PEKING
Tientsin
Huhehot
Yentai
Tsingtao
Nanking
Shanghai
Wuhan
Hangchow
Wenchow
Foochow
Taipei
Kiuchuan
Lanchow
Sian
Wanhsien
Chungking
Changsha
Kweilin
Kunming
Mengtsz
Kwangchow
Hong Kong (Br.)
Macau (Port.)
LHASA
BHUTAN
Sadiya
Myitkyina
Lashio
Mandalay
RANGOON
Chieng Mai
BANGKOK
VIENTIANE
Hanoi
N. VIET NAM
Hue
Binh Dinh
S. VIET NAM
SAIGON
MANILA
Iloilo
Davao
Ussuriysk
Vladivostok
Sapporo
Aomori
Sendai
TOKYO
Yokohama
Kyoto
Kobe
Nagoya
Osaka
Pyongyang
SEOUL
Pusan
Nagasaki
BRUNEI
Penang
Ipoh
KUALA LUMPUR
Medan
SINGAPORE
Manado
Balikpapan
Serang
Buru
Ambon
Bandjarmasin
Macassar
Padang
Palembang
Benkulen
Telukbetung
JAKARTA
Bandung
Surabaya
Darwin
Andaman Is. (Ind.)
Nicobar Is. (Ind.)
Amur
Lena
Hwang
Yangtze
Mekong
Brahmaputra
120 140 160 180 100 120 140
F G H J K
b c d e
40 20 0

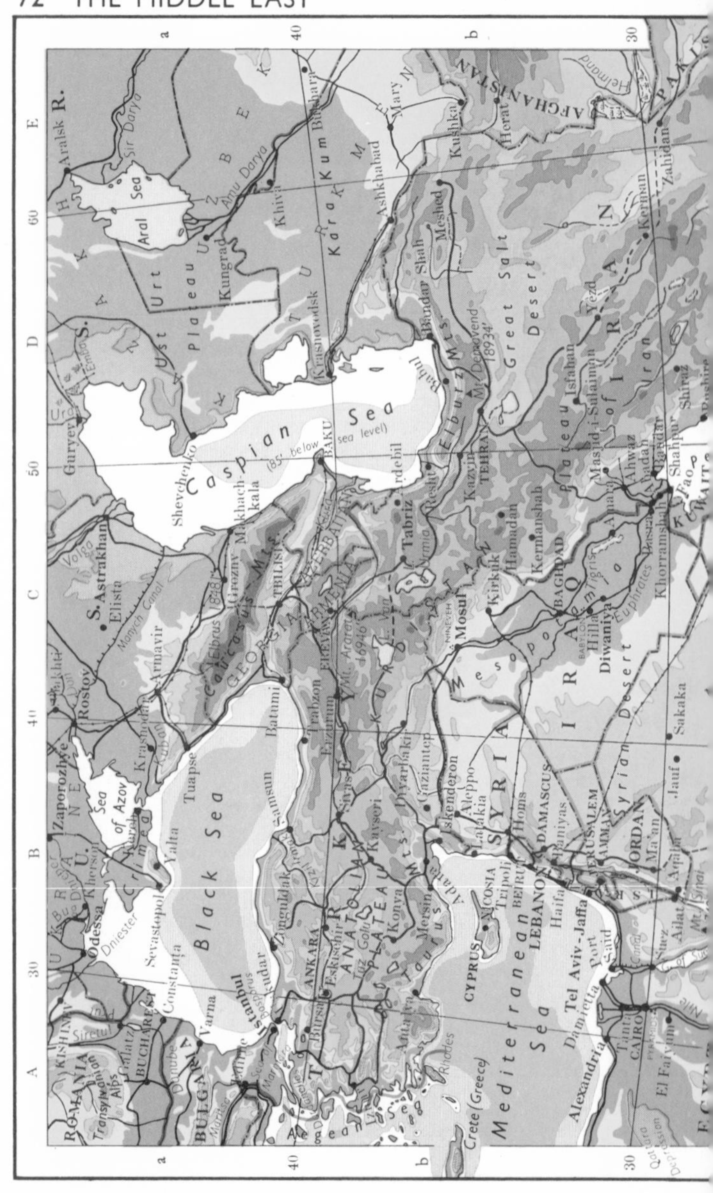
Black Sea
Caspian Sea
(85' below sea level)
Aral Sea
Sea of Azov
Mediterranean Sea
Great Salt Desert
Syrian Desert
Plateau of Iran
Anatolian Plateau
Ust Urt Plateau
Kara Kum
Caucasus Mts.
Elburz Mts.
Taurus Mts.
Mesopotamia
U.S.S.R.
TURKEY
IRAN
IRAQ
SYRIA
LEBANON
JORDAN
AFGHANISTAN
GEORGIA
ARMENIA
AZERBAIJAN
KURDISTAN
ROMANIA
BULGARIA
CYPRUS
Crete (Greece)
Rhodes
ANKARA
TEHRAN
BAGHDAD
DAMASCUS
BEIRUT
NICOSIA
JERUSALEM
AMMAN
BAKU
TBILISI
EREVAN
BUCHAREST
CAIRO
Istanbul
Odessa
Sevastopol
Yalta
Kherson
Zaporozhye
Rostov
Krasnodar
Tuapse
Armavir
Astrakhan
Elista
Grozny
Makhachkala
Shevchenko
Guryev
Krasnovodsk
Ashkhabad
Khiva
Kungrad
Aralsk
Bukhara
Mary
Kushka
Herat
Meshed
Bandar Shah
Babul
Resht
Kazvin
Tabriz
Ardebil
Hamadan
Kermanshah
Isfahan
Yezd
Kerman
Zahidan
Shiraz
Abadan
Ahwaz
Khorramshahr
Basra
Fao
Amara
Diwaniya
Hilla
BABYLON
Kirkuk
Mosul
NINEVEH
Erzurum
Trabzon
Batumi
Samsun
Sivas
Kayseri
Konya
Eskişehir
Bursa
Zonguldak
Üsküdar
Adana
Mersin
Antalya
Iskenderon
Aleppo
Gaziantep
Diyarbakir
Latakia
Homs
Tripoli
Baniyas
Haifa
Tel Aviv-Jaffa
Port Said
Suez
Damietta
Alexandria
Tanta
El Faiyum
Ailat
Aqaba
Ma'an
Jauf
Sakaka
Varna
Constanta
Galatz
Mt. Ararat 16946'
Mt. Elbrus 18481'
Mt. Demavend 18934'
Mt. Sinai
L. Van
L. Urmia
Tuz Gölü
Volga
Don
Dnieper
Dniester
Danube
Kuban
Manych Canal
Amu Darya
Sir Darya
Emba
Ural
Tigris
Euphrates
Nile
Helmand
Siretul
Maritsa
Bosphorus
Sea of Marmara
Aegean Sea
Transylvanian Alps
Qattara Depression
Suez Canal
G. of Suez
a
b
A
B
C
D
E
30
40
50
60

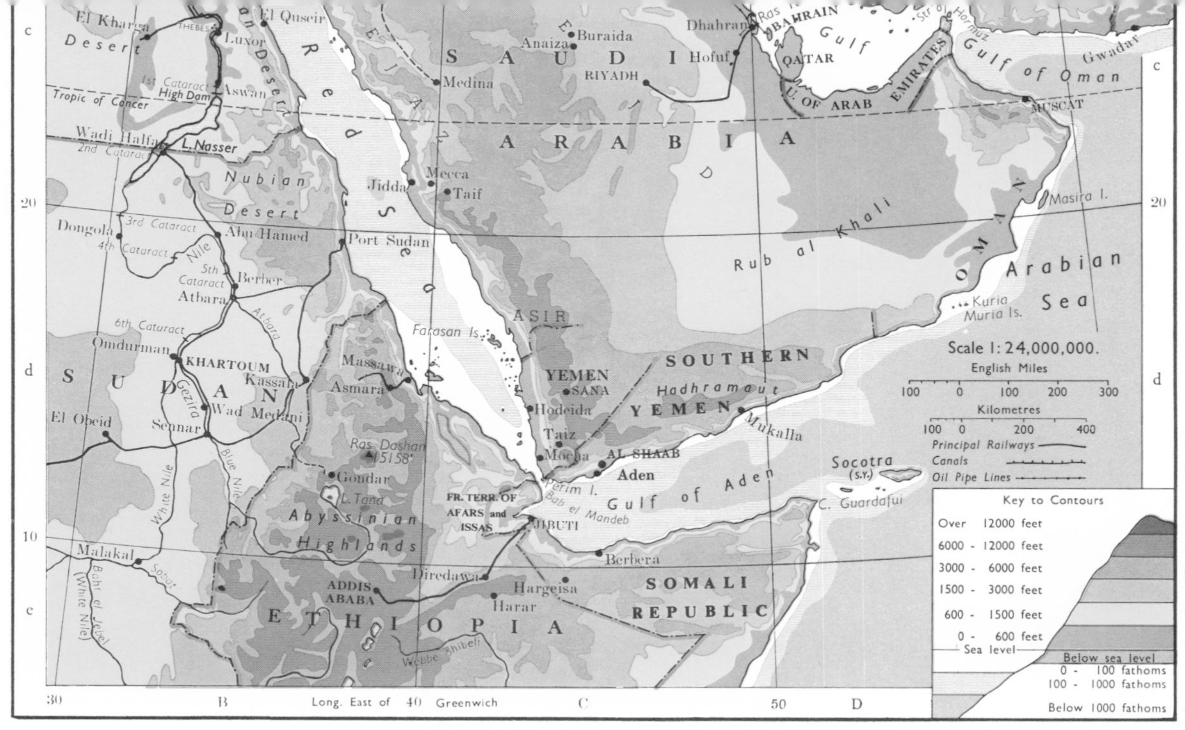
SAUDI ARABIA
Rub al Khali
OMAN
Arabian Sea
Gulf of Oman
Gulf of Aden
Red Sea
Gulf
Str. of Hormuz
Gwadar
SOUTHERN YEMEN
YEMEN
SANA
Hadhramaut
SOMALI REPUBLIC
ETHIOPIA
SUDAN
Nubian Desert
Abyssinian Highlands
FR. TERR. OF AFARS and ISSAS
U. OF ARAB EMIRATES
QATAR
BAHRAIN
MUSCAT
Masira I.
Kuria Muria Is.
Socotra (S.Y.)
C. Guardafui
Mukalla
Aden
AL SHAAB
Perim I.
Bab el Mandeb
Berbera
Hargeisa
Harar
Diredawa
ADDIS ABABA
Gondar
L. Tana
Ras Dashan 15158
Asmara
Massawa
Farasan Is.
Hodeida
Taiz
Mocha
ASIR
Jidda
Mecca
Taif
Medina
Buraida
Anaiza
RIYADH
Hofuf
Dhahran
Port Sudan
Kassala
Wad Medani
KHARTOUM
Omdurman
Atbara
Berber
Abu Hamed
Dongola
Wadi Halfa
L. Nasser
High Dam
Aswan
Luxor
THEBES
El Quseir
El Kharga Desert
Tropic of Cancer
Blue Nile
White Nile
Gezira
Sennar
El Obeid
Malakal
Sobat
Bahr el Jebel (White Nile)
Webbe Shibeli
1st Cataract
2nd Cataract
3rd Cataract
4th Cataract
5th Cataract
6th Cataract
Nile
Scale 1: 24,000,000.
English Miles
100 0 100 200 300
Kilometres
100 0 200 400
Principal Railways
Canals
Oil Pipe Lines
Key to Contours
Over 12000 feet
6000 - 12000 feet
3000 - 6000 feet
1500 - 3000 feet
600 - 1500 feet
0 - 600 feet
Sea level
Below sea level
0 - 100 fathoms
100 - 1000 fathoms
Below 1000 fathoms
Long. East of 40 Greenwich
30
B
C
50
D
c
d
e
10
20

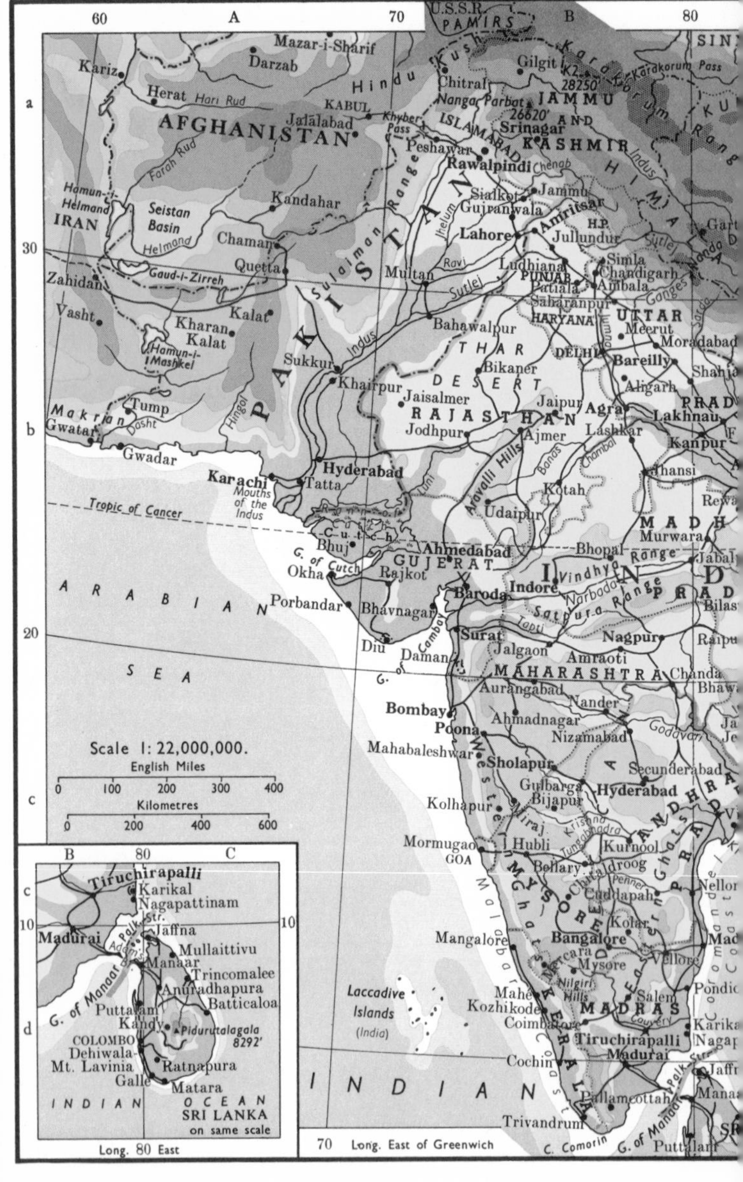
AFGHANISTAN
PAKISTAN
IRAN
U.S.S.R.
PAMIRS
JAMMU AND KASHMIR
RAJASTHAN
GUJERAT
MAHARASHTRA
MYSORE
KERALA
MADRAS
ANDHRA PRADESH
UTTAR PRADESH
MADHYA PRADESH
PUNJAB
HARYANA
DELHI
INDIA
ARABIAN SEA
INDIAN OCEAN
Tropic of Cancer
Mazar-i-Sharif
Darzab
Kariz
Herat
Hari Rud
KABUL
Jalalabad
Khyber Pass
Hindu Kush
Chitral
Gilgit
K2 28250'
Nanga Parbat 26620'
Karakorum Pass
Srinagar
ISLAMABAD
Peshawar
Rawalpindi
Chenab
Indus
HIMALAYA
Farah Rud
Hamun-i-Helmand
Seistan Basin
Helmand
Kandahar
Chaman
Quetta
Gaud-i-Zirreh
Zahidan
Vasht
Kharan
Kalat
Hamun-i-Mashkel
Sulaiman Range
Multan
Jhelum
Ravi
Sutlej
Sialkot
Jammu
Gujranwala
Amritsar
Lahore
Jullundur
Ludhiana
Patiala
Simla
Chandigarh
Ambala
Saharanpur
Ganges
Meerut
Moradabad
Bareilly
Aligarh
Agra
Lakhnau
Kanpur
Jhansi
Bahawalpur
THAR DESERT
Bikaner
Sukkur
Khairpur
Jaisalmer
Jaipur
Jodhpur
Ajmer
Lashkar
Aravalli Hills
Banas
Chambal
Kotah
Udaipur
Makran
Tump
Dasht
Gwatar
Gwadar
Hingol
Hyderabad
Karachi
Tatta
Mouths of the Indus
Rann of Cutch
Bhuj
G. of Cutch
Okha
Rajkot
Ahmedabad
Bhopal
Vindhya Range
Indore
Baroda
Narbada
Satpura Range
Porbandar
Bhavnagar
G. of Cambay
Diu
Daman
Surat
Tapti
Jalgaon
Amraoti
Nagpur
Aurangabad
Nander
Bombay
Poona
Ahmadnagar
Nizamabad
Godavari
Mahabaleshwar
Sholapur
Secunderabad
Hyderabad
Gulbarga
Bijapur
Kolhapur
Miraj
Krishna
Tungabhadra
Mormugao
GOA
Hubli
Kurnool
Bellary
Chitaldroog
Penner
Cuddapah
Kolar
Mangalore
Bangalore
Mercara
Mysore
Vellore
Nilgiri Hills
Salem
Mahe
Kozhikode
Coimbatore
Cauvery
Tiruchirapalli
Madurai
Cochin
Palamcottah
Trivandrum
C. Comorin
G. of Manaar
Western Ghats
Eastern Ghats
Malabar Coast
Coromandel Coast
Laccadive Islands (India)
Murwara
Rewa
Chanda
Sutlej
Gartok
Nanda Devi
Sarda
Jumna
Scale 1: 22,000,000.
English Miles
0 100 200 300 400
Kilometres
0 200 400 600
70 Long. East of Greenwich
60
70
80
30
20
A
B
a
b
c
d
Tiruchirapalli
Karikal
Nagapattinam
Palk Str.
Jaffna
Madurai
Adam's Bridge
Mullaittivu
Manaar
Trincomalee
Anuradhapura
G. of Manaar
Batticaloa
Puttalam
Kandy
Pidurutalagala 8292'
COLOMBO
Dehiwala-Mt. Lavinia
Ratnapura
Galle
Matara
INDIAN OCEAN
SRI LANKA on same scale
Long. 80 East
10
C

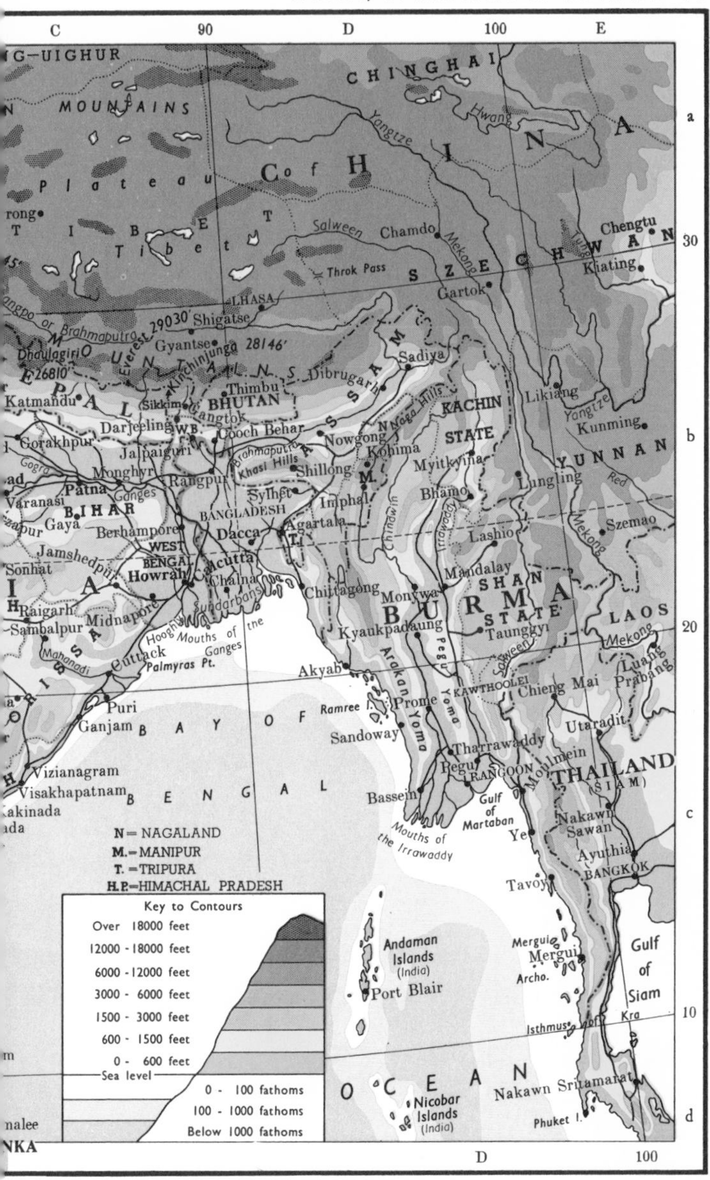
C
90
D
100
E
CHINGHAI
MOUNTAINS
Plateau
Tibet
TIBET
CHINA
Hwang
Yangtze
Salween
Chamdo
Mekong
Chengtu
Kiating
SZECHWAN
Throk Pass
Gartok
LHASA
Shigatse
Gyantse
Everest 29030'
Kinchinjunga 28146'
Dhaulagiri
26810'
Brahmaputra
HIMALAYA MOUNTAINS
Sadiya
Dibrugarh
ASSAM
Thimbu
BHUTAN
Katmandu
NEPAL
Sikkim
Gangtok
Darjeeling
W.B.
Cooch Behar
Gorakhpur
Jalpaiguri
Nowgong
Naga Hills
Kohima
KACHIN STATE
Likiang
Kunming
YUNNAN
Khasi Hills
Shillong
Myitkyina
Lungling
Red
Monghyr
Rangpur
M.
Patna
Ganges
Gogra
Sylhet
Imphal
Bhamo
Varanasi
BIHAR
Gaya
BANGLADESH
Agartala
Chindwin
Irrawaddy
Szemao
Berhampore
Dacca
T.
Lashio
Jamshedpur
WEST BENGAL
Calcutta
Howrah
Chalna
Sundarbans
Chittagong
Monywa
Mandalay
SHAN STATE
Sonhat
Raigarh
Sambalpur
Midnapore
ORISSA
Mahanadi
Hooghly
Mouths of the Ganges
Cuttack
Palmyras Pt.
BURMA
Kyaukpadaung
Pegu
Taunggyi
LAOS
Mekong
Luang Prabang
Akyab
Arakan Yoma
Pegu Yoma
KAWTHOOLEI
Salween
Chieng Mai
Puri
Ganjam
BAY OF BENGAL
Ramree I.
Prome
Sandoway
Utaradit
Tharrawaddy
Pegu
RANGOON
Moulmein
THAILAND (SIAM)
Vizianagram
Visakhapatnam
Kakinada
Bassein
Gulf of Martaban
Ye
Nakawn Sawan
Mouths of the Irrawaddy
Ayuthia
BANGKOK
Tavoy
N = NAGALAND
M. = MANIPUR
T. = TRIPURA
H.P. = HIMACHAL PRADESH
Key to Contours
Over 18000 feet
12000 - 18000 feet
6000 - 12000 feet
3000 - 6000 feet
1500 - 3000 feet
600 - 1500 feet
0 - 600 feet
Sea level
0 - 100 fathoms
100 - 1000 fathoms
Below 1000 fathoms
Andaman Islands (India)
Port Blair
Mergui Archo.
Mergui
Gulf of Siam
Isthmus of Kra
OCEAN
Nicobar Islands (India)
Nakawn Sritamarat
Phuket I.
a
b
c
d
30
20
10
D
100

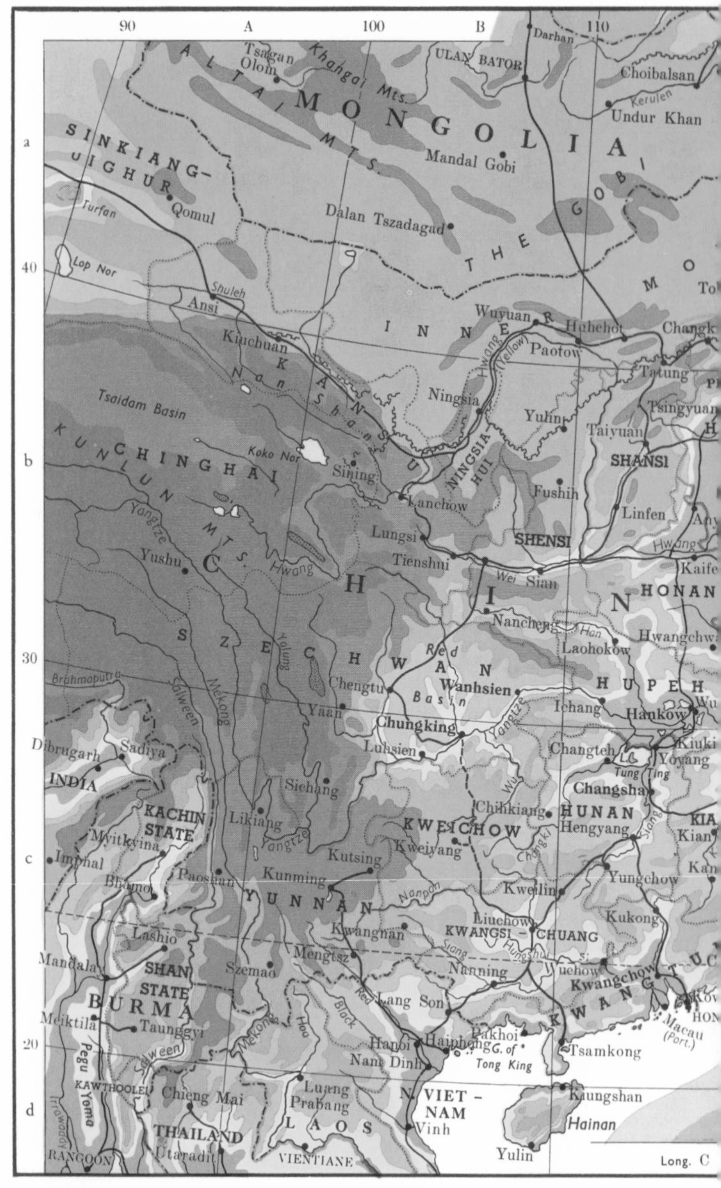

MONGOLIA
ULAN BATOR
Choibalsan
Undur Khan
Mandal Gobi
Dalan Tszadagad
THE GOBI
Khangai Mts.
ALTAI MTS.
Tsagan Olom
SINKIANG-UIGHUR
Qomul
Turfan
Lop Nor
Shuleh
Ansi
Kiuchuan
KANSU
Nan Shan
INNER MONGOLIA
Wuyuan
Huhehot
Paotow
Changk
Tatung
Tsingyuan
Ningsia
Yulin
Taiyuan
SHANSI
NINGSIA HUI
Fushih
Linfen
Tsaidam Basin
KUNLUN MTS.
CHINGHAI
Koko Nor
Sining
Lanchow
Lungsi
Tienshui
SHENSI
Wei
Sian
Kaife
HONAN
Yangtze
Yushu
Hwang
CHINA
Nancheng
Han
Hwangchw
Laohokow
SZECHWAN
Red Basin
Wanhsien
Chengtu
Yaan
Chungking
Ichang
HUPEH
Hankow
Brahmaputra
Salween
Mekong
Yalung
Luhsien
Changteh
Tung Ting
Kiuki
Yoyang
Changsha
Dibrugarh
Sadiya
INDIA
Sichang
KACHIN STATE
Likiang
Chihkiang
HUNAN
KWEICHOW
Kweiyang
Hengyang
Siang
Kian
Myitkyina
Imphal
Bhamo
Paoshan
Kutsing
Kunming
YUNNAN
Nanpan
Kweilin
Yungchow
Kukong
Liuchow
KWANGSI - CHUANG
Kwangnan
Lashio
Mandalay
SHAN STATE
BURMA
Szemao
Mengtsz
Nanning
Kwangchow
KWANGTUNG
Meiktila
Taunggyi
Lang Son
Red
Black
Hoa
Macau (Port.)
Hanoi
Haiphong
Pakhoi
G. of Tong King
Nam Dinh
Tsamkong
Pegu Yoma
KAWTHOOLEI
Chieng Mai
Luang Prabang
VIET - NAM
Kaungshan
Hainan
Irrawaddy
THAILAND
LAOS
Vinh
RANGOON
Utaradit
VIENTIANE
Yulin
Long. C
90
A
100
B
110
a
40
b
30
c
20
d

Hulun
Nunkiang
Pehanchen
Great Khingan Mts.
Lungkiang
HEILUNG-KIANG
Fuchin
Kiamusz
Ussuri
Suihwa
Pinkiang
Sungari
L. Khanka
Sikhote Alin
U. S. S. R.
Taoan
Mutankiang
Spassk
Dalniy
Olga
Yungki
Ussuriysk
Changchun
Tunhwa
KIRIN
Vladivostok
Szepingkai
Chaoyangchen
Shenyang
Chongjin
LIAONING
Chinhsien
Yalu
Kanggye
Yingkow
NORTH KOREA
Antung
Hungnam
Wonsan
Pyongyang
Nampo
Taku
G. of Chihli
Lüta
Chorwon
SEOUL
Weihai
Yentai
Ongjin
Inchon
SOUTH KOREA
Taejon
Taegu
Yellow Sea
Kunsan
Kwangju
Pusan
Korea Str.
Tsingtao
Mokpo
Haichow
KIANGSU
Yencheng
Quelpart
Soochow
Shanghai
Kahsing
Hangchow
Ningpo
CHEKIANG
Kinhwa
Taichow
Wenchow
Chungan
Min
Foochow
Keelung
Taipei
Hsiamen
Taichung
FORMOSA
(TAIWAN)
Tainan
Bashi Channel
Batan Is
Babuyan Is.
Laoag
East China Sea
Tropic of Cancer
Ryukyu Islands
Okinawa
Naha
Amami
Osumi Is
Kagoshima
Nagasaki
Sasebo
Kumamoto
KYUSHU
Fukuoka
Kitakyushu
Hiroshima
Inland Sea
Kochi
SHIKOKU
Takamatsu
Yonago
Kobe
Osaka
Kyoto
Hamamatsu
Nagoya
Yokosuka
Yokohama
TOKYO
Mt. Fuji 12388
Kanazawa
Toyama
HONSHU
Niigata
Koriyama
Sendai
JAPAN
Sea of Japan
Akita
Morioka
Aomori
Hakodate
Muroran
Sapporo
Otaru
HOKKAIDO
Asahigawa
Abashiri
Kushiro
La Perouse Str.
PACIFIC OCEAN
140
130
40
30
D
E
F
a
b
c
Key to Contours
Over 18000 feet
12000 - 18000 feet
6000 - 12000 feet
3000 - 6000 feet
1500 - 3000 feet
600 - 1500 feet
0 - 600 feet
Sea level
Below sea level
0 - 100 fathoms
100 - 1000 fathoms
Below 1000 fathoms
Scale 1 : 23,000,000
Miles
0 100 200 300 400
Kilometres
0 200 400 600

BURMA
RANGOON
Moulmein
Tak
G. of Martaban
Ye
Tavoy
Mergui
Mergui Archo.
Isthmus of Kra
THAILAND (SIAM)
Nakawn Sawan
Ayuthia
BANGKOK
Korat
VIENTIANE
Udon Thani
Ubon Ratchathani
LAOS
Mekong
Vinh
N. VIET NAM
INDO-CHINA
Hue
Da Nang
Pakse
SOUTH VIET NAM
Binh Dinh
Battambang
Tonle Sap
CAMBODIA
Pursat
PHNOM PENH
Nha Trang
SAIGON
Cholon
Long Xuyen
Gulf of Siam
Pt. de Camau
Surat Thani
Nakawn Sritamarat
Phuket
Songkhla
Bandar Atjeh
Alor Star
George Tn.
Penang
Kota Bharu
Kuala Trengganu
Taiping
Ipoh
WEST
MALAYSIA
Kuantan
KUALA LUMPUR
Malacca
Strait of Malacca
Medan
SINGAPORE
Riouw Archo.
Sibolga
Nias
SUMATRA
Kampar
Lingga Archo.
Padang
Siberut
Mentawai Islands
Hari
Telanaipura
Bangka
Billiton
Musi
Palembang
Telukbetung
Enggano
Natuna Is
C. Datu
Kuching
Pontianak
Kapuas
KALIMANTAN
Raja 7474'
Tandjung
Sampit
Matua
Bandjarmasin
Kota Kinabalu
Labuan
BRUNEI (Br.)
Miri
Sibu
Rajang
SOUTH CHINA SEA
INDONESIA
Java Sea
Sunda Str.
JAKARTA
Serang
Bogor
Bandung
Semarang
Madura
Surabaya
Bali
JAVA
Tjilatjap
Djokjakarta
Malang
Denpasar
INDIAN OCEAN
Christmas I. (Br.)
Scale, 1: 23,000,000
English Miles
0 100 200 300 400 500
Kilometres
0 200 400 600 800
A B C
100 110
a b c d
10 0 10

D
130
E
Key to Contours
Over 12000 feet
6000 - 12000 feet
3000 - 6000 feet
1500 - 3000 feet
600 - 1500 feet
0 - 600 feet
Sea level
0 - 100 fathoms
100 - 1000 fathoms
Below 1000 fathoms
Oil Pipe Lines
Laoag
Baguio
Dagupan
Luzon
Quezon City
MANILA
PHILIPPINES
Calapan
Mindoro
Legaspi
Masbate
Samar
Tacloban
Panay
Iloilo
Cebu
Leyte
Palawan
Cebu
Negros
Bohol
Emden Deep
35410'
PACIFIC
Dipolog
Cagayan
Sulu Sea
Mindanao
Palau Is.
Zamboanga
Davao
Sandakan
Jolo
Sulu Archipelago
OCEAN
Talaud Is.
Celebes
Sea
Tarakan
Sangihe
Is.
Pitu
Manado
Halmahera
Ternate
Molucca
Strait
Gorontalo
Waigeo
Equator
Samarinda
G. of Tomini
Poh
Toboli
Schouten Is.
Macassar
Sula Is.
Obi Is.
Misool
SULAWESI
Ceram
NEW GUINEA
G. of Bone
Madjene
Buru
Amboina
E S I A
Macassar
Butung
Muna
Banda Sea
Kei Is.
Aru Is.
Raba
Ruteng
Lomblen
Alor
Wetar
Babar
Tanimbar Is.
Pantar
Dili (Port.)
Sumbawa
Flores
Waingapu
Savu Sea
Timor
Sumba
Arafura Sea
Savu
Kupang
Roti
Timor Sea
Melville I.
Bathurst I.
Darwin
AUSTRALIA
Long. 120 East
D
a
10
b
0
c
10
d
H
A

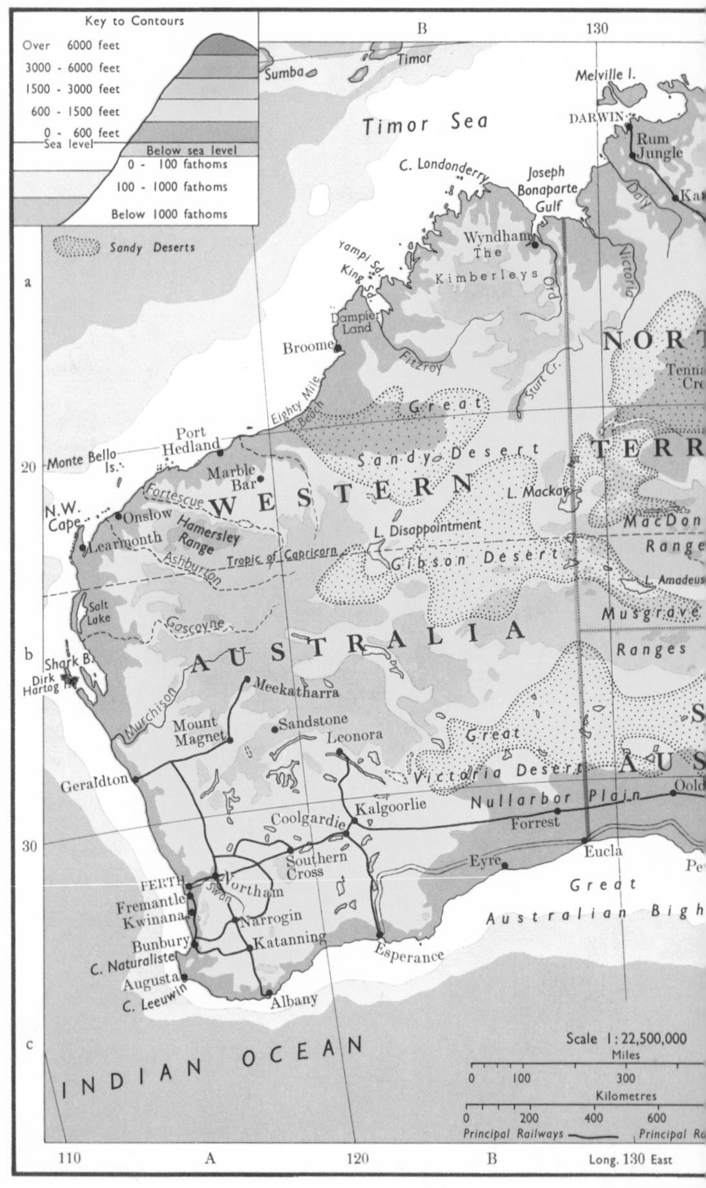
Key to Contours
Over 6000 feet
3000 - 6000 feet
1500 - 3000 feet
600 - 1500 feet
0 - 600 feet
Sea level
Below sea level
0 - 100 fathoms
100 - 1000 fathoms
Below 1000 fathoms
Sandy Deserts
Timor
Sumba
Timor Sea
Melville I.
DARWIN
Rum Jungle
C. Londonderry
Joseph Bonaparte Gulf
Daly
Wyndham
The Kimberleys
Ord
Victoria
Yampi Sd.
King Sd.
Dampier Land
Broome
Fitzroy
Sturt Cr.
Eighty Mile Beach
Great Sandy Desert
Port Hedland
Monte Bello Is.
Marble Bar
WESTERN AUSTRALIA
L. Mackay
N.W. Cape
Onslow
Fortescue
Hamersley Range
Learmonth
Ashburton
Tropic of Capricorn
L. Disappointment
Gibson Desert
Range
L. Amadeus
Salt Lake
Gascoyne
Musgrave Ranges
Shark B.
Dirk Hartog I.
Meekatharra
Murchison
Mount Magnet
Sandstone
Leonora
Great Victoria Desert
Geraldton
Nullarbor Plain
Kalgoorlie
Coolgardie
Forrest
Southern Cross
Eucla
Eyre
PERTH
Northam
Swan
Fremantle
Kwinana
Narrogin
Great Australian Bight
Bunbury
Katanning
Esperance
C. Naturaliste
Augusta
C. Leeuwin
Albany
INDIAN OCEAN
Scale 1:22,500,000
Miles
0 100 300
Kilometres
0 200 400 600
Principal Railways
110 A 120 B Long. 130 East
B 130
a b c
20 30

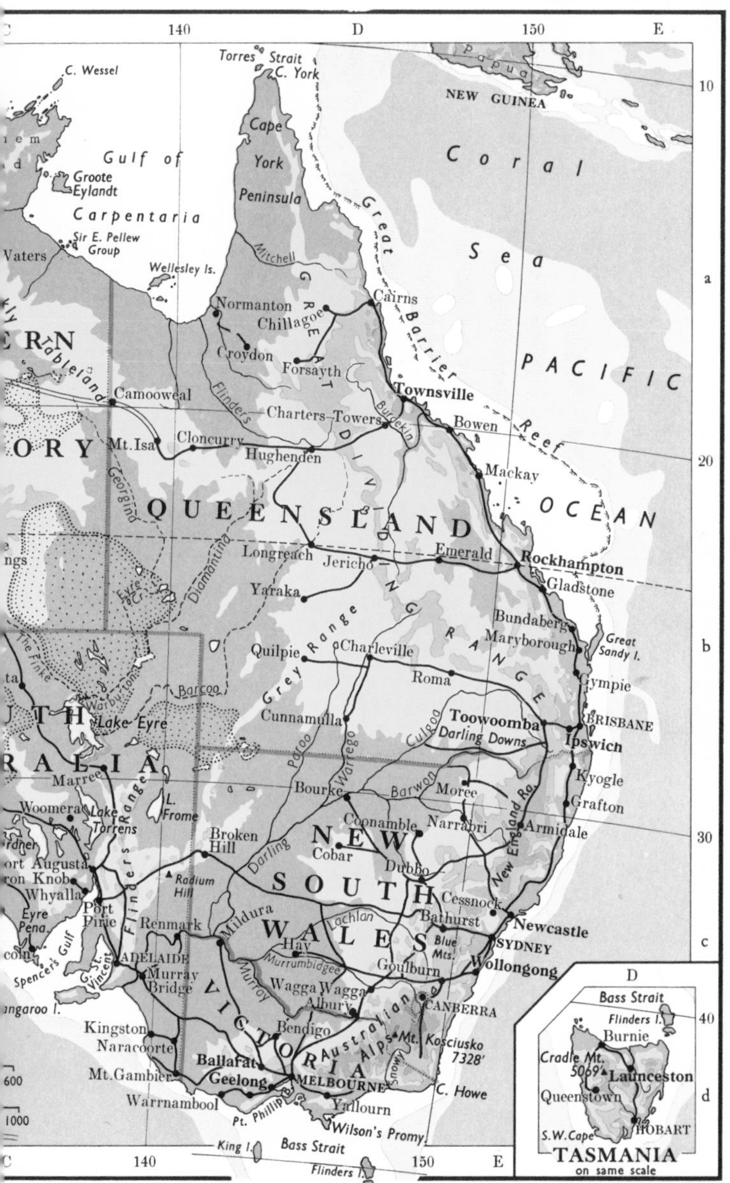

Torres Strait
C. York
C. Wessel
Gulf of Carpentaria
Groote Eylandt
Sir E. Pellew Group
Wellesley Is.
Cape York Peninsula
NEW GUINEA
Papua
Coral Sea
PACIFIC OCEAN
Great Barrier Reef
Mitchell
Normanton
Chillagoe
Croydon
Forsayth
Cairns
Townsville
Bowen
Mackay
Camooweal
Flinders
Charters Towers
Burdekin
Cloncurry
Mt. Isa
Hughenden
Georgina
QUEENSLAND
GREAT DIVIDING RANGE
Diamantina
Longreach
Jericho
Emerald
Rockhampton
Gladstone
Yaraka
Bundaberg
Maryborough
Great Sandy I.
Gympie
Quilpie
Charleville
Grey Range
Roma
Barcoo
Cunnamulla
Toowoomba
Darling Downs
Culgoa
BRISBANE
Ipswich
Lake Eyre
Warburton
The Finke
Eyre Cr.
Paroo
Warrego
Bourke
Barwon
Moree
Kyogle
Grafton
Marree
Flinders Ranges
L. Frome
Woomera
Lake Torrens
Broken Hill
Darling
Coonamble
Narrabri
Armidale
New England Ra.
NEW SOUTH WALES
Cobar
Dubbo
Port Augusta
Whyalla
Radium Hill
Cessnock
Newcastle
Port Pirie
Eyre Pena.
Renmark
Mildura
Lachlan
Bathurst
Blue Mts.
SYDNEY
Spencer's Gulf
G. St. Vincent
ADELAIDE
Hay
Murrumbidgee
Goulburn
Wollongong
Murray Bridge
Murray
Wagga Wagga
Albury
CANBERRA
VICTORIA
Kingston
Naracoorte
Bendigo
Australian Alps
Mt. Kosciusko 7328'
Ballarat
Geelong
MELBOURNE
Snowy
Mt. Gambier
C. Howe
Warrnambool
Pt. Phillip
Yallourn
Wilson's Promy.
King I.
Bass Strait
Flinders I.
140
150
D
E
10
20
30
40
a
b
c
d
600
1000
Bass Strait
Flinders I.
Burnie
Cradle Mt. 5069'
Launceston
Queenstown
HOBART
S.W. Cape
TASMANIA
on same scale

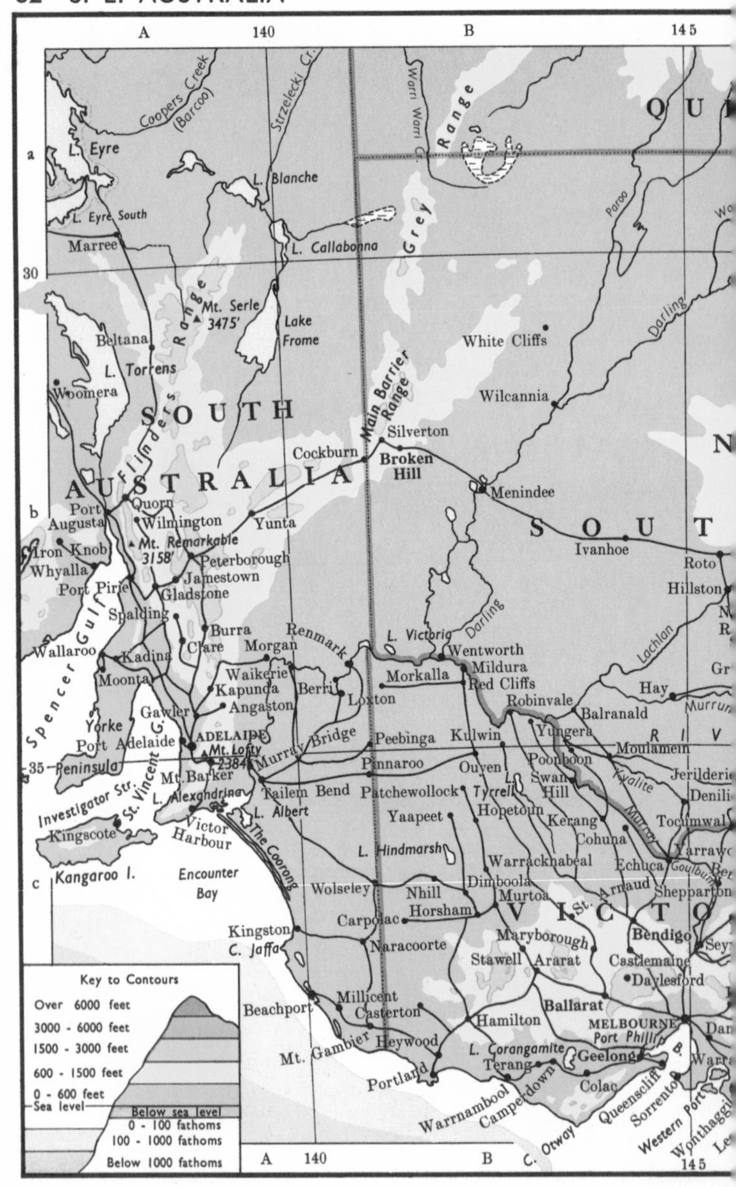

A
140
B
145
a
b
c
30
35
L. Eyre
Coopers Creek (Barcoo)
Strzelecki Cr.
Warri Warri Cr.
Grey Range
L. Eyre South
L. Blanche
L. Callabonna
Marree
Mt. Serle 3475'
Flinders Range
Lake Frome
Beltana
L. Torrens
Woomera
SOUTH AUSTRALIA
Main Barrier Range
White Cliffs
Wilcannia
Silverton
Cockburn
Broken Hill
Menindee
Paroo
Darling
Port Augusta
Quorn
Wilmington
Yunta
Mt. Remarkable 3158'
Iron Knob
Whyalla
Peterborough
Jamestown
Port Pirie
Gladstone
Spalding
Burra
Clare
Morgan
Renmark
Spencer Gulf
Wallaroo
Kadina
Moonta
Waikerie
Kapunda
Berri
Loxton
Angaston
Gawler
Yorke Peninsula
Port Adelaide
ADELAIDE
Mt. Lofty 2384
St. Vincent G.
Murray Bridge
Mt. Barker
L. Alexandrina
Investigator Str.
Kingscote
Kangaroo I.
Victor Harbour
Encounter Bay
Tailem Bend
L. Albert
The Coorong
Pinnaroo
Peebinga
Patchewollock
Yaapeet
L. Hindmarsh
Wolseley
Nhill
Horsham
Kingston
C. Jaffa
Carpolac
Naracoorte
Beachport
Millicent
Casterton
Mt. Gambier
Heywood
Portland
L. Victoria
Wentworth
Mildura
Red Cliffs
Morkalla
Robinvale
Balranald
Kulwin
Ouyen
Yungera
Poonboon
Swan Hill
L. Tyrrell
Hopetoun
Kerang
Cohuna
Warracknabeal
Dimboola
Murtoa
VICTO
St. Arnaud
Maryborough
Stawell
Ararat
Bendigo
Castlemaine
Daylesford
Ballarat
Hamilton
L. Corangamite
Terang
Camperdown
Warrnambool
Colac
Geelong
MELBOURNE
Port Phillip B.
Queenscliff
Sorrento
C. Otway
Western Port
Wonthaggi
S O U T
Ivanhoe
Roto
Hillston
Lachlan
Hay
Murrum
R I V
Moulamein
Kyalite
Murray
Jerilderie
Deniliquin
Tocumwal
Echuca
Goulburn
Shepparton
Yarrawonga
Seymour
Q U
N
Key to Contours
Over 6000 feet
3000 - 6000 feet
1500 - 3000 feet
600 - 1500 feet
0 - 600 feet
Sea level
Below sea level
0 - 100 fathoms
100 - 1000 fathoms
Below 1000 fathoms

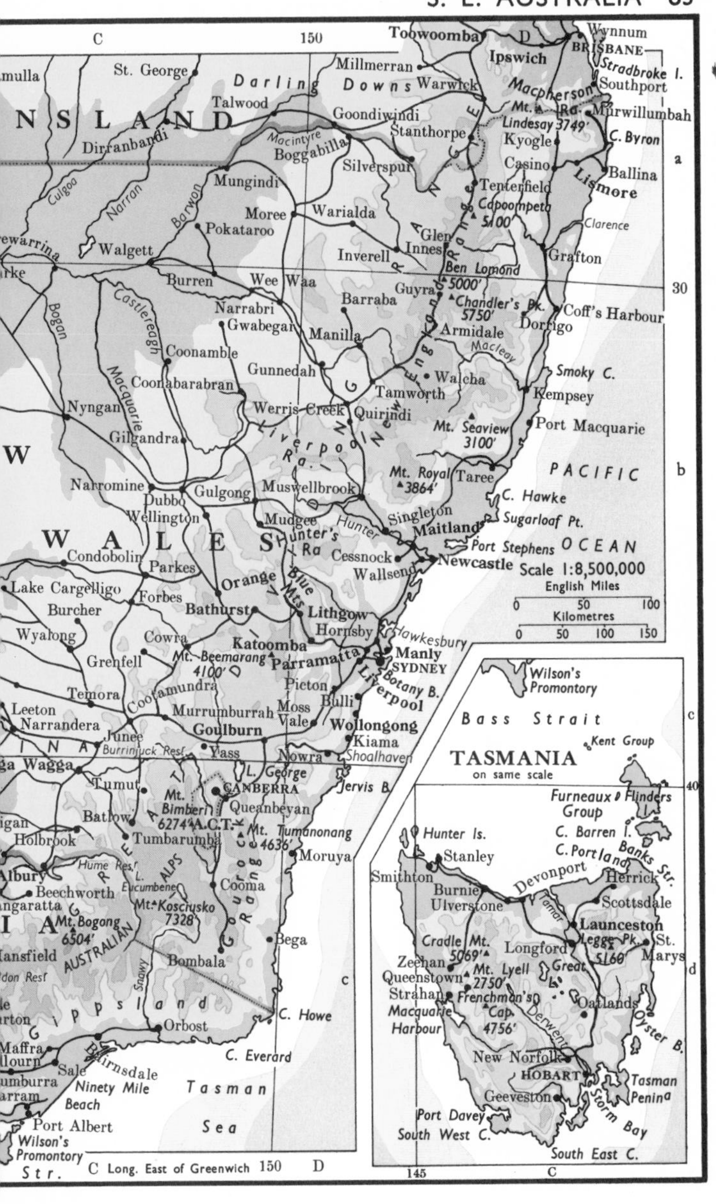

Toowoomba
Wynnum
BRISBANE
Ipswich
Stradbroke I.
Southport
Millmerran
Warwick
Darling Downs
St. George
Talwood
QUEENSLAND
Goondiwindi
Macpherson Ra.
Mt. Lindesay 3749'
Murwillumbah
C. Byron
Stanthorpe
Kyogle
Dirranbandi
Macintyre
Boggabilla
Silverspur
Casino
Ballina
Lismore
Mungindi
Tenterfield
Capoompeta 5100'
Culgoa
Narran
Barwon
Moree
Warialda
Pokataroo
Clarence
Glen Innes
Walgett
Inverell
Grafton
Ben Lomond 5000'
Burren
Wee Waa
Guyra
Chandler's Pk. 5750'
Castlereagh
Narrabri
Barraba
Coff's Harbour
Dorrigo
Bogan
Gwabegar
Manilla
Armidale
Macleay
Coonamble
Gunnedah
Walcha
Smoky C.
Macquarie
Coonabarabran
Tamworth
Kempsey
Nyngan
Werris Creek
Quirindi
New England Range
Mt. Seaview 3100'
Port Macquarie
Gilgandra
Liverpool Ra.
Mt. Royal 3864'
Taree
PACIFIC OCEAN
Narromine
Dubbo
Gulgong
Muswellbrook
C. Hawke
Wellington
Mudgee
Hunter
Singleton
Maitland
Sugarloaf Pt.
NEW SOUTH WALES
Hunter's Ra
Port Stephens
Condobolin
Cessnock
Newcastle
Parkes
Wallsend
Scale 1:8,500,000
English Miles
0 50 100
Kilometres
0 50 100 150
Lake Cargelligo
Orange
Blue Mts
Forbes
Burcher
Bathurst
Lithgow
Hornsby
Hawkesbury
Wyalong
Cowra
Katoomba
Manly
Mt. Beemarang 4100'
Parramatta
SYDNEY
Grenfell
Great Dividing Range
Botany B.
Picton
Liverpool
Temora
Cootamundra
Bulli
Leeton
Narrandera
Murrumburrah
Moss Vale
Wollongong
Goulburn
Junee
Kiama
Burrinjuck Resr.
Yass
Nowra
Shoalhaven
Wagga Wagga
L. George
Jervis B.
Tumut
CANBERRA
Mt. Bimberi 6274'
A.C.T.
Queanbeyan
Batlow
Mt. Tumanonang 4636'
Holbrook
Tumbarumba
Moruya
Hume Resr.
Albury
Australian Alps
L. Eucumbene
Cooma
Beechworth
Gourock Range
Mt. Kosciusko 7328'
Wangaratta
Mt. Bogong 6504'
Mansfield
Snowy
Bombala
Bega
Gippsland
C. Howe
Orbost
Maffra
Sale
Bairnsdale
C. Everard
Ninety Mile Beach
Tasman Sea
Port Albert
Wilson's Promontory
Str.
C Long. East of Greenwich 150 D
Wilson's Promontory
Bass Strait
Kent Group
TASMANIA
on same scale
Furneaux Group
Flinders I.
C. Barren I.
C. Portland
Banks Str.
Hunter Is.
Stanley
Smithton
Devonport
Herrick
Burnie
Ulverstone
Tamar
Scottsdale
Launceston
Cradle Mt. 5069'
Legge Pk. 5160'
St. Marys
Longford
Zeehan
Queenstown
Mt. Lyell 2750'
Great L.
Strahan
Frenchman's Cap 4756'
Oatlands
Macquarie Harbour
Derwent
Oyster B.
New Norfolk
HOBART
Tasman Penin.
Geeveston
Storm Bay
Port Davey
South West C.
South East C.
145

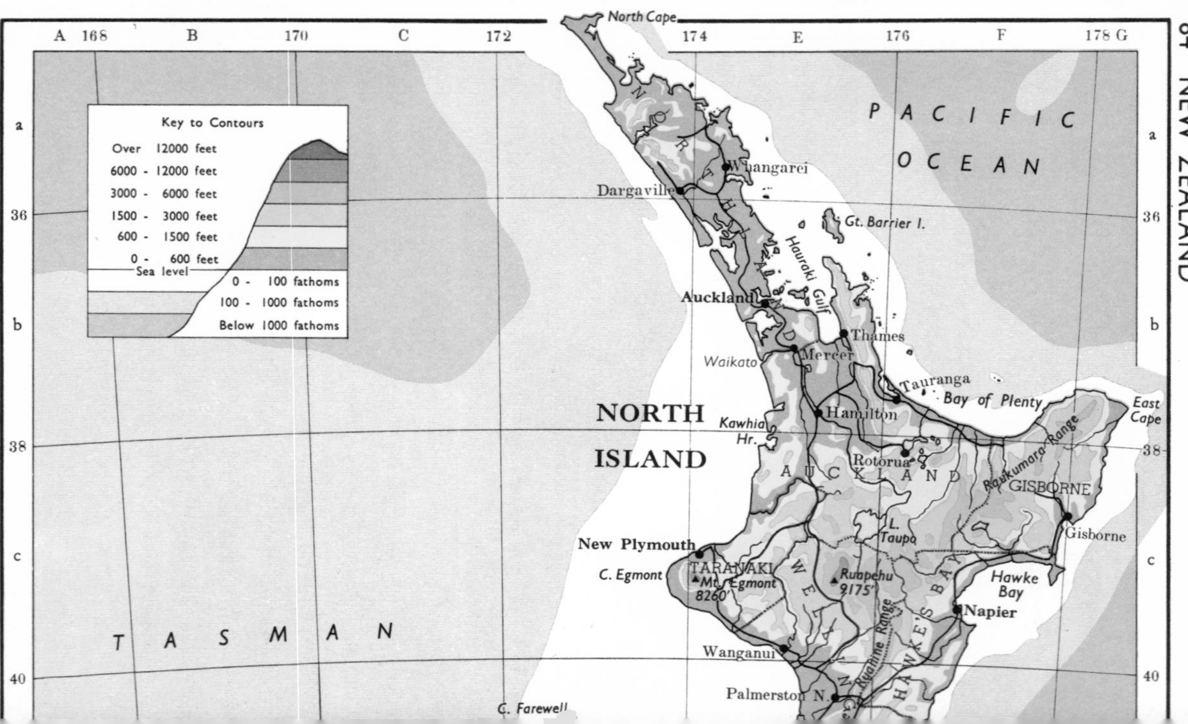
Key to Contours
Over 12000 feet
6000 - 12000 feet
3000 - 6000 feet
1500 - 3000 feet
600 - 1500 feet
0 - 600 feet
Sea level
0 - 100 fathoms
100 - 1000 fathoms
Below 1000 fathoms
PACIFIC
OCEAN
TASMAN
NORTH
ISLAND
North Cape
NORTHLAND
Dargaville
Whangarei
Gt. Barrier I.
Hauraki Gulf
Auckland
Thames
Mercer
Waikato
Hamilton
Tauranga
Bay of Plenty
East Cape
Kawhia Hr.
Rotorua
AUCKLAND
L. Taupo
Raukumara Range
GISBORNE
Gisborne
Hawke Bay
Napier
HAWKES BAY
Ruahine Range
Ruapehu 9175'
WELLINGTON
TARANAKI
Mt. Egmont 8260'
New Plymouth
C. Egmont
Wanganui
Palmerston N.
C. Farewell
A
B
C
E
F
G
168
170
172
174
176
178
a
b
c
36
38
40

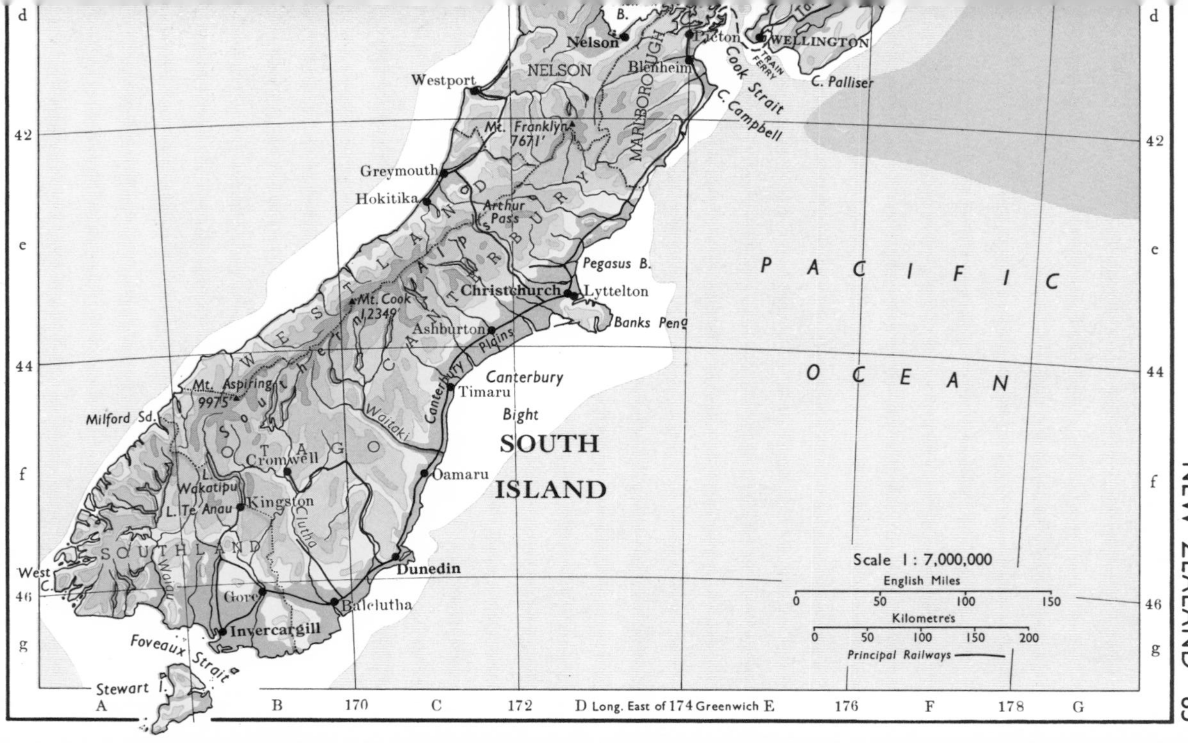
PACIFIC
OCEAN
SOUTH
ISLAND
WELLINGTON
C. Palliser
Cook Strait
TRAIN FERRY
C. Campbell
Picton
Blenheim
MARLBOROUGH
Nelson
NELSON
B.
Westport
Greymouth
Hokitika
Mt. Franklyn 7671'
Arthur Pass
CANTERBURY
WESTLAND
Southern Alps
OTAGO
SOUTHLAND
Pegasus B.
Lyttelton
Christchurch
Banks Peng
Canterbury Plains
Canterbury Bight
Ashburton
Timaru
Oamaru
Dunedin
Waitaki
Mt. Cook 12349'
Mt. Aspiring 9975'
Milford Sd.
Cromwell
L. Wakatipu
L. Te Anau
Kingston
Clutha
Balclutha
Gore
Invercargill
Waiau
West C.
Foveaux Strait
Stewart I.
Scale 1 : 7,000,000
English Miles
0 50 100 150
Kilometres
0 50 100 150 200
Principal Railways
A B 170 C 172 D Long. East of 174 Greenwich E 176 F 178 G
d 42 e 44 f 46 g

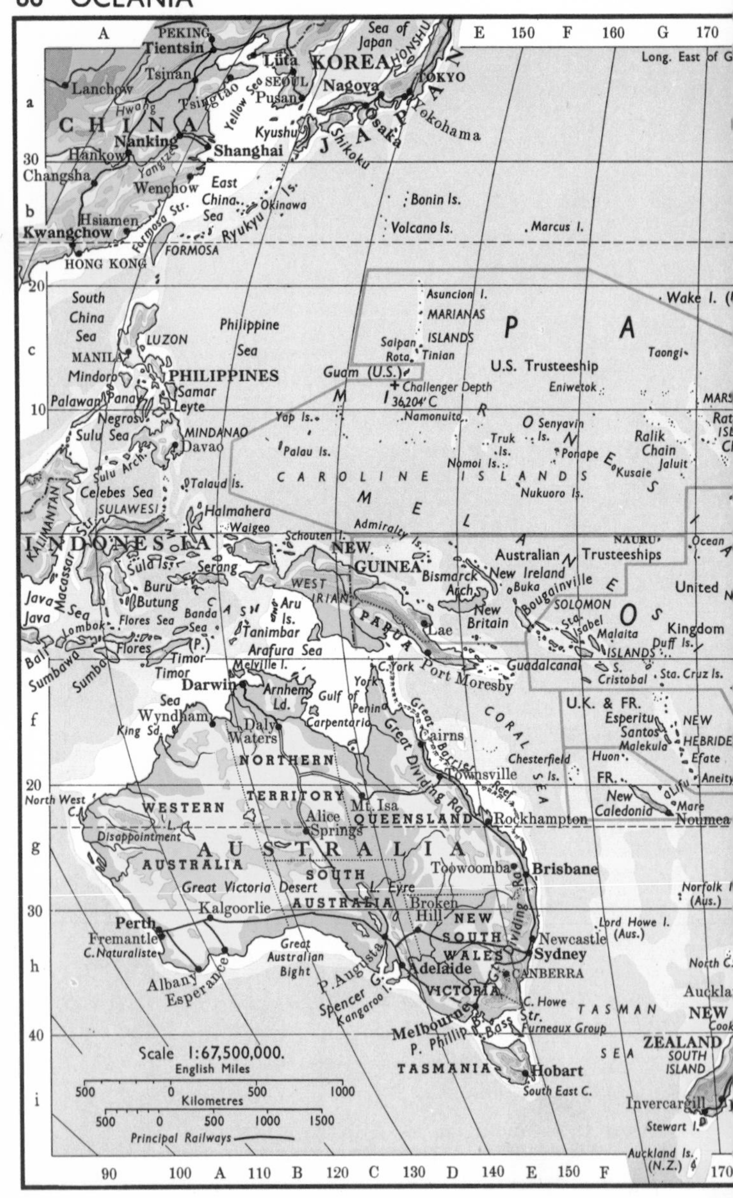
PEKING
Tientsin
Lanchow
Tsinan
Tsingtao
Yellow Sea
SEOUL
Pusan
Lüta
KOREA
Sea of Japan
HONSHU
Nagoya
TOKYO
Yokohama
Osaka
JAPAN
Kyushu
Shikoku
CHINA
Hwang
Nanking
Shanghai
Hankow
Yangtze
Changsha
Wenchow
East China Sea
Okinawa
Ryukyu Is.
Bonin Is.
Volcano Is.
Marcus I.
Hsiamen
Kwangchow
Formosa Str.
FORMOSA
HONG KONG
South China Sea
LUZON
MANILA
Mindoro
PHILIPPINES
Samar
Leyte
Palawan
Panay
Negros
Sulu Sea
MINDANAO
Davao
Sulu Arch.
Philippine Sea
Asuncion I.
MARIANAS ISLANDS
Saipan
Rota
Tinian
Guam (U.S.)
Challenger Depth 36,204' C
PA
U.S. Trusteeship
Wake I.
Taongi
Eniwetok
Yap Is.
Palau Is.
Namonuito
Truk Is.
Senyavin Is.
Ponape
Nomoi Is.
Ralik Chain
Jaluit
Kusaie
MICRONESIA
CAROLINE ISLANDS
Nukuoro Is.
Talaud Is.
Celebes Sea
KALIMANTAN
SULAWESI
Halmahera
Waigeo
Schouten I.
Admiralty Is.
MELANESIA
INDONESIA
NAURU
Ocean I.
Macassar Str.
Sula Is.
Serang
NEW GUINEA
Bismarck Arch.
New Ireland
Buka
Australian Trusteeships
Buru
WEST IRIAN
Bougainville
United Kingdom
Java Sea
Java
Butung
Flores Sea
Banda Sea
Aru Is.
Tanimbar
PAPUA
Lae
New Britain
SOLOMON ISLANDS
Sta. Isabel
Malaita
Duff Is.
Lombok
Bali
Sumbawa
Sumba
Flores
Timor
Arafura Sea
Melville I.
C. York
Port Moresby
Guadalcanal
S. Cristobal
Sta. Cruz Is.
Timor Sea
Darwin
Arnhem Ld.
Gulf of Carpentaria
York Penin.
CORAL SEA
U.K. & FR.
Espiritu Santos
Malekula
NEW HEBRIDES
Efate
Aneityum
Wyndham
King Sd.
Daly Waters
NORTHERN TERRITORY
Great Barrier Reef
Great Dividing Ra.
Cairns
Townsville
Chesterfield Is.
Huon
FR.
New Caledonia
Loyalty Is.
Mare
Noumea
North West C.
WESTERN AUSTRALIA
Mt. Isa
Alice Springs
QUEENSLAND
Rockhampton
L. Disappointment
AUSTRALIA
Toowoomba
Brisbane
SOUTH AUSTRALIA
Great Victoria Desert
L. Eyre
Broken Hill
Norfolk I. (Aus.)
Kalgoorlie
Perth
Fremantle
C. Naturaliste
NEW SOUTH WALES
Lord Howe I. (Aus.)
Newcastle
Sydney
Great Australian Bight
P. Augusta
Adelaide
CANBERRA
North C.
Auckland
Albany
Esperance
Spencer G.
Kangaroo I.
VICTORIA
C. Howe
TASMAN SEA
NEW ZEALAND
Melbourne
P. Phillip B.
Bass Str.
Furneaux Group
Cook
SOUTH ISLAND
TASMANIA
Hobart
South East C.
Invercargill
Stewart I.
Auckland Is. (N.Z.)
Long. East of G
Scale 1:67,500,000.
English Miles
500 0 500 1000
Kilometres
500 0 500 1000 1500
Principal Railways

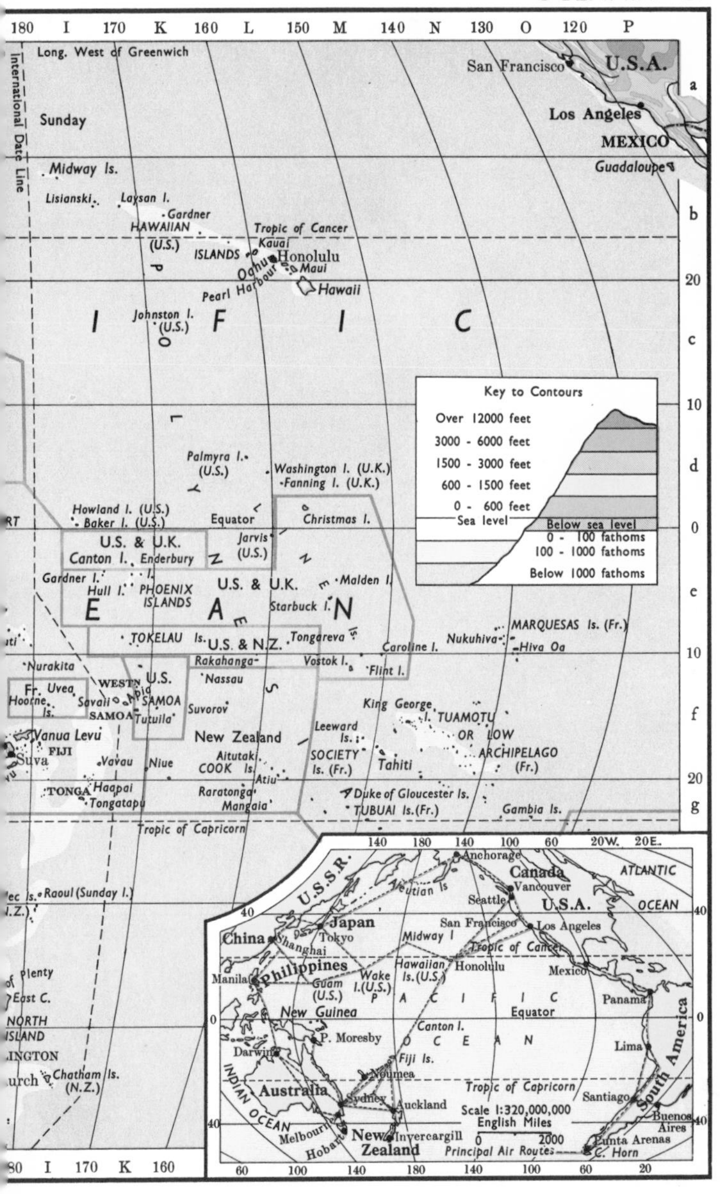
Long. West of Greenwich
International Date Line
Sunday
Midway Is.
Lisianski
Laysan I.
Gardner
HAWAIIAN (U.S.) ISLANDS
Tropic of Cancer
Kauai
Oahu
Honolulu
Maui
Pearl Harbour
Hawaii
San Francisco
U.S.A.
Los Angeles
MEXICO
Guadaloupe
Johnston I. (U.S.)
PACIFIC OCEAN
POLYNESIA
Key to Contours
Over 12000 feet
3000 - 6000 feet
1500 - 3000 feet
600 - 1500 feet
0 - 600 feet
Sea level
Below sea level
0 - 100 fathoms
100 - 1000 fathoms
Below 1000 fathoms
Palmyra I. (U.S.)
Washington I. (U.K.)
Fanning I. (U.K.)
Howland I. (U.S.)
Baker I. (U.S.)
Equator
Christmas I.
Jarvis (U.S.)
U.S. & U.K.
Canton I.
Enderbury I.
Gardner I.
Hull I.
PHOENIX ISLANDS
U.S. & U.K.
Malden I.
Starbuck I.
MARQUESAS Is. (Fr.)
Nukuhiva
Hiva Oa
TOKELAU Is.
U.S. & N.Z.
Tongareva Is.
Caroline I.
Nurakita
Rakahanga
Vostok I.
Flint I.
Nassau
Fr. Uvea
Hoorne Is.
WEST SAMOA
Savaii
Apia
U.S. SAMOA
Tutuila
Suvorov
King George I.
TUAMOTU OR LOW ARCHIPELAGO (Fr.)
Vanua Levu
FIJI
Suva
New Zealand
Leeward Is.
SOCIETY Is. (Fr.)
Tahiti
Vavau
Niue
Aitutaki
COOK Is.
Atiu
TONGA
Haapai
Tongatapu
Raratonga
Mangaia
Duke of Gloucester Is.
TUBUAI Is. (Fr.)
Gambia Is.
Tropic of Capricorn
Raoul (Sunday I.)
Chatham Is. (N.Z.)
NORTH ISLAND
East C.
U.S.S.R.
Anchorage
Canada
Aleutian Is
Vancouver
Seattle
U.S.A.
ATLANTIC OCEAN
Japan
Tokyo
China
Shanghai
San Francisco
Los Angeles
Midway I
Tropic of Cancer
Honolulu
Hawaiian Is. (U.S.)
Mexico
Manila
Philippines
Guam (U.S.)
Wake I. (U.S.)
PACIFIC OCEAN
Panama
Equator
New Guinea
Canton I.
P. Moresby
Lima
Darwin
Fiji Is.
Noumea
South America
INDIAN OCEAN
Australia
Sydney
Auckland
Tropic of Capricorn
Santiago
Scale 1:320,000,000
English Miles
0 2000
Buenos Aires
Melbourne
Hobart
New Zealand
Invercargill
Principal Air Routes
Punta Arenas
C. Horn

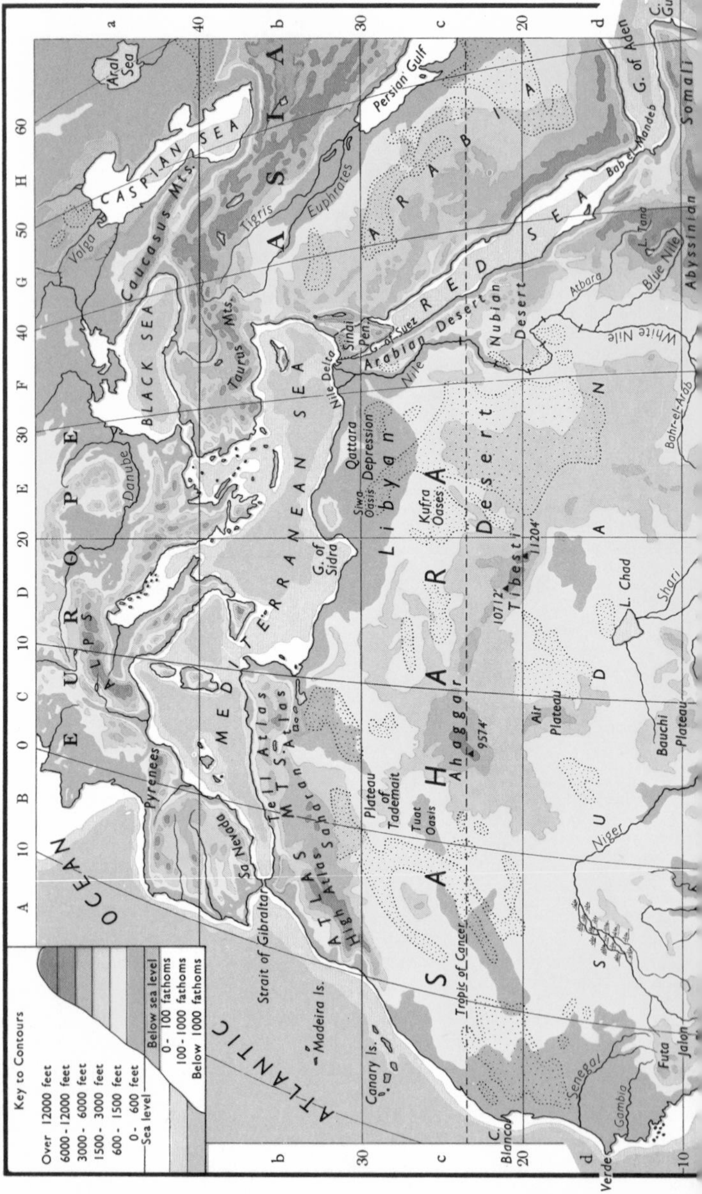

Key to Contours

Over 12000 feet
6000 - 12000 feet
3000 - 6000 feet
1500 - 3000 feet
600 - 1500 feet
0 - 600 feet
Sea level
Below sea level
0 - 100 fathoms
100 - 1000 fathoms
Below 1000 fathoms

EUROPE
ASIA
ATLANTIC OCEAN
MEDITERRANEAN SEA
BLACK SEA
CASPIAN SEA
RED SEA
Aral Sea
Persian Gulf
G. of Aden
Socotra
C. Guardafui
Somali
Abyssinian
Bab el Mandeb
L. Tana
Blue Nile
Atbara
White Nile
Bahr-el-Arab
Volga
Caucasus Mts.
Tigris
Euphrates
ARABIA
Taurus Mts.
Danube
ALPS
Pyrenees
Sa Nevada
Strait of Gibraltar
Madeira Is.
Canary Is.
Tell Atlas
Saharan Atlas
High Atlas
ATLAS MTS.
G. of Sidra
Nile Delta
Sinai Pen.
G. of Suez
Arabian Desert
Nubian Desert
Nile
Qattara Depression
Siwa Oasis
Libyan Desert
Kufra Oases
SAHARA
Plateau of Tademait
Tuat Oasis
Ahaggar
9574'
Tibesti
10712'
11204'
Tropic of Cancer
Air Plateau
L. Chad
Shari
SUDAN
Bauchi Plateau
Niger
Senegal
Gambia
Futa Jalon
C. Blanco
C. Verde

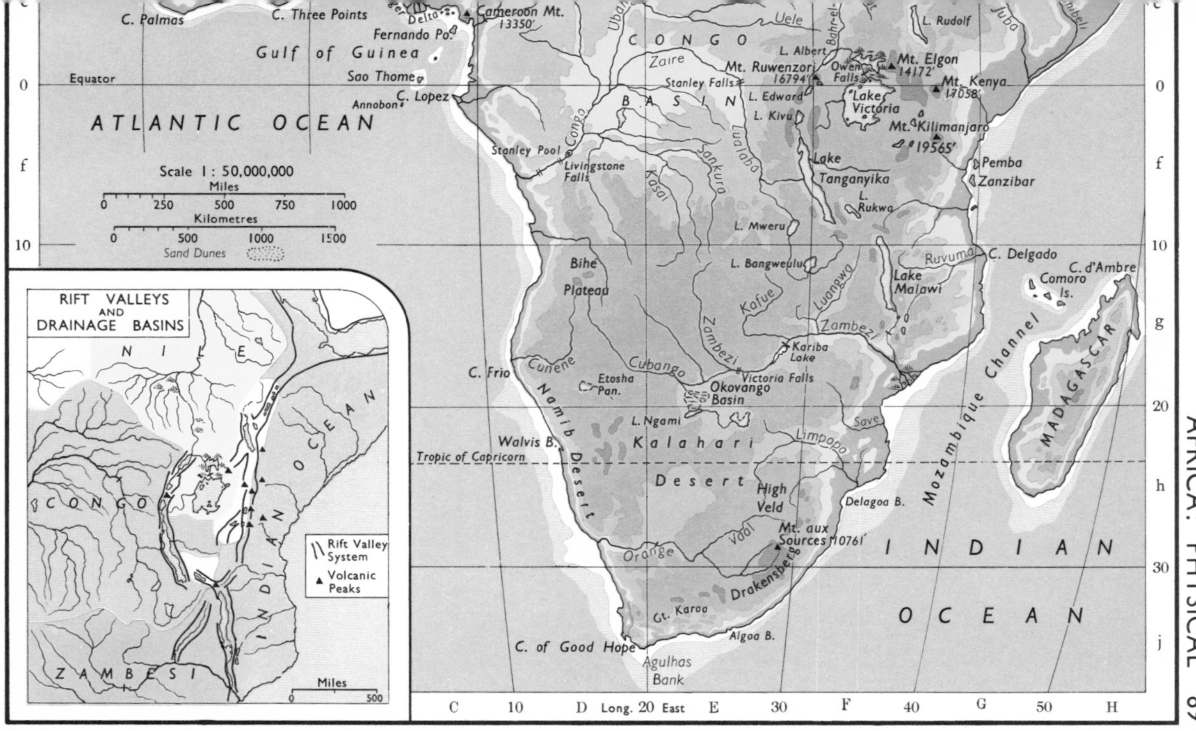

C. Palmas
C. Three Points
Cameroon Mt. 13350'
Delta
Fernando Po
Gulf of Guinea
Equator
Sao Thome
Annobon
C. Lopez
ATLANTIC OCEAN
Scale 1 : 50,000,000
Miles
0 250 500 750 1000
Kilometres
0 500 1000 1500
Sand Dunes
CONGO BASIN
Uele
Zaire
Stanley Falls
Stanley Pool
Congo
Livingstone Falls
Kasai
Sankura
Lualaba
Bahr-el-
L. Rudolf
Juba
L. Albert
Mt. Ruwenzori 16794'
Owen Falls
Mt. Elgon 14172'
Mt. Kenya 17058'
L. Edward
Lake Victoria
L. Kivu
Mt. Kilimanjaro 19565'
Lake Tanganyika
L. Rukwa
Pemba
Zanzibar
L. Mweru
L. Bangweulu
Ruvuma
C. Delgado
Lake Malawi
Comoro Is.
C. d'Ambre
Bihe Plateau
Kafue
Luangwa
Zambezi
Kariba Lake
MADAGASCAR
Mozambique Channel
C. Frio
Cunene
Etosha Pan.
Cubango
Victoria Falls
Okovango Basin
L. Ngami
Kalahari Desert
Namib Desert
Walvis B.
Tropic of Capricorn
Save
Limpopo
High Veld
Delagoa B.
Vaal
Mt. aux Sources 10761'
Orange
Drakensberg
Gt. Karoo
Algoa B.
C. of Good Hope
Agulhas Bank
INDIAN OCEAN
C 10 D Long. 20 East E 30 F 40 G 50 H
RIFT VALLEYS AND DRAINAGE BASINS
NILE
CONGO
INDIAN OCEAN
ZAMBESI
Rift Valley System
Volcanic Peaks
Miles
0 500

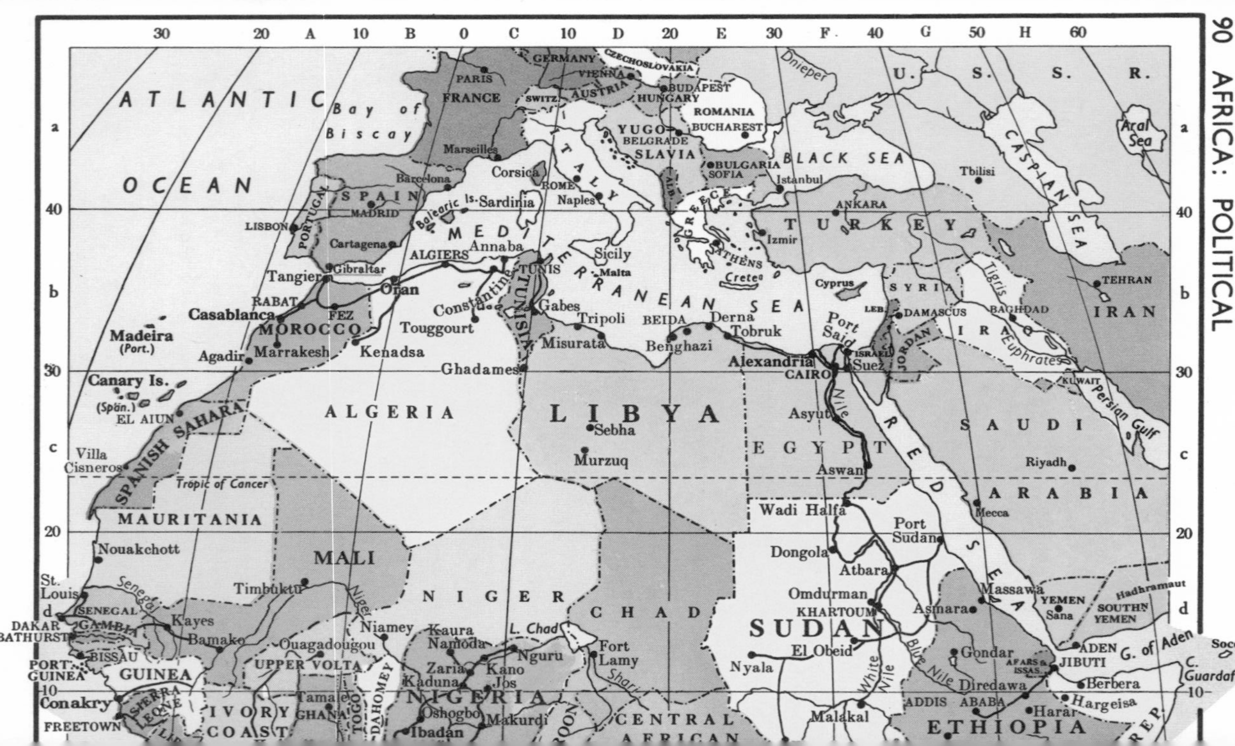
ATLANTIC
OCEAN
Bay of Biscay
FRANCE
PARIS
Marseilles
SPAIN
MADRID
Barcelona
Cartagena
Gibraltar
PORTUGAL
LISBON
Madeira (Port.)
Canary Is. (Spän.)
EL AIUN
SPANISH SAHARA
Villa Cisneros
Tropic of Cancer
MAURITANIA
Nouakchott
St. Louis
DAKAR
SENEGAL
GAMBIA
BATHURST
BISSAU
PORT. GUINEA
GUINEA
Conakry
FREETOWN
SIERRA LEONE
MOROCCO
RABAT
Casablanca
Marrakesh
Agadir
Tangier
FEZ
Oran
ALGIERS
Kenadsa
Touggourt
Constantine
Annaba
Ghadames
ALGERIA
MALI
Timbuktu
Bamako
Kayes
Senegal
Niger
UPPER VOLTA
Ouagadougou
Niamey
DAHOMEY
TOGO
GHANA
Tamale
IVORY COAST
NIGERIA
Kaura Namoda
Kano
Zaria
Kaduna
Jos
Ibadan
Oshogbo
Makurdi
Nguru
NIGER
L. Chad
Fort Lamy
Shari
CHAD
CENTRAL AFRICAN
TUNISIA
TUNIS
Gabes
Tripoli
Misurata
LIBYA
Sebha
Murzuq
BEIDA
Benghazi
Derna
Tobruk
Alexandria
CAIRO
Port Said
Suez
Asyut
Aswan
EGYPT
Nile
Wadi Halfa
Dongola
Atbara
Omdurman
KHARTOUM
Port Sudan
SUDAN
El Obeid
Nyala
Malakal
White Nile
Blue Nile
ETHIOPIA
ADDIS ABABA
Asmara
Gondar
Massawa
Diredawa
Harar
Hargeisa
Berbera
JIBUTI
AFARS & ISSAS
ADEN
G. of Aden
C. Guardafui
Socotra
SOUTHN. YEMEN
YEMEN
Sana
Hadhramaut
RED SEA
SAUDI ARABIA
Mecca
Riyadh
KUWAIT
Persian Gulf
IRAN
TEHRAN
IRAQ
BAGHDAD
Tigris
Euphrates
SYRIA
DAMASCUS
LEB.
ISRAEL
JORDAN
Cyprus
TURKEY
ANKARA
Istanbul
Izmir
Tbilisi
CASPIAN SEA
Aral Sea
U. S. S. R.
BLACK SEA
Dnieper
ROMANIA
BUCHAREST
BULGARIA
SOFIA
YUGOSLAVIA
BELGRADE
ALB.
GREECE
ATHENS
Crete
HUNGARY
BUDAPEST
CZECHOSLOVAKIA
AUSTRIA
VIENNA
GERMANY
SWITZ.
ITALY
ROME
Naples
Sicily
Malta
Corsica
Sardinia
Balearic Is.
MEDITERRANEAN SEA

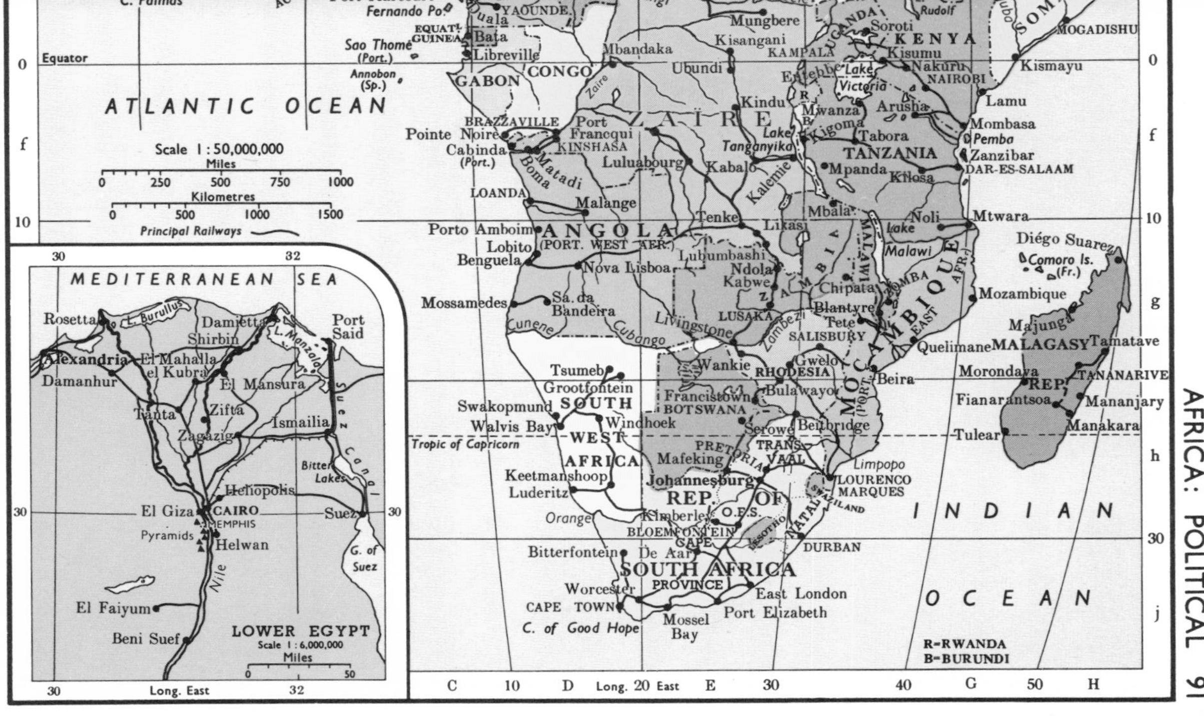
ATLANTIC OCEAN
INDIAN OCEAN
Scale 1 : 50,000,000
Miles
0 250 500 750 1000
Kilometres
0 500 1000 1500
Principal Railways
Equator
Tropic of Capricorn
Long. 20 East
R=RWANDA
B=BURUNDI
ZAÏRE
ANGOLA
(PORT. WEST AFR.)
KENYA
UGANDA
TANZANIA
ZAMBIA
MALAWI
MOÇAMBIQUE
(PORT. EAST AFR.)
RHODESIA
BOTSWANA
SOUTH WEST AFRICA
REP. OF SOUTH AFRICA
MALAGASY REP.
CONGO
GABON
EQUAT. GUINEA
LESOTHO
SWAZILAND
NATAL
O.F.S.
TRANSVAAL
CAPE PROVINCE
Sao Thomé (Port.)
Annobon (Sp.)
Fernando Po
Comoro Is. (Fr.)
KINSHASA
BRAZZAVILLE
NAIROBI
KAMPALA
DAR-ES-SALAAM
LUSAKA
SALISBURY
ZOMBA
LOANDA
PRETORIA
TANANARIVE
LOURENCO MARQUES
DURBAN
CAPE TOWN
BLOEMFONTEIN
YAOUNDE
MOGADISHU
Kismayu
Lamu
Mombasa
Pemba
Zanzibar
Kisumu
Nakuru
Soroti
Arusha
Entebbe
Lake Victoria
Lake Tanganyika
Lake Malawi
Kigoma
Tabora
Mwanza
Kindu
Kisangani
Mungbere
Mbandaka
Ubundi
Kabalo
Kalemie
Mpanda
Kilosa
Mbala
Noli
Mtwara
Tenke
Likasi
Lubumbashi
Ndola
Kabwe
Chipata
Blantyre
Tete
Livingstone
Wankie
Gwelo
Bulawayo
Francistown
Serowe
Beitbridge
Beira
Mozambique
Quelimane
Diégo Suarez
Majunga
Tamatave
Morondava
Fianarantsoa
Mananjary
Manakara
Tulear
Tsumeb
Grootfontein
Windhoek
Walvis Bay
Swakopmund
Keetmanshoop
Luderitz
Porto Amboim
Lobito
Benguela
Mossamedes
Sa. da Bandeira
Nova Lisboa
Malange
Luluabourg
Port Francqui
Matadi
Boma
Cabinda (Port.)
Pointe Noire
Libreville
Bata
Duala
Johannesburg
Mafeking
Kimberley
De Aar
Bitterfontein
Worcester
Mossel Bay
East London
Port Elizabeth
C. of Good Hope
Orange
Limpopo
Zambezi
Cubango
Cunene
Zaire
MEDITERRANEAN SEA
LOWER EGYPT
Scale 1 : 6,000,000
Miles
0 50
Alexandria
Rosetta
L. Burullus
Damietta
L. Manzala
Port Said
Shirbin
El Mahalla el Kubra
Damanhur
El Mansura
Tanta
Zifta
Zagazig
Ismailia
Suez Canal
Bitter Lakes
Heliopolis
CAIRO
MEMPHIS
El Giza
Pyramids
Helwan
Suez
G. of Suez
El Faiyum
Beni Suef
Nile
Long. East

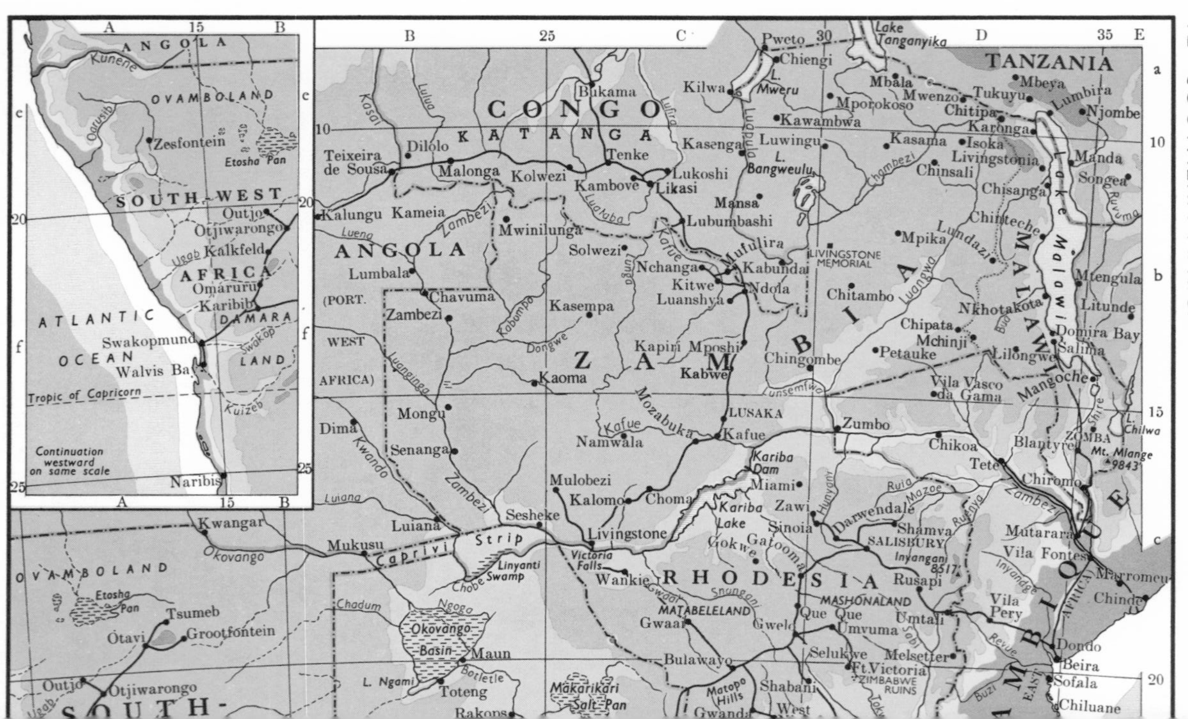
TANZANIA
MALAWI
Lake Malawi
CONGO
KATANGA
ANGOLA
ZAMBIA
RHODESIA
MOZAMBIQUE
SOUTH-WEST AFRICA
(PORT. WEST AFRICA)
Caprivi Strip
Lake Tanganyika
L. Mweru
L. Bangweulu
Kariba Dam
Kariba Lake
Victoria Falls
Linyanti Swamp
Okovango Basin
Makarikari Salt Pan
Etosha Pan
L. Ngami
LIVINGSTONE MEMORIAL
ZIMBABWE RUINS
LUSAKA
SALISBURY
ZOMBA
MASHONALAND
MATABELELAND
OVAMBOLAND
DAMARALAND
ATLANTIC OCEAN
Tropic of Capricorn
Continuation westward on same scale
Mbeya
Tukuyu
Chitipa
Karonga
Livingstonia
Nkhotakota
Lilongwe
Blantyre
Mangoche
Chiromo
Tete
Beira
Sofala
Chiluane
Dondo
Vila Pery
Vila Fontes
Mutarara
Chinde
Marromeu
Umtali
Rusapi
Melsetter
Ft. Victoria
Shabani
Bulawayo
Gwanda
Gwaai
Wankie
Livingstone
Kalomo
Choma
Mazabuka
Kafue
Kabwe
Ndola
Kitwe
Luanshya
Mufulira
Nchanga
Lubumbashi
Likasi
Kolwezi
Mongu
Senanga
Sesheke
Mulobezi
Maun
Toteng
Tsumeb
Grootfontein
Otavi
Otjiwarongo
Outjo
Swakopmund
Walvis Bay
Karibib
Omaruru
Kalkfeld
Zesfontein
Naribis
Kwangar
Mukusu
Dilolo
Teixeira de Sousa
Malonga
Kasai
Zambezi
Luapula
Luangwa
Chambezi
Ruvuma
Shire
Okovango
Kunene
Mt. Mlange 9843
Inyangani 8517

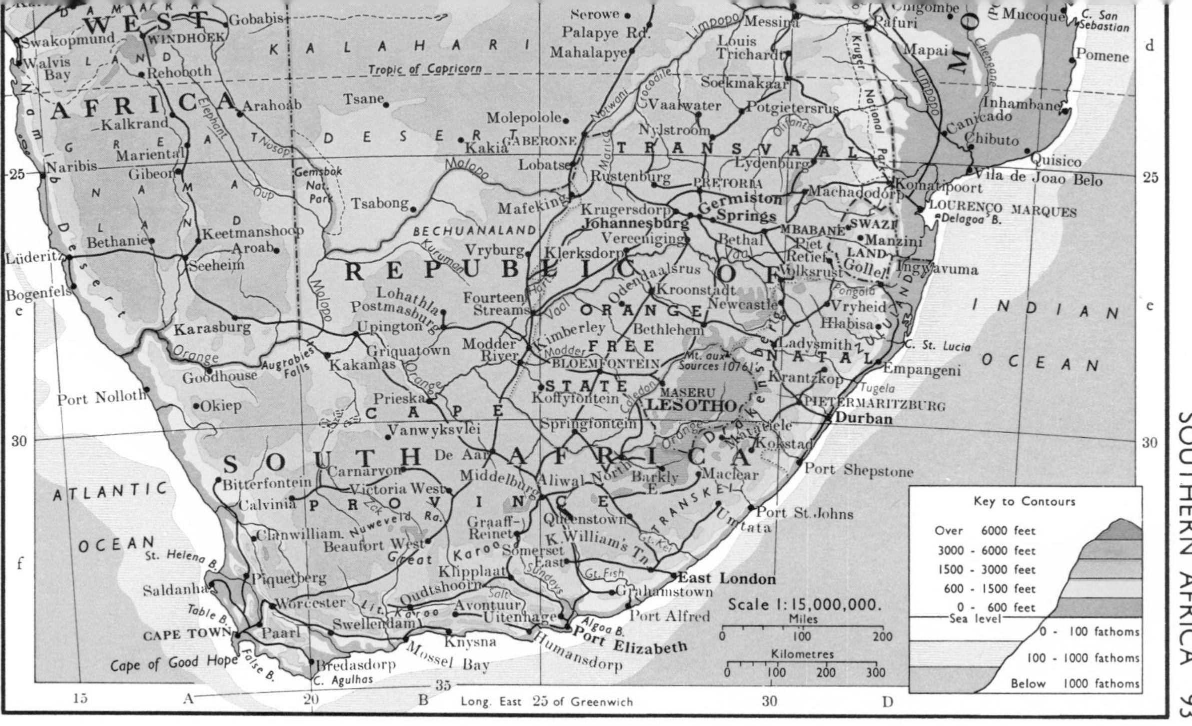
WEST AFRICA
DAMARALAND
NAMALAND
Namib Desert
KALAHARI DESERT
Tropic of Capricorn
REPUBLIC OF SOUTH AFRICA
TRANSVAAL
ORANGE FREE STATE
CAPE PROVINCE
NATAL
ZULULAND
LESOTHO
SWAZILAND
BECHUANALAND
TRANSKEI
INDIAN OCEAN
ATLANTIC OCEAN
Kruger National Park
Gemsbok Nat. Park
Limpopo
Orange
Vaal
Molopo
Modder
Caledon
Tugela
Pongola
Olifants
Crocodile
Notwani
Marico
Hartz
Kuruman
Elephant
Nosop
Oup
Augrabies Falls
Great Karoo
Lit. Karoo
Nuweveld Ra.
Drakensberg
Sundays
Gt. Fish
Gt. Kei
Salt
Mt. aux Sources 10761
Swakopmund
Walvis Bay
WINDHOEK
Rehoboth
Gobabis
Arahoab
Kalkrand
Mariental
Gibeon
Naribis
Keetmanshoop
Aroab
Bethanie
Seeheim
Lüderitz
Bogenfels
Karasburg
Goodhouse
Okiep
Port Nolloth
Tsane
Tsabong
Kakia
Molepolole
GABERONE
Lobatse
Mafeking
Serowe
Palapye Rd.
Mahalapye
Messina
Louis Trichardt
Soekmakaar
Vaalwater
Potgietersrus
Nylstroom
Lydenburg
Rustenburg
PRETORIA
Germiston
Springs
Krugersdorp
Johannesburg
Vereeniging
Klerksdorp
Bethal
Machadodorp
Komatipoort
MBABANE
Manzini
Piet Retief
Volksrust
Vryburg
Fourteen Streams
Lohathla
Postmasburg
Upington
Kakamas
Griquatown
Modder River
Kimberley
Odendaalsrus
Kroonstadt
Bethlehem
Newcastle
Vryheid
Hlabisa
Ladysmith
Krantzkop
BLOEMFONTEIN
Koffyfontein
MASERU
Prieska
Vanwyksvlei
Springfontein
De Aar
Middelburg
Carnarvon
Victoria West
Bitterfontein
Calvinia
Clanwilliam
Beaufort West
Graaff-Reinet
Aliwal North
Barkly E.
Maclear
Matatiele
Kokstad
Queenstown
Somerset East
Klipplaat
K. William's Tn
Umtata
Port St. Johns
Port Shepstone
PIETERMARITZBURG
Durban
Empangeni
C. St. Lucia
Ingwavuma
East London
Grahamstown
Port Alfred
Port Elizabeth
Algoa B.
Humansdorp
Uitenhage
Avontuur
Oudtshoorn
Knysna
Mossel Bay
Swellendam
Bredasdorp
C. Agulhas
Worcester
Paarl
Piquetberg
Saldanha
St. Helena B.
Table B.
CAPE TOWN
False B.
Cape of Good Hope
Pafuri
Mapai
Chengane
Canicado
Chibuto
Inhambane
Quisico
Vila de Joao Belo
LOURENÇO MARQUES
Delagoa B.
Mucoque
C. San Sebastian
Pomene
Scale 1:15,000,000.
Miles
0 100 200
Kilometres
0 100 200 300
Key to Contours
Over 6000 feet
3000 - 6000 feet
1500 - 3000 feet
600 - 1500 feet
0 - 600 feet
Sea level
0 - 100 fathoms
100 - 1000 fathoms
Below 1000 fathoms
Long. East 25 of Greenwich
15
20
25
30
35
A
B
D
d
e
f

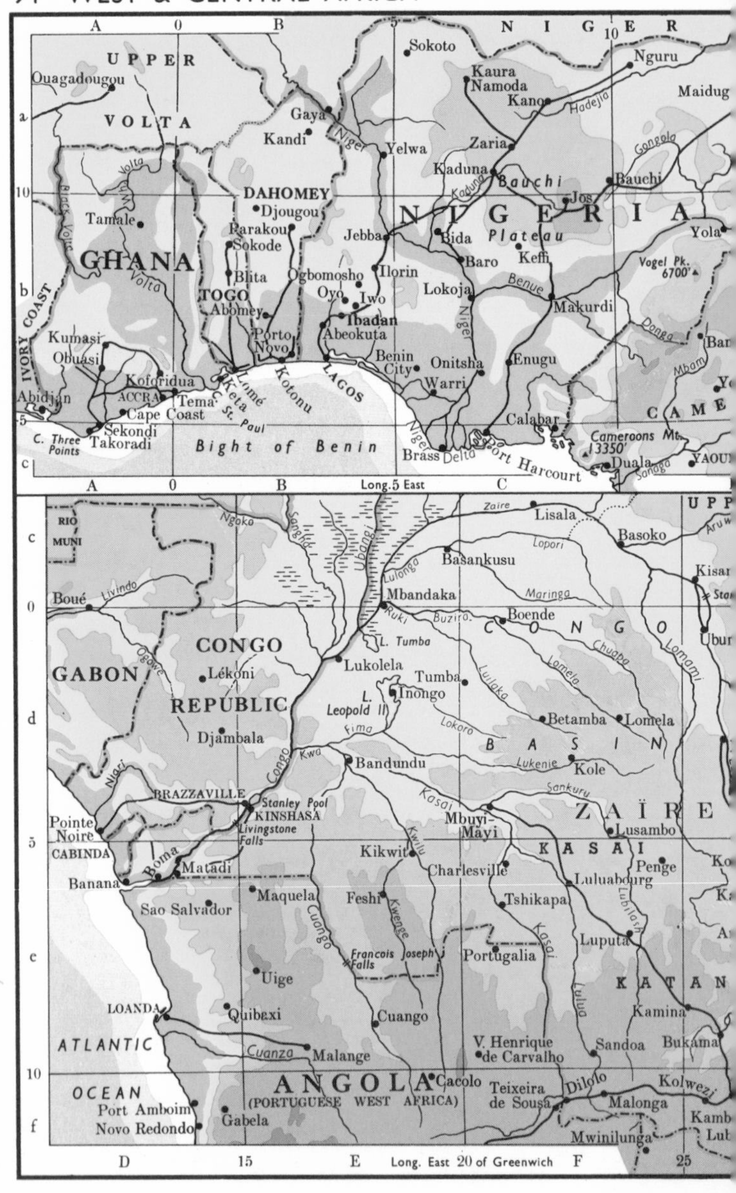

NIGER
UPPER VOLTA
Ouagadougou
Sokoto
Nguru
Kaura Namoda
Kano
Maidug
Hadejia
Gaya
Kandi
Niger
Yelwa
Zaria
Gongola
Kaduna
Bauchi
Bauchi
Jos
Black Volta
Volta
White Volta
DAHOMEY
Djougou
Tamale
NIGERIA
Plateau
Yola
Parakou
Sokode
Jebba
Bida
Keffi
GHANA
Baro
Vogel Pk. 6700'
Blita
Ogbomosho
Ilorin
Lokoja
Benue
TOGO
Oyo
Iwo
Makurdi
IVORY COAST
Abomey
Ibadan
Abeokuta
Donga
Kumasi
Porto Novo
Obuasi
Benin City
Onitsha
Enugu
Mbam
Koforidua
Lomé
Kotonu
LAGOS
Warri
Abidjan
ACCRA
Tema
Keta
C. St. Paul
Cape Coast
CAMEROONS
Calabar
Sekondi
Takoradi
C. Three Points
Bight of Benin
Brass
Niger Delta
Port Harcourt
Cameroons Mt. 13350'
Duala
Sanaga
YAOUNDE
Long. 5 East
RIO MUNI
Ngoko
Sangha
Ubangi
Zaïre
Lisala
Lopori
Basoko
Aruwimi
Basankusu
Lulonga
Kisangani
Boué
Livindo
Mbandaka
Maringa
Ruki
Busira
Boende
Stanley Falls
CONGO
L. Tumba
CONGO
Chuapa
Lomami
Ubundu
Ogowe
Lukolela
GABON
Lékoni
Tumba
Lomela
Lulaka
L. Leopold II
Inongo
REPUBLIC
Betamba
Lomela
Lokoro
Fima
Djambala
BASIN
Kwa
Bandundu
Lukenie
Kole
Congo
Niari
Kasai
Sankuru
BRAZZAVILLE
Stanley Pool
KINSHASA
Livingstone Falls
ZAÏRE
Mbuyi-Mayi
Pointe Noire
Lusambo
CABINDA
KASAI
Boma
Matadi
Kikwit
Kwilu
Charlesville
Penge
Banana
Luluabourg
Maquela
Feshi
Sao Salvador
Tshikapa
Cuango
Kwenge
Lubilash
Luputa
Kasai
Francois Joseph Falls
Portugalia
Uige
KATANGA
LOANDA
Quibaxi
Kamina
Cuango
Lulua
ATLANTIC
V. Henrique de Carvalho
Sandoa
Bukama
Cuanza
Malange
ANGOLA
(PORTUGUESE WEST AFRICA)
Cacolo
Teixeira de Sousa
Dilolo
Kolwezi
Malonga
OCEAN
Port Amboim
Novo Redondo
Gabela
Mwinilunga
Long. East 20 of Greenwich

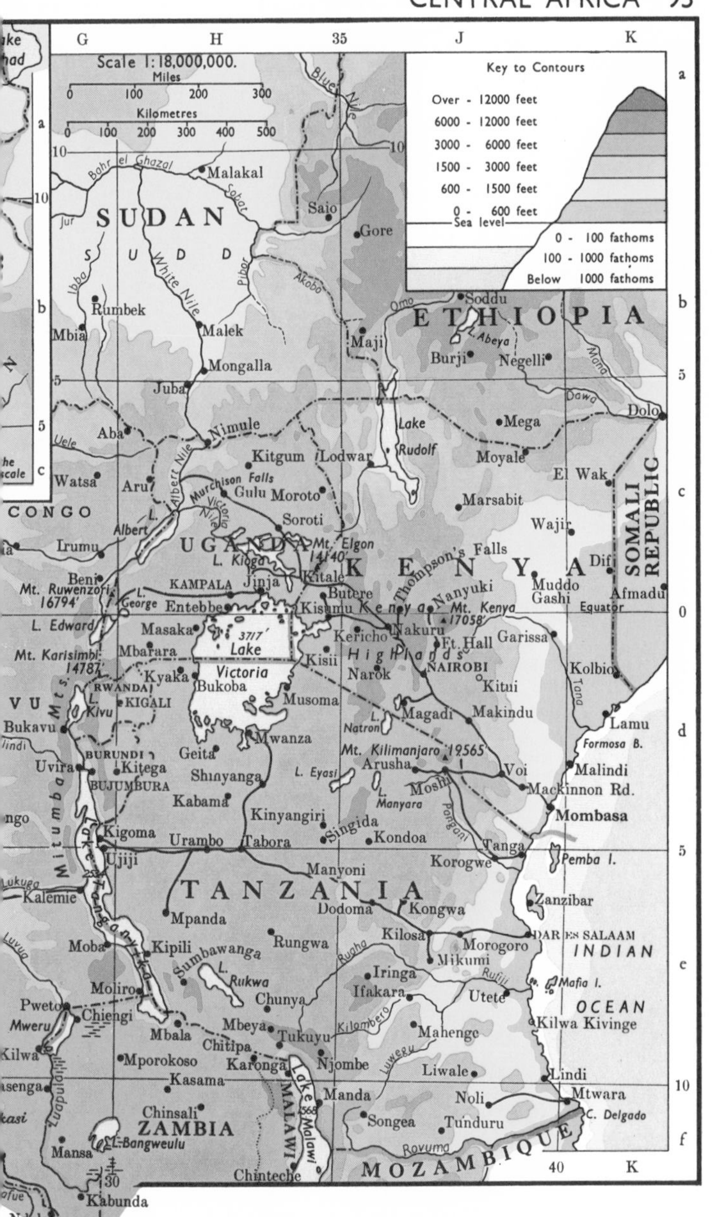
Scale 1:18,000,000.
Miles
Kilometres
Key to Contours
Over - 12000 feet
6000 - 12000 feet
3000 - 6000 feet
1500 - 3000 feet
600 - 1500 feet
0 - 600 feet
Sea level
0 - 100 fathoms
100 - 1000 fathoms
Below 1000 fathoms
SUDAN
SUDD
ETHIOPIA
UGANDA
KENYA
SOMALI REPUBLIC
TANZANIA
ZAMBIA
MALAWI
MOZAMBIQUE
CONGO
RWANDA
BURUNDI
INDIAN OCEAN
Malakal
Saio
Gore
Rumbek
Mbia
Malek
Mongalla
Juba
Nimule
Aba
Watsa
Aru
Kitgum
Lodwar
Gulu
Moroto
Soroti
Maji
Soddu
Burji
Negelli
Mega
Moyale
Dolo
El Wak
Marsabit
Wajir
Dif
Muddo Gashi
Afmadu
Irumu
Beni
KAMPALA
Jinja
Entebbe
Kitale
Butere
Kisumu
Nanyuki
Mt. Kenya 17058'
Nakuru
Ft. Hall
Garissa
Kericho
Kisii
Narok
NAIROBI
Kitui
Kolbio
Masaka
Mbarara
Kyaka
Bukoba
KIGALI
Musoma
Magadi
Makindu
Lamu
Bukavu
Mwanza
Geita
Kitega
BUJUMBURA
Uvira
Shinyanga
Arusha
Moshi
Voi
Malindi
Mackinnon Rd.
Mombasa
Kabama
Kinyangiri
Singida
Kondoa
Kigoma
Ujiji
Urambo
Tabora
Tanga
Korogwe
Pemba I.
Manyoni
Kalemie
Mpanda
Dodoma
Kongwa
Zanzibar
Rungwa
Kilosa
Morogoro
Mikumi
DAR ES SALAAM
Moba
Kipili
Sumbawanga
Iringa
Ifakara
Utete
Mafia I.
Moliro
Pweto
Chiengi
Chunya
Mbala
Mbeya
Tukuyu
Mahenge
Kilwa Kivinge
Kilwa
Chitipa
Mporokoso
Karonga
Njombe
Liwale
Lindi
Kasama
Manda
Noli
Mtwara
C. Delgado
Chinsali
Songea
Tunduru
Mansa
L. Bangweulu
Chinteche
Kabunda
Ndola
Bahr el Ghazal
Sobat
Jur
Ibba
White Nile
Pibor
Akobo
Blue Nile
Omo
L. Abeya
Mana
Dawa
Lake Rudolf
Uele
Albert Nile
Murchison Falls
Victoria Nile
L. Albert
L. Kioga
Mt. Elgon 14140'
Thompson's Falls
Kenya Highlands
Equator
Mt. Ruwenzori 16794'
L. George
L. Edward
3717' Lake Victoria
Mt. Karisimbi 14787'
L. Kivu
Mitumba Mts.
L. Natron
Mt. Kilimanjaro 19565'
Tana
Formosa B.
L. Eyasi
L. Manyara
Pangani
Lake Tanganyika
Lukuga
Luvua
L. Rukwa
Rugha
Rufiji
Kilombero
Luwegu
Mweru
Luapula
Lake Malawi
Rovuma
G
H
J
K
35
40
10
5
0
a
b
c
d
e
f

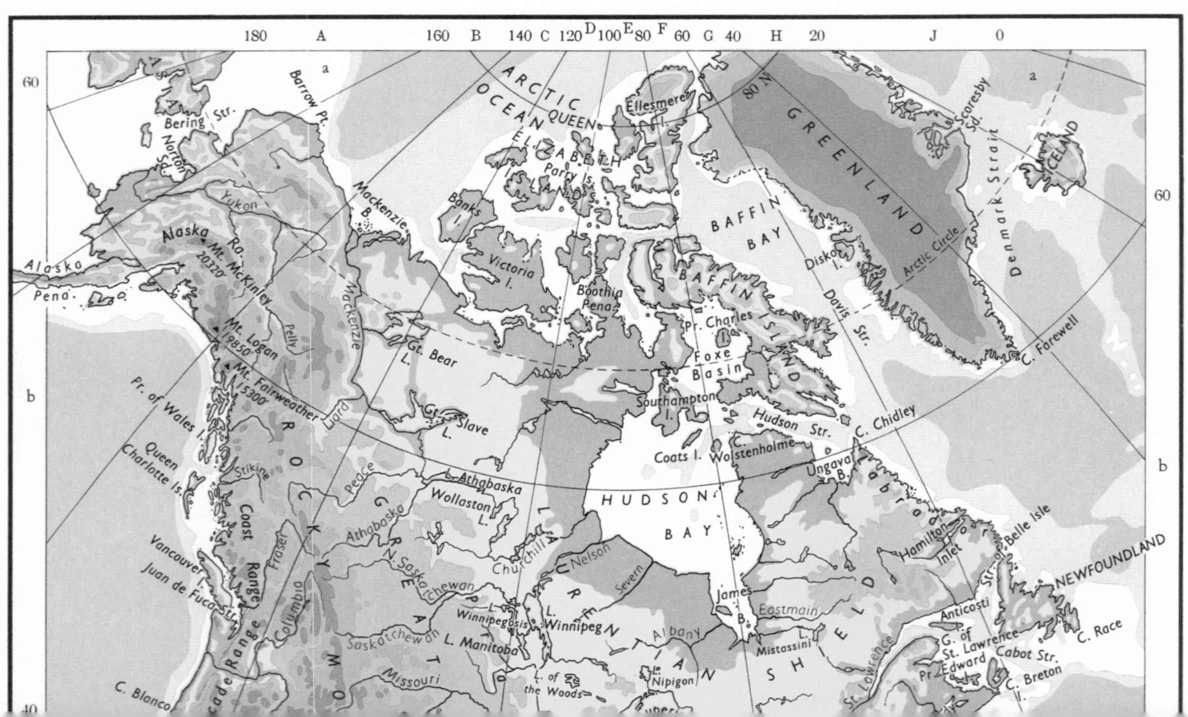
ASIA
Bering Str.
Norton Sd.
Barrow Pt.
ARCTIC OCEAN
QUEEN ELIZABETH ISLANDS
Parry Is.
Ellesmere I.
GREENLAND
80 N
Scoresby Sd.
ICELAND
Denmark Strait
Arctic Circle
Disko I.
Davis Str.
C. Farewell
BAFFIN BAY
BAFFIN ISLAND
Pr. Charles I.
Foxe Basin
Boothia Pena.
Banks I.
Victoria I.
Mackenzie B.
Mackenzie
Yukon
Alaska Ra.
Mt. McKinley 20320'
Alaska Pena.
Pelly
Mt. Logan 19850'
Mt. Fairweather 15300'
Liard
Gt. Bear L.
Gt. Slave L.
Southampton I.
Hudson Str.
C. Chidley
Coats I.
C. Wolstenholme
Ungava B.
Labrador
Pr. of Wales I.
Queen Charlotte Is.
Stikine
ROCKY MOUNTAINS
Peace
L. Athabaska
Wollaston L.
HUDSON BAY
Coast Range
Vancouver I.
Juan de Fuca Str.
Fraser
Columbia
Cascade Range
Athabaska
N. Saskatchewan
Saskatchewan
GREAT PLAINS
Churchill
Nelson
Severn
LAURENTIAN SHIELD
L. Winnipegosis
L. Winnipeg
L. Manitoba
Missouri
L. of the Woods
L. Nipigon
Albany
James B.
Eastmain
L. Mistassini
Hamilton Inlet
Str. of Belle Isle
NEWFOUNDLAND
C. Race
Anticosti I.
G. of St. Lawrence
Cabot Str.
Pr. Edward I.
C. Breton I.
St. Lawrence
C. Blanco
180
A
160
B
140
C
120
D
100
E
80
F
60
G
40
H
20
J
0
60
a
b
40

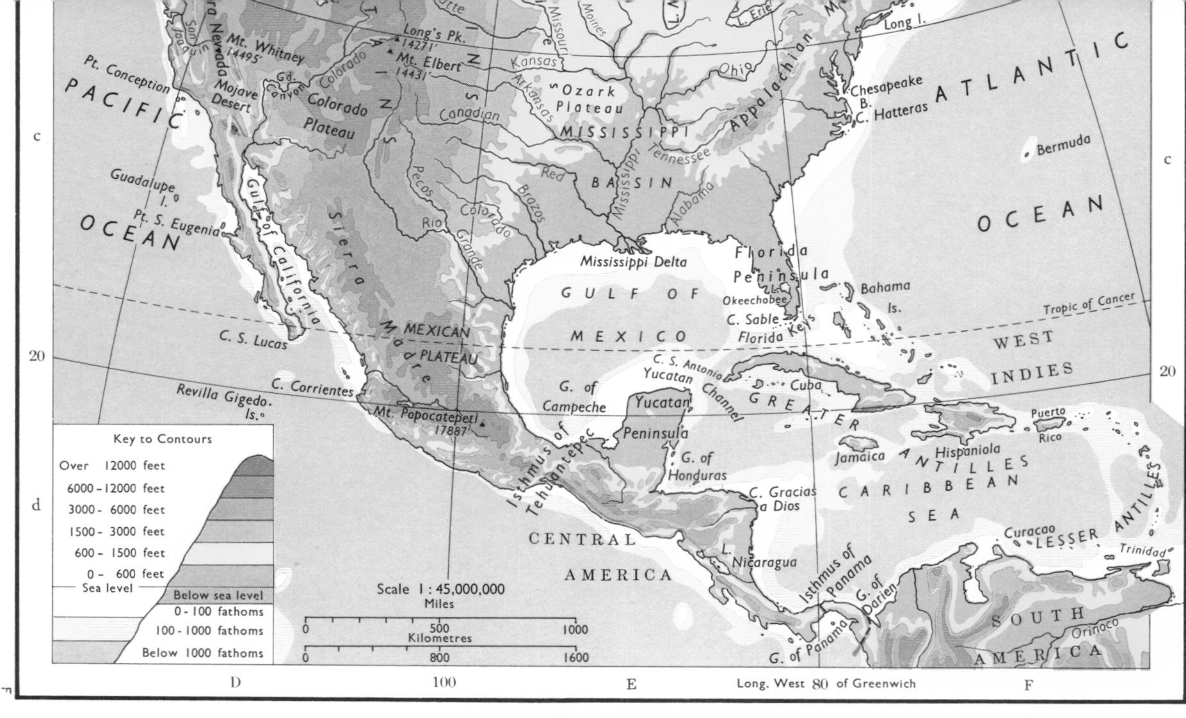
ATLANTIC
OCEAN
Bermuda
Long I.
Chesapeake B.
C. Hatteras
L. Erie
Appalachian
Ohio
Tennessee
Alabama
Mississippi
MISSISSIPPI
BASIN
Missouri
Moines
Kansas
Arkansas
Ozark Plateau
Red
Brazos
Colorado
Canadian
Pecos
Rio Grande
Long's Pk. 14271'
Mt. Elbert 14431'
Colorado
Colorado Plateau
Gd. Canyon
Mt. Whitney 14495'
Mojave Desert
San Joaquin
Pt. Conception
PACIFIC
OCEAN
Guadalupe I.
Pt. S. Eugenia
Gulf of California
C. S. Lucas
C. Corrientes
Revilla Gigedo. Is.
Sierra Madre
MEXICAN PLATEAU
Mt. Popocatepetl 17887'
Mississippi Delta
GULF OF
MEXICO
G. of Campeche
Isthmus of Tehuantepec
Florida Peninsula
Okeechobee
C. Sable
Florida Keys
Bahama Is.
Tropic of Cancer
WEST
INDIES
C. S. Antonio
Yucatan Channel
Yucatan Peninsula
Cuba
GREATER ANTILLES
Hispaniola
Jamaica
Puerto Rico
LESSER ANTILLES
Trinidad
Curacao
CARIBBEAN
SEA
G. of Honduras
C. Gracias a Dios
L. Nicaragua
CENTRAL
AMERICA
Isthmus of Panama
G. of Panama
G. of Darien
Orinoco
SOUTH
AMERICA
Scale 1 : 45,000,000
Miles
0 500 1000
Kilometres
0 800 1600
Key to Contours
Over 12000 feet
6000 - 12000 feet
3000 - 6000 feet
1500 - 3000 feet
600 - 1500 feet
0 - 600 feet
Sea level
Below sea level
0 - 100 fathoms
100 - 1000 fathoms
Below 1000 fathoms
Long. West 80 of Greenwich
100
20
c
d
D
E
F

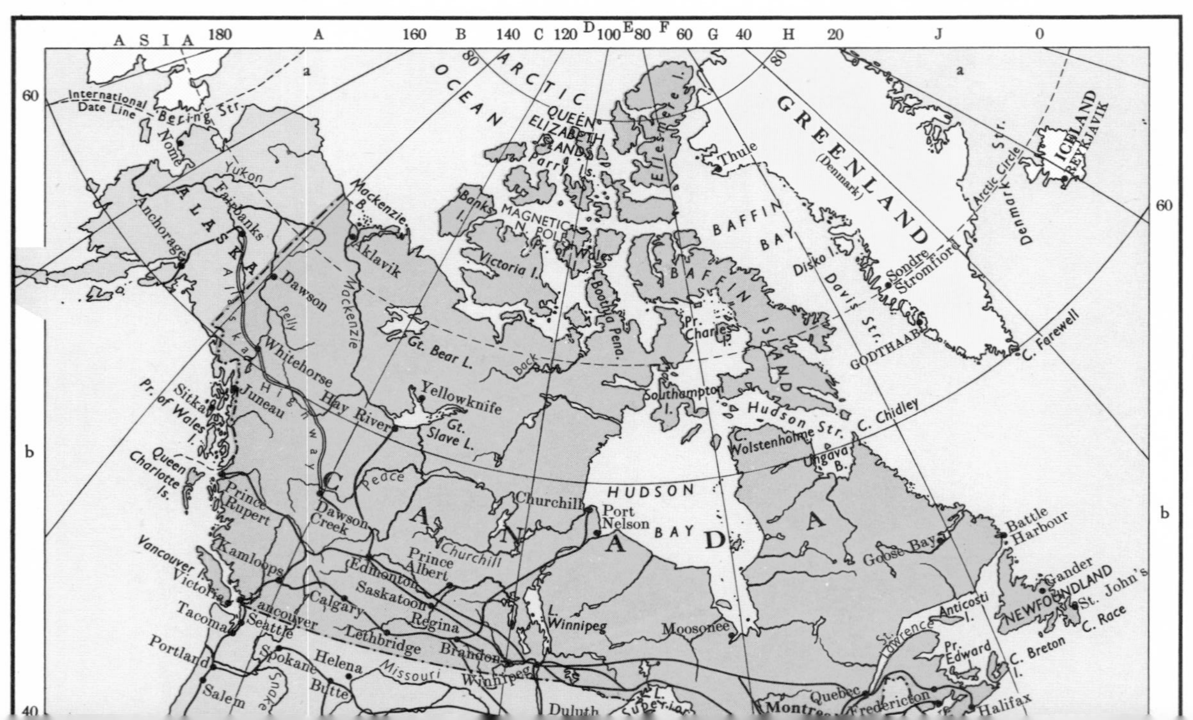
GREENLAND
(Denmark)
ICELAND
REYKJAVIK
Denmark Str.
Arctic Circle
Thule
Disko I.
Sondre Stromfiord
GODTHAAB
C. Farewell
Davis Str.
BAFFIN BAY
BAFFIN ISLAND
Pr. Charles I.
Southampton I.
Hudson Str.
C. Chidley
Ungava B.
C. Wolstenholme
HUDSON BAY
ARCTIC OCEAN
QUEEN ELIZABETH ISLANDS
Parry Is.
Ellesmere
MAGNETIC N. POLE
Banks I.
Victoria I.
Boothia Pena.
Pr. of Wales I.
Back
Mackenzie B.
Aklavik
Mackenzie
Gt. Bear L.
Yellowknife
Gt. Slave L.
Hay River
Peace
Dawson Creek
Dawson
Pelly
Whitehorse
Alaska Highway
Yukon
Fairbanks
ALASKA
Anchorage
Nome
Bering Str.
International Date Line
ASIA
Juneau
Sitka
Pr. of Wales I.
Queen Charlotte Is.
Prince Rupert
Kamloops
Vancouver I.
Vancouver
Victoria
Seattle
Tacoma
Portland
Salem
Spokane
Snake
Butte
Helena
Missouri
Calgary
Lethbridge
Edmonton
Saskatoon
Regina
Prince Albert
Churchill
Brandon
Winnipeg
L. Winnipeg
Port Nelson
Moosonee
Duluth
L. Superior
Montreal
Quebec
Fredericton
Halifax
Pr. Edward I.
C. Breton I.
Anticosti I.
St. Lawrence
Goose Bay
Battle Harbour
NEWFOUNDLAND
Gander
St. John's
C. Race
CANADA
60
0
20
40
60
80
100
120
140
160
180
80
40
a
b
A
B
C
D
E
F
G
H
J

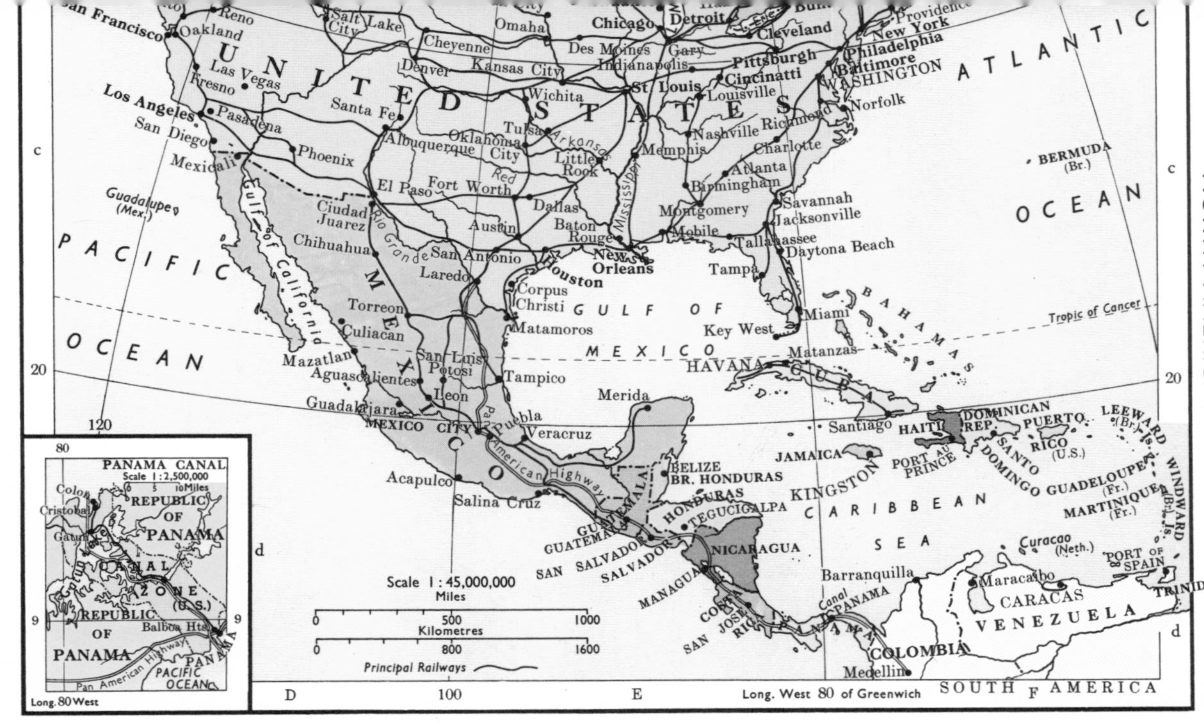
UNITED STATES
MEXICO
ATLANTIC OCEAN
PACIFIC OCEAN
GULF OF MEXICO
CARIBBEAN SEA
BAHAMAS
CUBA
BERMUDA (Br.)
Tropic of Cancer
San Francisco
Oakland
Reno
Fresno
Las Vegas
Los Angeles
Pasadena
San Diego
Mexicali
Guadalupe (Mex.)
Salt Lake City
Phoenix
Santa Fe
Albuquerque
El Paso
Denver
Cheyenne
Omaha
Kansas City
Wichita
Tulsa
Oklahoma City
Fort Worth
Dallas
Austin
San Antonio
Laredo
Corpus Christi
Houston
Baton Rouge
New Orleans
Little Rock
Memphis
Nashville
Birmingham
Montgomery
Mobile
Atlanta
Tallahassee
Tampa
Key West
Miami
Jacksonville
Daytona Beach
Savannah
Charlotte
Richmond
Norfolk
WASHINGTON
Baltimore
Philadelphia
New York
Providence
Pittsburgh
Cincinnati
Louisville
St Louis
Indianapolis
Gary
Chicago
Detroit
Cleveland
Erie
Des Moines
Arkansas
Red
Mississippi
Rio Grande
Gulf of California
Ciudad Juarez
Chihuahua
Torreon
Culiacan
Mazatlan
Aguascalientes
Guadalajara
San Luis Potosi
Leon
Matamoros
Tampico
MEXICO CITY
Puebla
Veracruz
Merida
Acapulco
Salina Cruz
Pan American Highway
HAVANA
Matanzas
Santiago
JAMAICA
KINGSTON
HAITI
PORT AU PRINCE
DOMINICAN REP.
SANTO DOMINGO
PUERTO RICO (U.S.)
LEEWARD Is. (Br.)
WINDWARD Is. (Br.)
GUADELOUPE (Fr.)
MARTINIQUE (Fr.)
Curacao (Neth.)
PORT OF SPAIN
TRINIDAD
BELIZE
BR. HONDURAS
HONDURAS
TEGUCIGALPA
GUATEMALA
SALVADOR
SAN SALVADOR
NICARAGUA
MANAGUA
COSTA RICA
SAN JOSE
PANAMA
Canal
Barranquilla
COLOMBIA
Medellin
Maracaibo
CARACAS
VENEZUELA
SOUTH AMERICA
Scale 1:45,000,000
Miles
0 500 1000
Kilometres
0 800 1600
Principal Railways
Long. West 80 of Greenwich
PANAMA CANAL
Scale 1:2,500,000
0 5 10 Miles
Colon
Cristobal
Gatun
REPUBLIC OF PANAMA
CANAL ZONE (U.S.)
Balboa Hts.
PANAMA
PACIFIC OCEAN
Pan American Highway
Long. 80 West

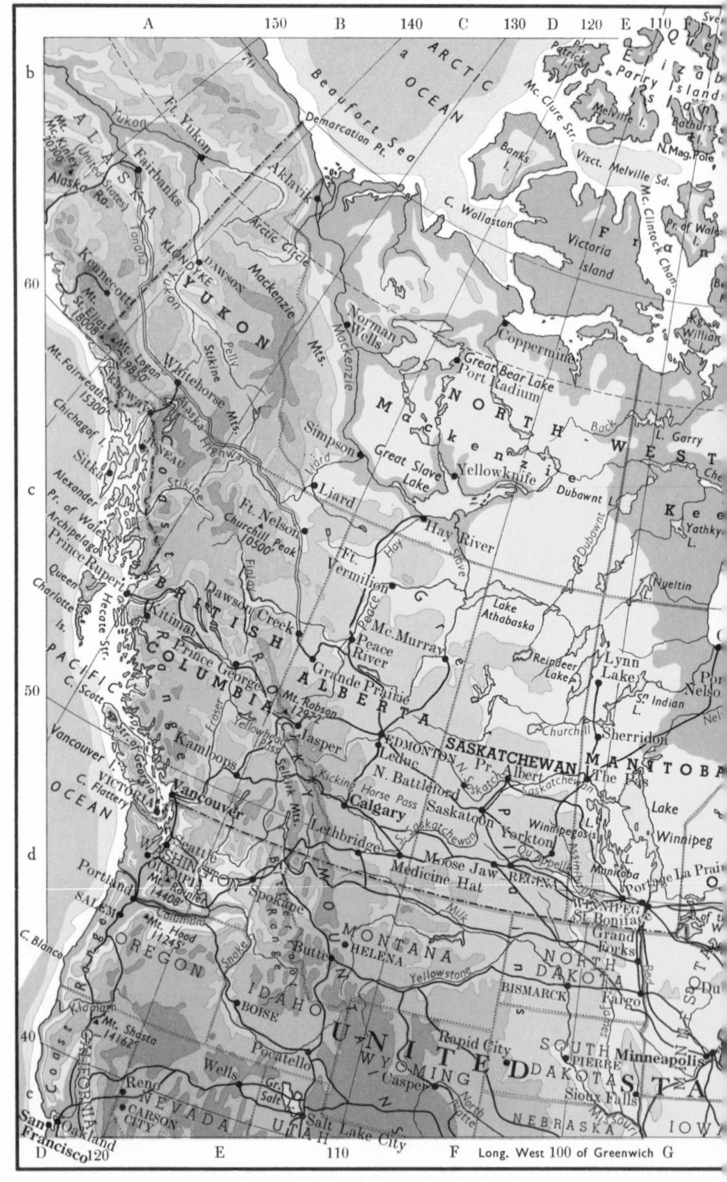
ARCTIC OCEAN
Beaufort Sea
Demarcation Pt.
Aklavik
ALASKA (United States)
Mt. McKinley 20300
Alaska Ra.
Fairbanks
Ft. Yukon
Yukon
Tanana
KLONDYKE
DAWSON
YUKON
Kennecott
Mt. St. Elias 18008
Mt. Logan 19850
Mt. Fairweather 15300
Skagway
Whitehorse
Mackenzie Mts.
Norman Wells
Great Bear Lake
Port Radium
Coppermine
Banks I.
Victoria Island
Mc. Clure Str.
Visct. Melville Sd.
Mc. Clintock Chan.
C. Wollaston
Arctic Circle
Elizabeth Islands
Melville I.
Bathurst I.
N.Mag.Pole
NORTH-WEST
Mackenzie
Simpson
Great Slave Lake
Yellowknife
Dubawnt L.
L. Garry
Back
Liard
Ft. Nelson
Churchill Peak 10500'
Hay River
Ft. Vermilion
Alaska Highway
Chichagof I.
JUNEAU
Sitka
Alexander Archipelago
Pr. of Wales I.
Prince Rupert
Queen Charlotte Is.
Hecate Str.
Kitimat
BRITISH COLUMBIA
Dawson Creek
Peace River
Mc.Murray
Lake Athabaska
Reindeer Lake
Lynn Lake
Prince George
Grande Prairie
ALBERTA
Mt. Robson 12972
Jasper
Yellowhead Pass
EDMONTON
Leduc
SASKATCHEWAN
MANITOBA
Sherridon
Churchill
The Pas
Pr. Albert
N. Battleford
Saskatoon
Kamloops
Vancouver
VICTORIA
Vancouver I.
C. Scott
PACIFIC OCEAN
C. Flattery
Kicking Horse Pass
Calgary
Selkirk Mts.
Lethbridge
Medicine Hat
Moose Jaw
REGINA
Yorkton
Lake Winnipegosis
Lake Winnipeg
L. Manitoba
Portage La Prairie
WINNIPEG
St. Boniface
Seattle
WASHINGTON
OLYMPIA
Mt. Rainier 14408'
Spokane
Portland
SALEM
Mt. Hood 11245'
OREGON
C. Blanco
MONTANA
HELENA
Butte
Milk
Yellowstone
NORTH DAKOTA
BISMARCK
Grand Forks
Fargo
IDAHO
BOISE
Snake
Mt. Shasta 14162'
Klamath
CALIFORNIA
Coast Range
Reno
CARSON CITY
NEVADA
Wells
Pocatello
Gr. Salt L.
Salt Lake City
UTAH
WYOMING
Casper
Rapid City
SOUTH DAKOTA
PIERRE
Sioux Falls
NEBRASKA
IOWA
Minneapolis
UNITED STATES
San Francisco
Oakland
Long. West 100 of Greenwich

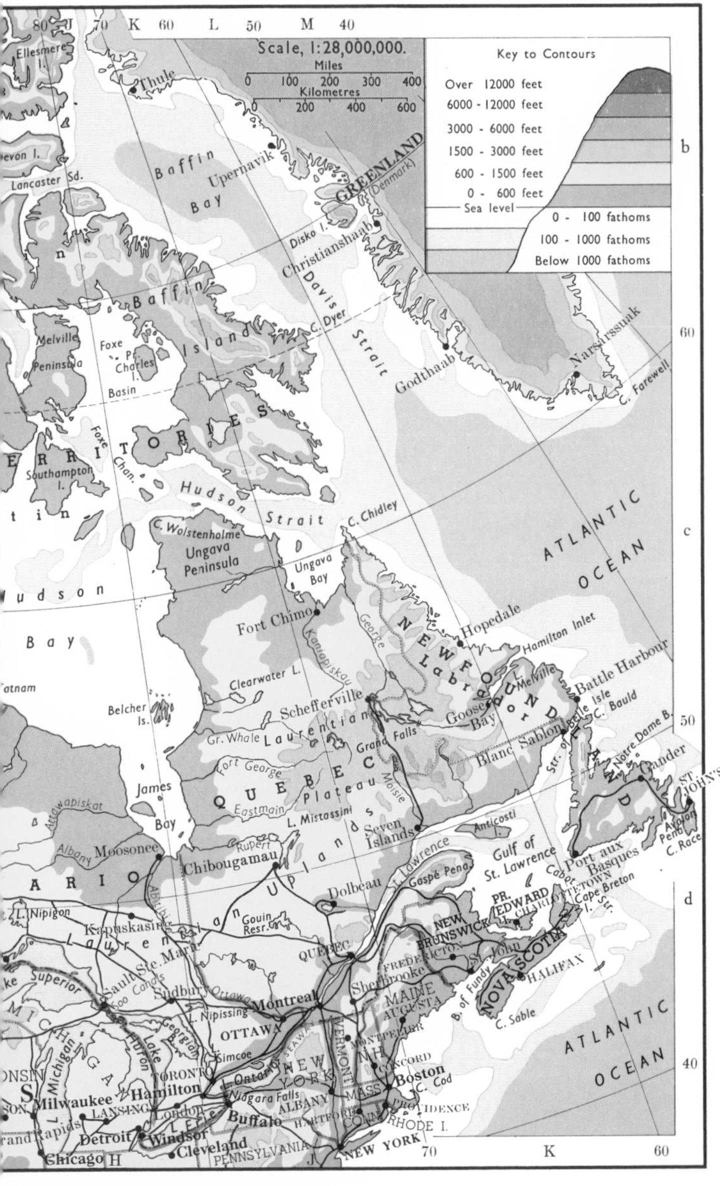
Scale, 1:28,000,000.
Miles
0 100 200 300 400
Kilometres
0 200 400 600
Key to Contours
Over 12000 feet
6000 - 12000 feet
3000 - 6000 feet
1500 - 3000 feet
600 - 1500 feet
0 - 600 feet
Sea level
0 - 100 fathoms
100 - 1000 fathoms
Below 1000 fathoms
Ellesmere I.
Thule
Baffin Bay
Upernavik
GREENLAND (Denmark)
Disko I.
Christianshaab
Davis Strait
C. Dyer
Godthaab
Narsarssuak
C. Farewell
Lancaster Sd.
Baffin Island
Melville Peninsula
Foxe Basin
Pr. Charles I.
Foxe Chan.
Southampton I.
Hudson Strait
C. Chidley
C. Wolstenholme
Ungava Peninsula
Ungava Bay
Hudson Bay
Fort Chimo
Kaniapiskau
George
Hopedale
Hamilton Inlet
Labrador
NEWFOUNDLAND
L. Melville
Goose Bay
Battle Harbour
Belle Isle
C. Bauld
Str. of Belle Isle
Blanc Sablon
Notre Dame B.
Gander
ST. JOHN'S
Avalon Pena.
C. Race
ATLANTIC OCEAN
Clearwater L.
Schefferville
Belcher Is.
Gr. Whale
Laurentian Plateau
Grand Falls
Fort George
QUEBEC
Moisie
James Bay
Eastmain
L. Mistassini
Seven Islands
Anticosti
Gulf of St. Lawrence
Attawapiskat
Albany
Moosonee
Rupert
Chibougamau
Port aux Basques
Cabot Str.
Dolbeau
Gaspé Pena.
PR. EDWARD I.
CHARLOTTETOWN
Cape Breton I.
L. Nipigon
Kapuskasing
Gouin Resr.
NEW BRUNSWICK
FREDERICTON
St. John
NOVA SCOTIA
HALIFAX
QUEBEC
Sherbrooke
B. of Fundy
C. Sable
Superior
Sault Ste. Marie
Soo Canals
Sudbury
Ottawa
Montreal
L. Nipissing
OTTAWA
MAINE
AUGUSTA
MONTPELIER
VERMONT
N.H.
CONCORD
Boston
C. Cod
MASS.
PROVIDENCE
RHODE I.
Georgian B.
Lake Huron
L. Michigan
Simcoe
TORONTO
L. Ontario
NEW YORK
Milwaukee
Hamilton
LANSING
London
Niagara Falls
ALBANY
Buffalo
HARTFORD
CONN.
Detroit
Windsor
L. Erie
Cleveland
PENNSYLVANIA
NEW YORK
Chicago
80 J 70 K 60 L 50 M 40
b
60
c
50
d
40
70 K 60

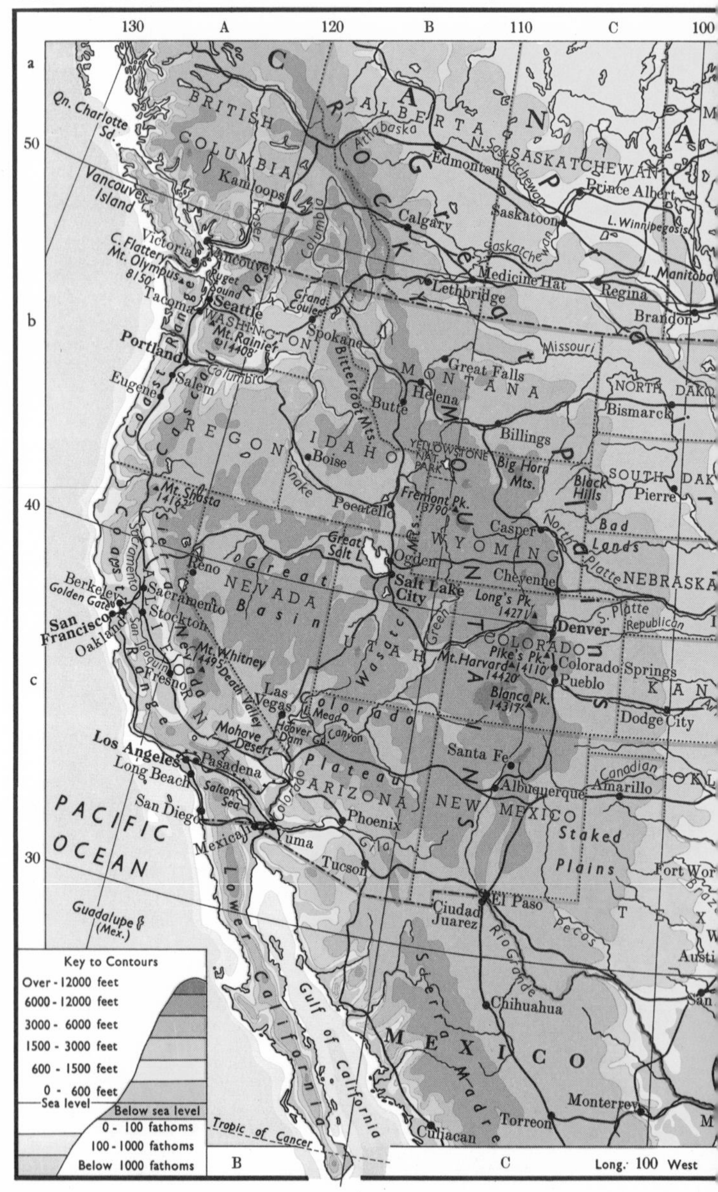
130
A
120
B
110
C
100
50
40
30
BRITISH COLUMBIA
ALBERTA
SASKATCHEWAN
CANADA
Qn. Charlotte Sd.
Vancouver Island
Kamloops
Edmonton
Prince Albert
Saskatoon
Calgary
L. Winnipegosis
Victoria
Vancouver
C. Flattery
Mt. Olympus 8150'
Medicine Hat
Lethbridge
Regina
L. Manitoba
Brandon
Tacoma
Seattle
Puget Sound
Grand Coulee
Spokane
WASHINGTON
Mt. Rainier 14408'
Portland
Salem
Eugene
Missouri
Great Falls
MONTANA
Helena
Butte
Bitterroot Mts.
Billings
NORTH DAKOTA
Bismarck
OREGON
IDAHO
Boise
YELLOWSTONE NAT. PARK
Big Horn Mts.
Black Hills
SOUTH DAKOTA
Pierre
Mt. Shasta 14162'
Pocatello
Fremont Pk. 13790'
Casper
Bad Lands
WYOMING
Great Salt L.
Ogden
Salt Lake City
Cheyenne
NEBRASKA
North Platte
S. Platte
Republican
Reno
Great Basin
NEVADA
Berkeley
Golden Gate
San Francisco
Oakland
Sacramento
Stockton
Long's Pk. 14271'
Denver
COLORADO
Pike's Pk. 14110'
Colorado Springs
Pueblo
Mt. Harvard 14420'
Blanca Pk. 14317'
KANSAS
Dodge City
UTAH
Wasatch Mts.
Mt. Whitney 14495'
Death Valley
Fresno
San Joaquin
Coast Range
Sierra Nevada
CALIFORNIA
Las Vegas
L. Mead
Hoover Dam
Gd. Canyon
Colorado Plateau
Mohave Desert
Los Angeles
Pasadena
Long Beach
Santa Fe
Albuquerque
Amarillo
Canadian
OKLAHOMA
Salton Sea
San Diego
ARIZONA
NEW MEXICO
Phoenix
Mexicali
Yuma
Gila
Tucson
Staked Plains
Fort Worth
PACIFIC OCEAN
El Paso
Ciudad Juarez
Pecos
Rio Grande
TEXAS
Austin
Guadalupe (Mex.)
Lower California
Gulf of California
Sierra Madre
Chihuahua
MEXICO
Monterrey
Torreon
Culiacan
San Antonio
Tropic of Cancer
ROCKY MOUNTAINS
Key to Contours
Over - 12000 feet
6000 - 12000 feet
3000 - 6000 feet
1500 - 3000 feet
600 - 1500 feet
0 - 600 feet
Sea level
Below sea level
0 - 100 fathoms
100 - 1000 fathoms
Below 1000 fathoms
Long. 100 West

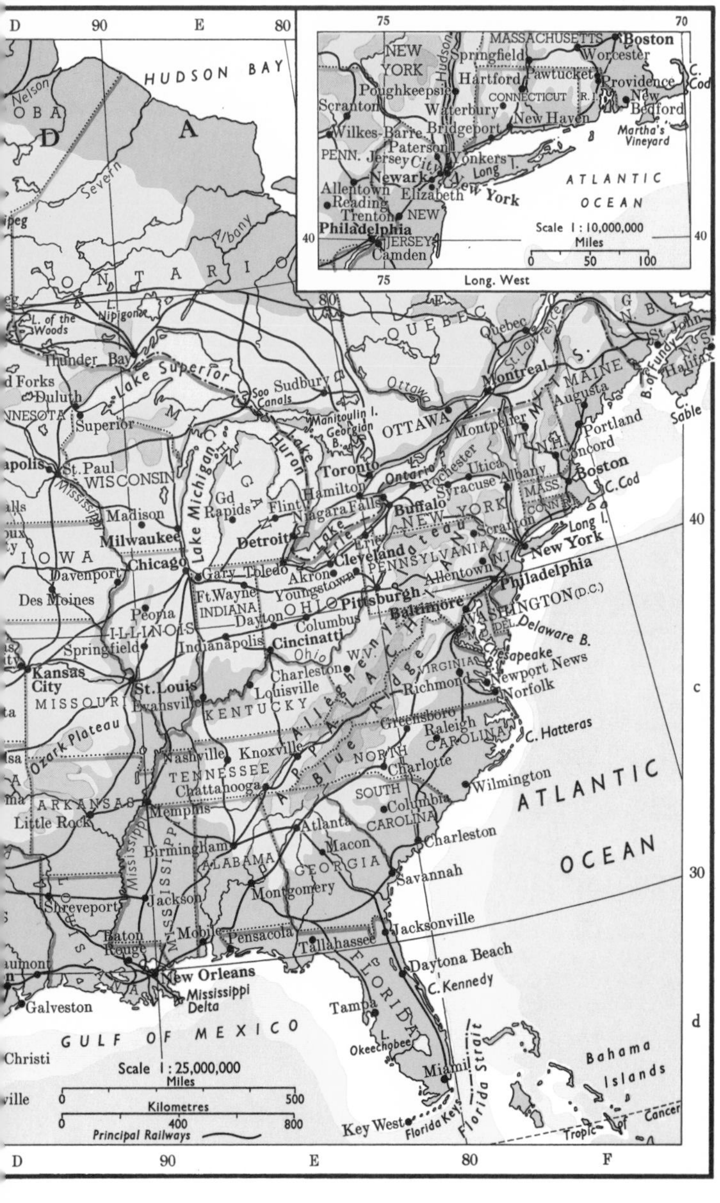
HUDSON BAY
ONTARIO
QUEBEC
Lake Superior
Lake Michigan
Lake Huron
Thunder Bay
Duluth
Superior
St. Paul
WISCONSIN
Madison
Milwaukee
Chicago
IOWA
Davenport
Des Moines
Peoria
ILLINOIS
Springfield
Kansas City
MISSOURI
St. Louis
Evansville
Ozark Plateau
Nashville
Knoxville
TENNESSEE
Chattanooga
ARKANSAS
Memphis
Little Rock
Birmingham
ALABAMA
Shreveport
Jackson
Baton Rouge
Mobile
Pensacola
New Orleans
Mississippi Delta
Galveston
GULF OF MEXICO
Soo Canals
Sudbury
Manitoulin I.
Georgian B.
OTTAWA
Toronto
Hamilton
Niagara Falls
Buffalo
Detroit
Flint
Gd Rapids
Toledo
Cleveland
Erie
Akron
Youngstown
Pittsburgh
Ft. Wayne
INDIANA
Indianapolis
Dayton
OHIO
Columbus
Cincinnati
Ohio
Charleston
W.V.
Louisville
KENTUCKY
Richmond
VIRGINIA
Greensboro
Raleigh
NORTH CAROLINA
Charlotte
SOUTH CAROLINA
Columbia
Atlanta
Macon
GEORGIA
Montgomery
Savannah
Charleston
Wilmington
Jacksonville
Tallahassee
Daytona Beach
C. Kennedy
FLORIDA
Tampa
L. Okeechobee
Miami
Key West
Florida Keys
Florida Strait
Bahama Islands
Tropic of Cancer
ATLANTIC OCEAN
C. Hatteras
Norfolk
Newport News
Chesapeake B.
Delaware B.
WASHINGTON (D.C.)
Baltimore
Philadelphia
Allentown
PENNSYLVANIA
NEW YORK
Scranton
New York
Long I.
Syracuse
Rochester
Utica
Albany
Ontario
Montreal
Quebec
St. Lawrence
Montpelier
VT.
N.H.
Concord
MASS.
Boston
C. Cod
MAINE
Augusta
Portland
St. John
Halifax
B. of Fundy
N.S.
C. Sable
Ottawa
Scale 1 : 25,000,000
Miles
Kilometres
Principal Railways
MASSACHUSETTS
Springfield
Worcester
Hartford
Pawtucket
Providence
CONNECTICUT
R.I.
New Bedford
Waterbury
New Haven
Bridgeport
Poughkeepsie
Scranton
Wilkes-Barre
Paterson
Jersey City
Yonkers
Newark
Elizabeth
Allentown
Reading
Trenton
NEW JERSEY
Philadelphia
Camden
Martha's Vineyard
Scale 1 : 10,000,000
Long. West

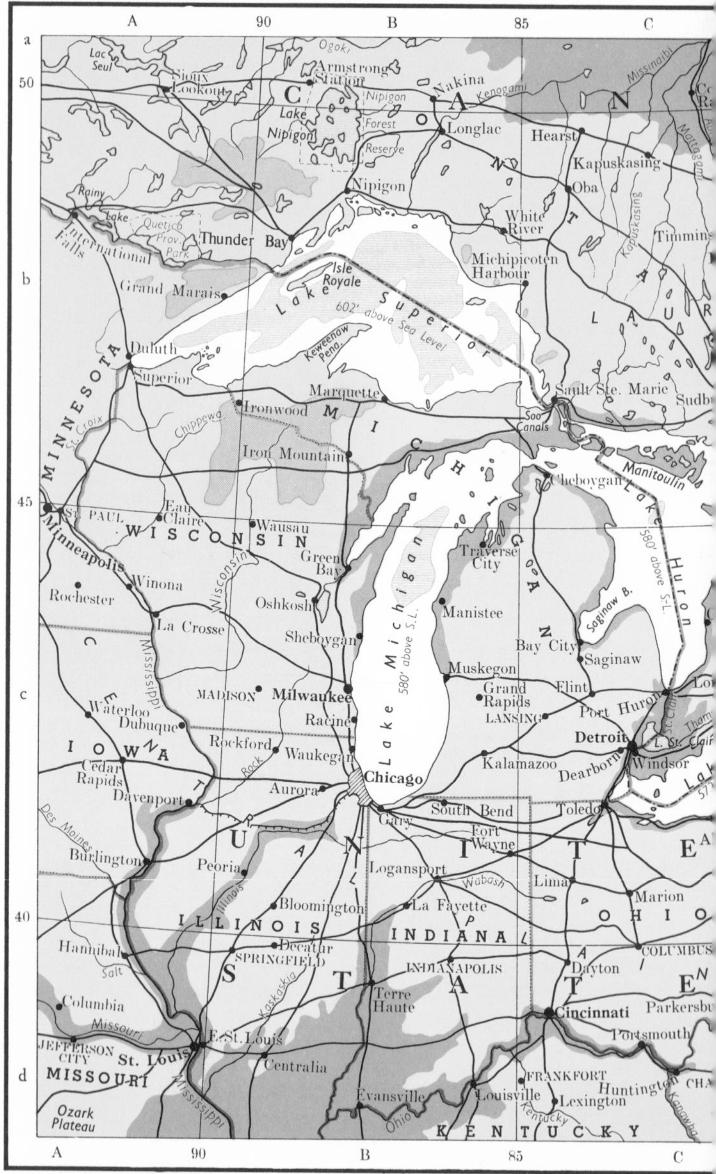

Lac Seul
Sioux Lookout
Armstrong Station
Ogoki
Nakina
Kenogami
Lake Nipigon
Nipigon Forest Reserve
Longlac
Hearst
Kapuskasing
Oba
Nipigon
Rainy Lake
Quetico Prov. Park
International Falls
Thunder Bay
White River
Timmins
Michipicoten Harbour
Isle Royale
Grand Marais
Lake Superior
602' above Sea Level
Keweenaw Pena.
Duluth
Superior
Marquette
Sault Ste. Marie
Sudbury
Soo Canals
Ironwood
Chippewa
St. Croix
MINNESOTA
Iron Mountain
Manitoulin
Cheboygan
ST. PAUL
Minneapolis
Eau Claire
Wausau
WISCONSIN
Traverse City
Green Bay
Lake Huron
580' above S.L.
Winona
Rochester
Wisconsin
Oshkosh
Manistee
Lake Michigan
580' above S.L.
La Crosse
Saginaw B.
Sheboygan
Bay City
Saginaw
Mississippi
Muskegon
MADISON
Milwaukee
Grand Rapids
Flint
Port Huron
LANSING
Waterloo
Dubuque
Racine
Detroit
L. St. Clair
Rockford
Waukegan
Kalamazoo
Dearborn
Windsor
IOWA
Cedar Rapids
Rock
Chicago
Aurora
Davenport
South Bend
Toledo
Gary
Des Moines
Fort Wayne
Burlington
Peoria
Logansport
Wabash
Lima
Marion
Bloomington
La Fayette
ILLINOIS
INDIANA
OHIO
Hannibal
Decatur
SPRINGFIELD
INDIANAPOLIS
COLUMBUS
Salt
Dayton
UNITED STATES
Terre Haute
Columbia
Kaskaskia
Cincinnati
Parkersburg
Missouri
JEFFERSON CITY
St. Louis
E. St. Louis
Portsmouth
Centralia
MISSOURI
FRANKFORT
Huntington
Mississippi
Evansville
Louisville
Lexington
Ozark Plateau
Ohio
Kentucky
KENTUCKY
Kanawha

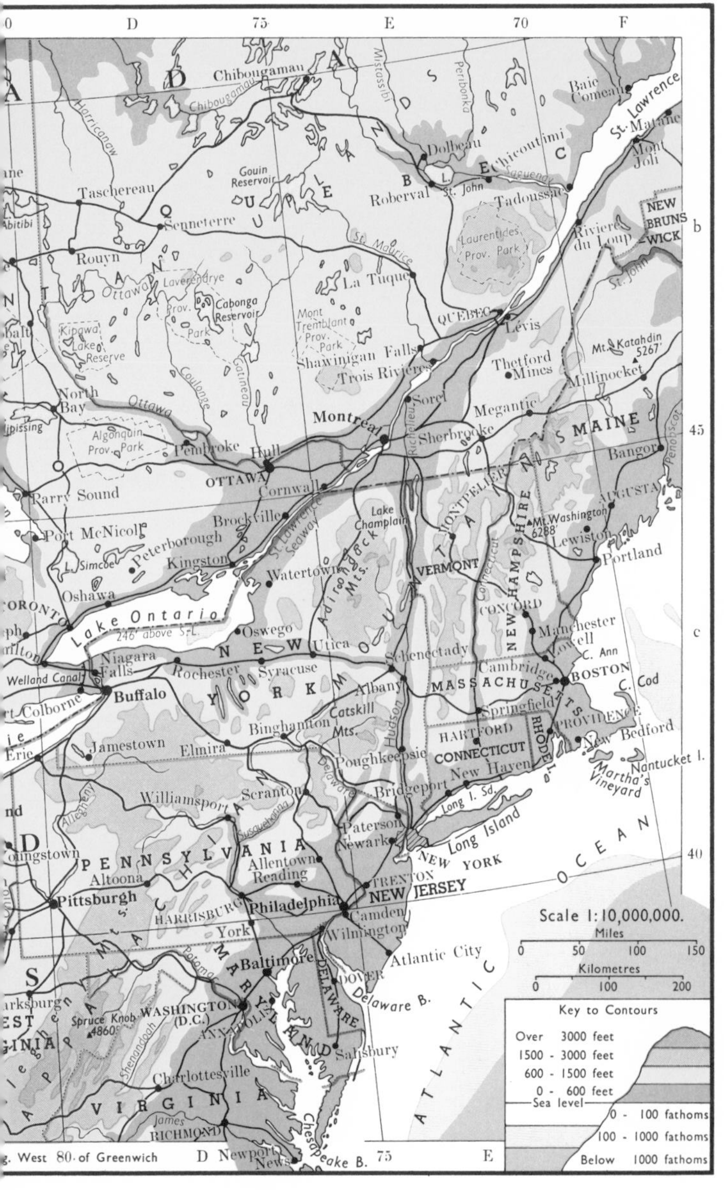
D
75
E
70
F
Chibougamau
Chibougamau
Harricanaw
Mistassibi
Peribonka
Baie Comeau
St. Lawrence
St. Matane
Mont Joli
Dolbeau
Chicoutimi
L. St. John
Saguenay
Roberval
Tadoussac
Gouin Reservoir
Taschereau
Senneterre
Abitibi
Rouyn
St. Maurice
La Tuque
Laurentides Prov. Park
Riviere du Loup
NEW BRUNSWICK
St. John
Laverendrye
Ottawa
Cabonga Reservoir
Prov. Park
Mont Tremblant Prov. Park
Kipawa Lake Reserve
Coulonge
Gatineau
Shawinigan Falls
Trois Rivieres
QUEBEC
Levis
Thetford Mines
Mt. Katahdin 5267'
Millinocket
North Bay
Nipissing
Algonquin Prov. Park
Ottawa
Sorel
Montreal
Megantic
Richelieu
Sherbrooke
MAINE
Penobscot
Bangor
Pembroke
Hull
OTTAWA
Cornwall
AUGUSTA
Parry Sound
Brockville
St. Lawrence Seaway
Lake Champlain
MONTPELIER
Mt. Washington 6288'
Lewiston
Port McNicoll
Peterborough
L. Simcoe
Kingston
Adirondack Mts.
VERMONT
NEW HAMPSHIRE
Portland
Watertown
Connecticut
Oshawa
TORONTO
Lake Ontario
246' above S.L.
Oswego
CONCORD
Manchester
Lowell
C. Ann
NEW YORK
Utica
Schenectady
Niagara Falls
Rochester
Syracuse
Welland Canal
Buffalo
Albany
MASSACHUSETTS
Cambridge
BOSTON
C. Cod
Port Colborne
Catskill Mts.
Hudson
Springfield
PROVIDENCE
Binghamton
HARTFORD
RHODE I.
New Bedford
L. Erie
Jamestown
Elmira
Delaware
Poughkeepsie
CONNECTICUT
New Haven
Nantucket I.
Martha's Vineyard
Allegheny
Williamsport
Scranton
Bridgeport
Long I. Sd.
Susquehanna
Paterson
Newark
Long Island
Youngstown
PENNSYLVANIA
Allentown
Reading
NEW YORK
ATLANTIC OCEAN
40
Altoona
TRENTON
NEW JERSEY
Pittsburgh
HARRISBURG
Philadelphia
Camden
Wilmington
York
Scale 1:10,000,000.
Miles
0 50 100 150
Kilometres
0 100 200
Potomac
Baltimore
Atlantic City
DELAWARE
DOVER
Delaware B.
Parkersburg
WEST VIRGINIA
Spruce Knob 4860'
WASHINGTON (D.C.)
ANNAPOLIS
MARYLAND
Shenandoah
Salisbury
Key to Contours
Over 3000 feet
1500 - 3000 feet
600 - 1500 feet
0 - 600 feet
Sea level
0 - 100 fathoms
100 - 1000 fathoms
Below 1000 fathoms
Charlottesville
VIRGINIA
James
RICHMOND
Chesapeake B.
Newport News
West 80 of Greenwich
D
75
E
45
b
c

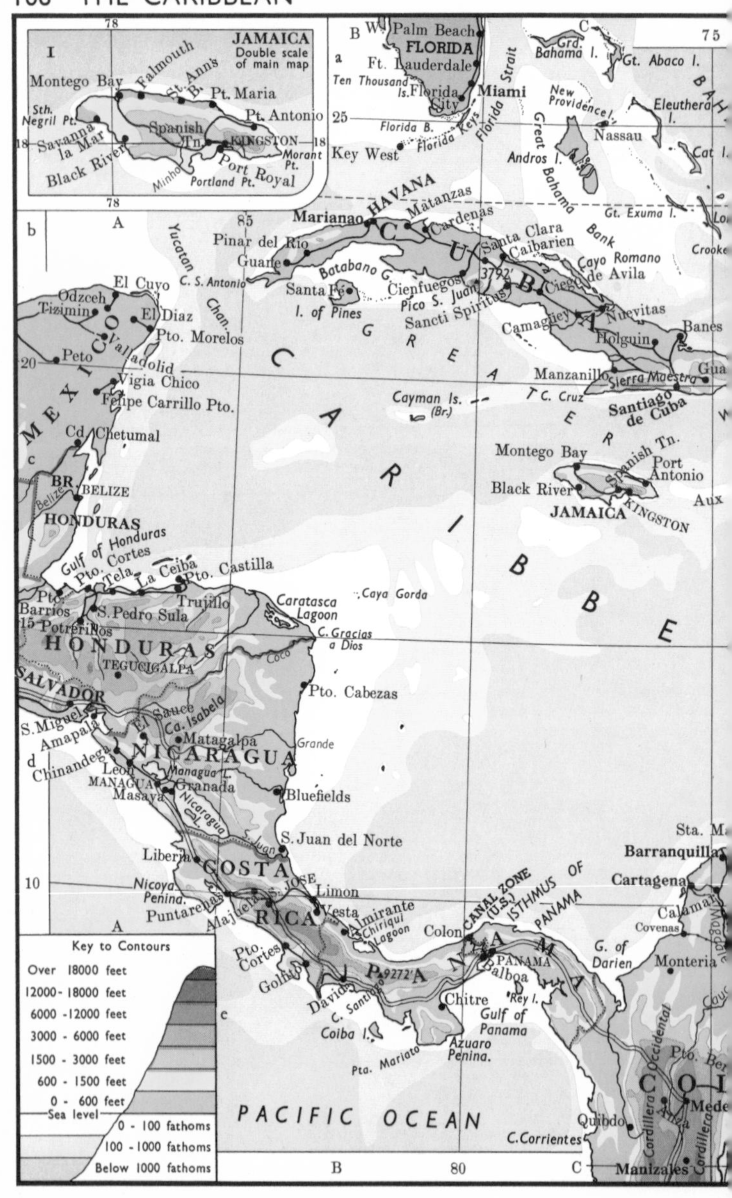
JAMAICA
Double scale of main map
Montego Bay
Falmouth
St. Ann's B.
Pt. Maria
Pt. Antonio
Sth. Negril Pt.
Savanna la Mar
Spanish Tn.
KINGSTON
Black River
Port Royal
Morant Pt.
Portland Pt.
Minho
FLORIDA
Palm Beach
Ft. Lauderdale
Ten Thousand Is.
Florida City
Miami
Florida B.
Florida Keys
Florida Strait
Key West
Grd. Bahama I.
Gt. Abaco I.
New Providence I.
Eleuthera I.
Nassau
Andros I.
Great Bahama Bank
Cat I.
Gt. Exuma I.
HAVANA
Matanzas
Marianao
Cardenas
Pinar del Rio
Guane
Santa Clara
Caibarien
CUBA
Cayo Romano
de Avila
Batabano G.
Santa Fé
I. of Pines
Cienfuegos
Pico S. Juan
3792'
Sancti Spiritus
Ciego
Nuevitas
Camaguey
Holguin
Banes
Manzanillo
Sierra Maestra
C. Cruz
Santiago de Cuba
Cayman Is. (Br.)
Yucatan Chan.
C. S. Antonio
El Cuyo
Odzceh
Tizimin
El Diaz
Pto. Morelos
Valladolid
Peto
MEXICO
Vigia Chico
Felipe Carrillo Pto.
Cd. Chetumal
BR. HONDURAS
BELIZE
Belize
GREATER
CARIBBEE
Montego Bay
Spanish Tn.
Port Antonio
Black River
JAMAICA
KINGSTON
Gulf of Honduras
Pto. Cortes
Tela
La Ceiba
Pto. Castilla
Trujillo
Pto. Barrios
S. Pedro Sula
Potrerillos
HONDURAS
TEGUCIGALPA
Caratasca Lagoon
Caya Gorda
C. Gracias a Dios
Coco
SALVADOR
Pto. Cabezas
S. Miguel
Amapala
El Sauce
Ca. Isabela
Matagalpa
NICARAGUA
Grande
Chinandega
Leon
Managua L.
MANAGUA
Masaya
Granada
Nicaragua L.
Bluefields
S. Juan
S. Juan del Norte
Liberia
COSTA RICA
Nicoya Penina.
Puntarenas
S. JOSE
Majuela
Limon
Vesta
Almirante
Chiriqui Lagoon
Colon
CANAL ZONE (U.S.)
ISTHMUS OF PANAMA
PANAMA
Balboa
Pto. Cortes
Golfito
David
9272'
C. Santiago
Chitre
Rey I.
Gulf of Panama
Coiba I.
Azuaro Penina.
Pta. Mariato
G. of Darien
Sta. M.
Barranquilla
Cartagena
Calamar
Covenas
Monteria
Magdale
Cauc
Pto. Ber
Cordillera Occidental
COL
Mede
Quibdo
C. Corrientes
Manizales
PACIFIC OCEAN
Key to Contours
Over 18000 feet
12000 - 18000 feet
6000 - 12000 feet
3000 - 6000 feet
1500 - 3000 feet
600 - 1500 feet
0 - 600 feet
Sea level
0 - 100 fathoms
100 - 1000 fathoms
Below 1000 fathoms

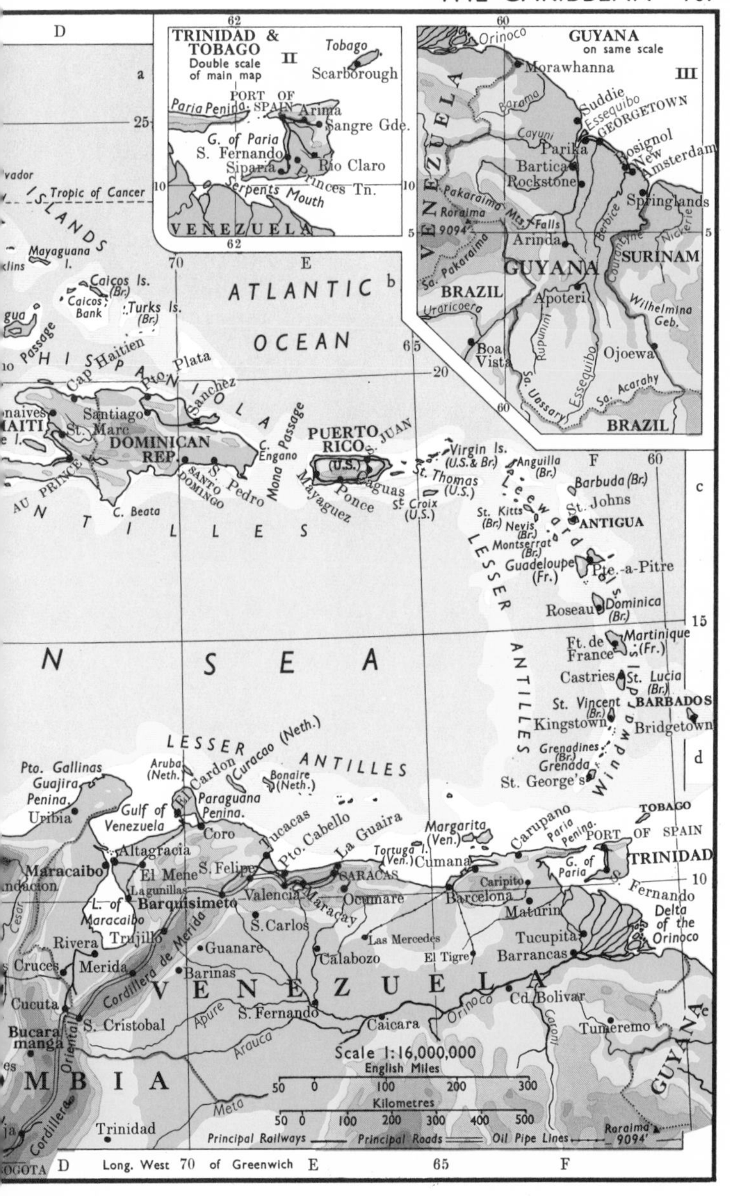
TRINIDAD & TOBAGO II
Double scale of main map
Tobago
Scarborough
PORT OF SPAIN
Arima
Sangre Gde.
Paria Penina.
G. of Paria
S. Fernando
Siparia
Rio Claro
Princes Tn.
Serpents Mouth
VENEZUELA
GUYANA on same scale III
Orinoco
Morawhanna
Barama
Suddie
Essequibo
GEORGETOWN
Cayuni
Parika
Rosignol
New Amsterdam
Bartica
Rockstone
Springlands
Pakaraima Mts.
Roraima 9094
Falls
Arinda
Berbice
Courantyne
Nickerie
SURINAM
GUYANA
Sa. Pakaraima
BRAZIL
Apoteri
Uraricoera
Wilhelmina Geb.
Rupununi
Boa Vista
Ojoewa
Essequibo
Sa. Uassary
Sa. Acarahy
BRAZIL
VENEZUELA
Tropic of Cancer
ISLANDS
Mayaguana I.
Caicos Is. (Br.)
Caicos Bank
Turks Is. (Br.)
ATLANTIC
OCEAN
HISPANIOLA
Cap Haitien
Pto. Plata
Sanchez
Santiago
St. Marc
HAITI
DOMINICAN REP.
PRINCE
SANTO DOMINGO
S. Pedro
C. Engano
Mona Passage
PUERTO RICO (U.S.)
JUAN
Mayaguez
Ponce
Caguas
Virgin Is. (U.S. & Br.)
St. Thomas (U.S.)
St. Croix (U.S.)
Anguilla (Br.)
Barbuda (Br.)
St. Johns
ANTIGUA
St. Kitts (Br.)
Nevis (Br.)
Montserrat (Br.)
Leeward Is.
LESSER
Guadeloupe (Fr.)
Pte.-a-Pitre
Roseau
Dominica (Br.)
C. Beata
ANTILLES
N SEA
Ft. de France
Martinique (Fr.)
ANTILLES
Castries
St. Lucia (Br.)
St. Vincent (Br.)
BARBADOS
Kingstown
Bridgetown
Grenadines (Br.)
Grenada
St. George's
Windward Is.
LESSER ANTILLES
Curacao (Neth.)
Aruba (Neth.)
Bonaire (Neth.)
Pto. Gallinas
Guajira Penina.
Uribia
Gulf of Venezuela
El Cardon
Paraguana Penina.
Coro
Tucacas
Pto. Cabello
La Guaira
Margarita (Ven.)
Tortuga I. (Ven.)
Carupano
Paria Penina.
PORT OF SPAIN
TOBAGO
TRINIDAD
G. of Paria
Altagracia
Maracaibo
El Mene
S. Felipe
CARACAS
Cumana
Caripito
Lagunillas
L. of Maracaibo
Barquisimeto
Valencia
Maracay
Ocumare
Barcelona
Maturin
S. Fernando
Delta of the Orinoco
Trujillo
S. Carlos
Las Mercedes
Tucupita
Rivera
Cordillera de Merida
Guanare
Calabozo
El Tigre
Barrancas
Cruces
Merida
Barinas
VENEZUELA
Cd. Bolivar
Cucuta
S. Cristobal
Apure
S. Fernando
Orinoco
Caicara
Caroni
Tumeremo
Bucaramanga
Arauca
Cordillera Oriental
GUYANA
MBIA
Meta
Trinidad
Roraima 9094'
Scale 1:16,000,000
English Miles
50 0 100 200 300
Kilometres
50 0 100 200 300 400 500
Principal Railways
Principal Roads
Oil Pipe Lines
Long. West 70 of Greenwich

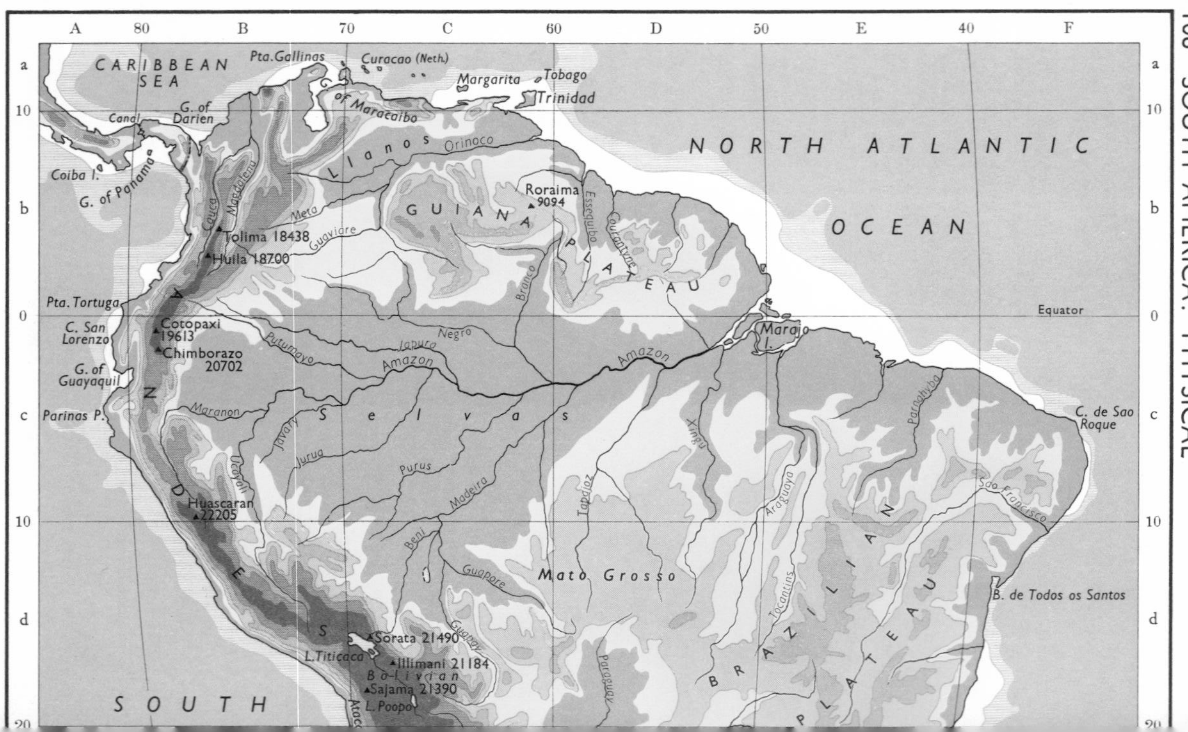
CARIBBEAN SEA
Pta. Gallinas
Curacao (Neth.)
Margarita
Tobago
Trinidad
G. of Maracaibo
Canal
G. of Darien
Coiba I.
G. of Panama
Llanos
Orinoco
NORTH ATLANTIC
OCEAN
Roraima 9094
GUIANA PLATEAU
Essequibo
Courantyne
Branco
Cauca
Magdalena
Meta
Guaviare
Tolima 18438
Huila 18700
Pta. Tortuga
Equator
C. San Lorenzo
Cotopaxi 19613
Chimborazo 20702
G. of Guayaquil
Negro
Japura
Putumayo
Amazon
Marajo I.
Parinas P.
Maranon
Selvas
Xingu
Parnahyba
C. de Sao Roque
Javary
Jurua
Ucayali
Purus
Madeira
Tapajoz
Araguaya
Sao Francisco
Huascaran 22205
ANDES
Beni
Guapore
Mato Grosso
Tocantins
BRAZILIAN PLATEAU
B. de Todos os Santos
Sorata 21490
L. Titicaca
Illimani 21184
Bolivian
Sajama 21390
L. Poopo
Guapay
Paraguay
Atac
SOUTH
A B C D E F
80 70 60 50 40
a b c d
10 0 10 20

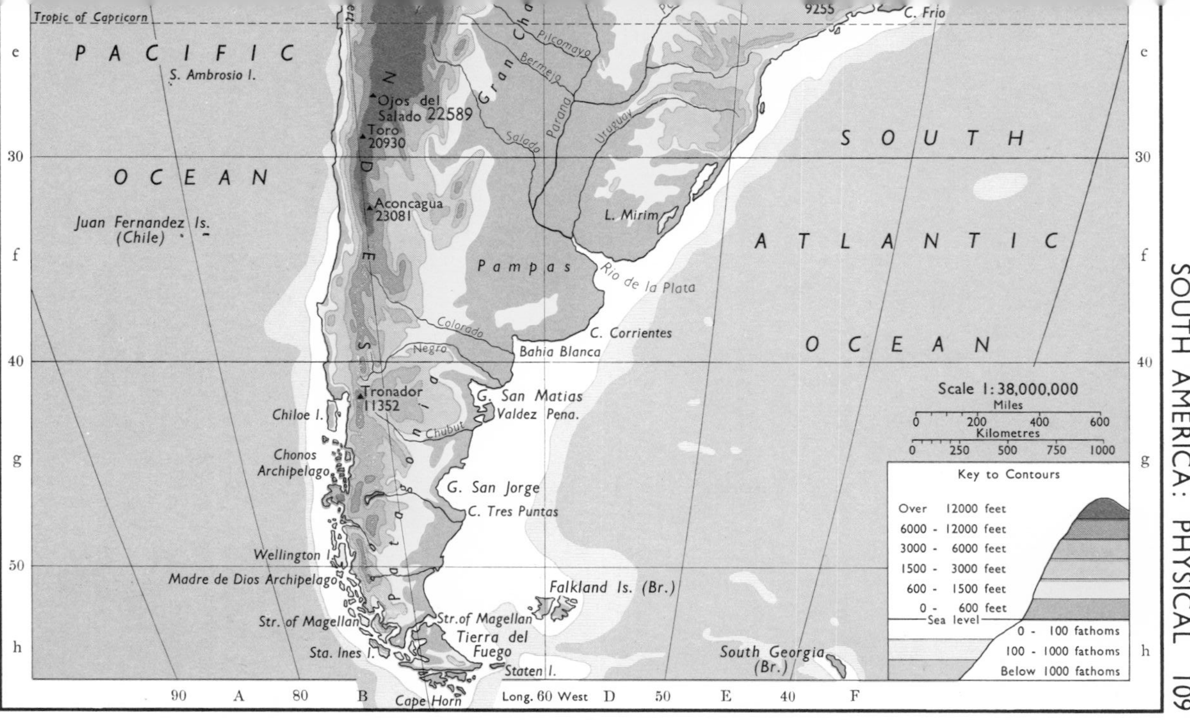

Tropic of Capricorn
PACIFIC
S. Ambrosio I.
OCEAN
Juan Fernandez Is. (Chile)
Ojos del Salado 22589
Toro 20930
Aconcagua 23081
Tronador 11352
Gran Chaco
Pilcomayo
Bermejo
Salado
Parana
Uruguay
L. Mirim
Pampas
Rio de la Plata
C. Corrientes
Colorado
Negro
Bahia Blanca
G. San Matias
Valdez Pena.
Chubut
Chiloe I.
Chonos Archipelago
G. San Jorge
C. Tres Puntas
Wellington I.
Madre de Dios Archipelago
Falkland Is. (Br.)
Str. of Magellan
Str. of Magellan
Tierra del Fuego
Sta. Ines I.
Staten I.
Cape Horn
South Georgia (Br.)
9255
C. Frio
SOUTH
ATLANTIC
OCEAN
Scale 1:38,000,000
Miles
0 200 400 600
Kilometres
0 250 500 750 1000
Key to Contours
Over 12000 feet
6000 - 12000 feet
3000 - 6000 feet
1500 - 3000 feet
600 - 1500 feet
0 - 600 feet
Sea level
0 - 100 fathoms
100 - 1000 fathoms
Below 1000 fathoms
90 A 80 B Long. 60 West D 50 E 40 F
e 30 f 40 g 50 h

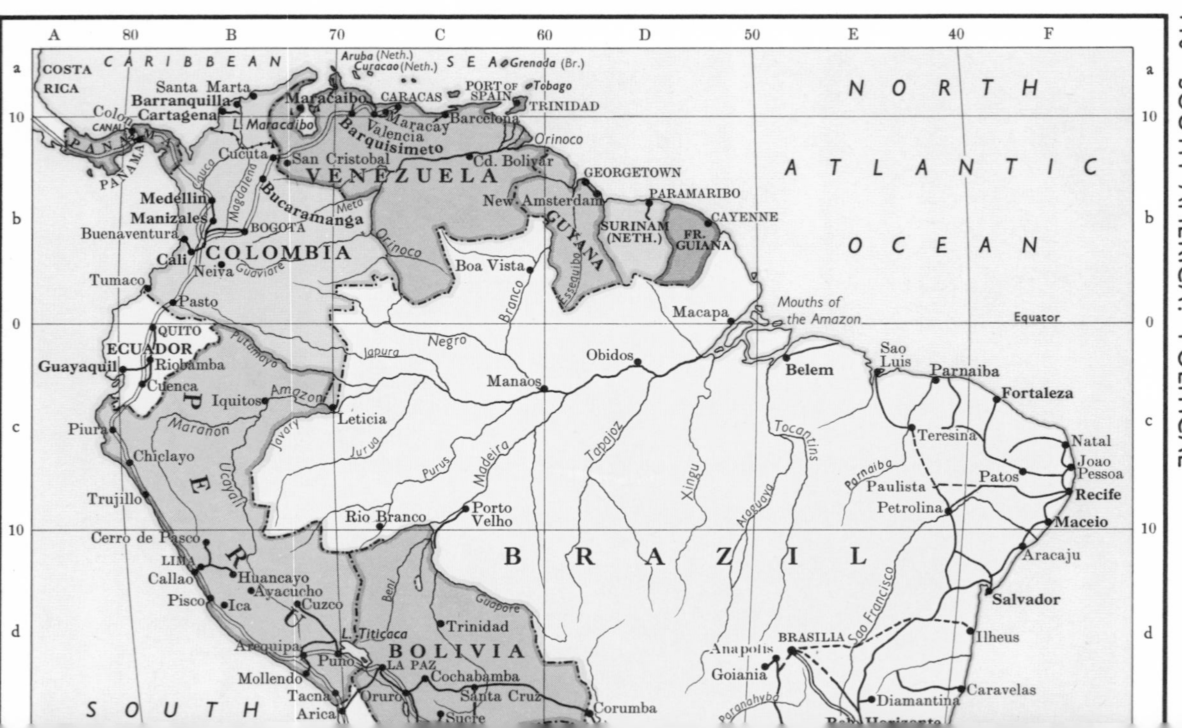
A
80
B
70
C
60
D
50
E
40
F
a
b
c
d
10
0
COSTA RICA
CARIBBEAN SEA
Aruba (Neth.)
Curacao (Neth.)
Grenada (Br.)
Tobago
PORT OF SPAIN
TRINIDAD
NORTH
ATLANTIC
OCEAN
Equator
Santa Marta
Barranquilla
Cartagena
Colon
CANAL
PANAMA
Maracaibo
L. Maracaibo
CARACAS
Valencia
Maracay
Barquisimeto
Barcelona
Orinoco
Cucuta
San Cristobal
Cd. Bolivar
VENEZUELA
GEORGETOWN
New Amsterdam
PARAMARIBO
CAYENNE
Medellin
Manizales
Magdalena
Cauca
Bucaramanga
Meta
BOGOTA
Buenaventura
GUYANA
SURINAM (NETH.)
FR. GUIANA
Cali
COLOMBIA
Neiva
Guaviare
Boa Vista
Essequibo
Tumaco
Pasto
Branco
Macapa
Mouths of the Amazon
QUITO
ECUADOR
Guayaquil
Riobamba
Cuenca
Putumayo
Japura
Negro
Obidos
Manaos
Belem
Sao Luis
Parnaiba
Fortaleza
Iquitos
Amazon
Leticia
PERU
Piura
Maranon
Chiclayo
Ucayali
Javary
Jurua
Purus
Madeira
Tapajoz
Xingu
Tocantins
Teresina
Natal
Joao Pessoa
Patos
Parnaiba
Paulista
Recife
Petrolina
Araguaya
Trujillo
Rio Branco
Porto Velho
Maceio
Cerro de Pasco
BRAZIL
Aracaju
LIMA
Callao
Huancayo
Ayacucho
Cuzco
Pisco
Ica
Beni
Guapore
Sao Francisco
Salvador
Trinidad
L. Titicaca
BOLIVIA
BRASILIA
Ilheus
Arequipa
Puno
LA PAZ
Anapolis
Goiania
Mollendo
Cochabamba
Caravelas
Tacna
Oruro
Santa Cruz
Paranahyba
Diamantina
SOUTH
Arica
Sucre
Corumba

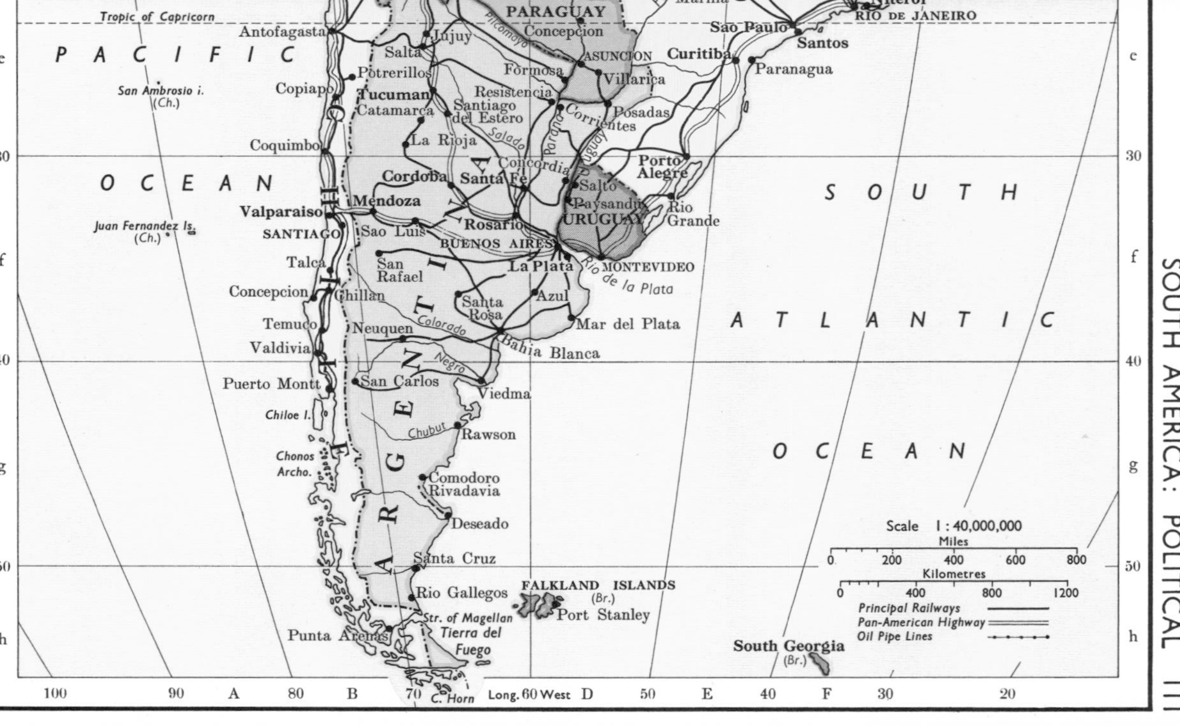
Tropic of Capricorn
PACIFIC
OCEAN
San Ambrosio i. (Ch.)
Juan Fernandez Is. (Ch.)
PARAGUAY
Concepcion
Pilcomayo
ASUNCION
Villarica
Formosa
Resistencia
Corrientes
Posadas
Antofagasta
Jujuy
Salta
Potrerillos
Copiapo
Tucuman
Catamarca
Santiago del Estero
Salado
La Rioja
Coquimbo
Parana
Uruguay
Concordia
Cordoba
Santa Fe
Mendoza
Valparaiso
SANTIAGO
Sao Luis
Rosario
BUENOS AIRES
Salto
Paysandu
URUGUAY
MONTEVIDEO
Rio de la Plata
La Plata
Talca
San Rafael
Concepcion
Chillan
Santa Rosa
Azul
Temuco
Neuquen
Colorado
Mar del Plata
Valdivia
Bahia Blanca
Negro
Puerto Montt
San Carlos
Viedma
Chiloe I.
Chubut
Rawson
Chonos Archo.
Comodoro Rivadavia
Deseado
Santa Cruz
Rio Gallegos
FALKLAND ISLANDS (Br.)
Port Stanley
Str. of Magellan
Punta Arenas
Tierra del Fuego
C. Horn
CHILE
ARGENTINA
Marilia
Niteroi
RIO DE JANEIRO
Sao Paulo
Santos
Curitiba
Paranagua
Porto Alegre
Rio Grande
SOUTH
ATLANTIC
OCEAN
Scale 1 : 40,000,000
Miles
0 200 400 600 800
Kilometres
0 400 800 1200
Principal Railways
Pan-American Highway
Oil Pipe Lines
South Georgia (Br.)
100 90 A 80 B 70 Long. 60 West D 50 E 40 F 30 20
c 30 f 40 g 50 h

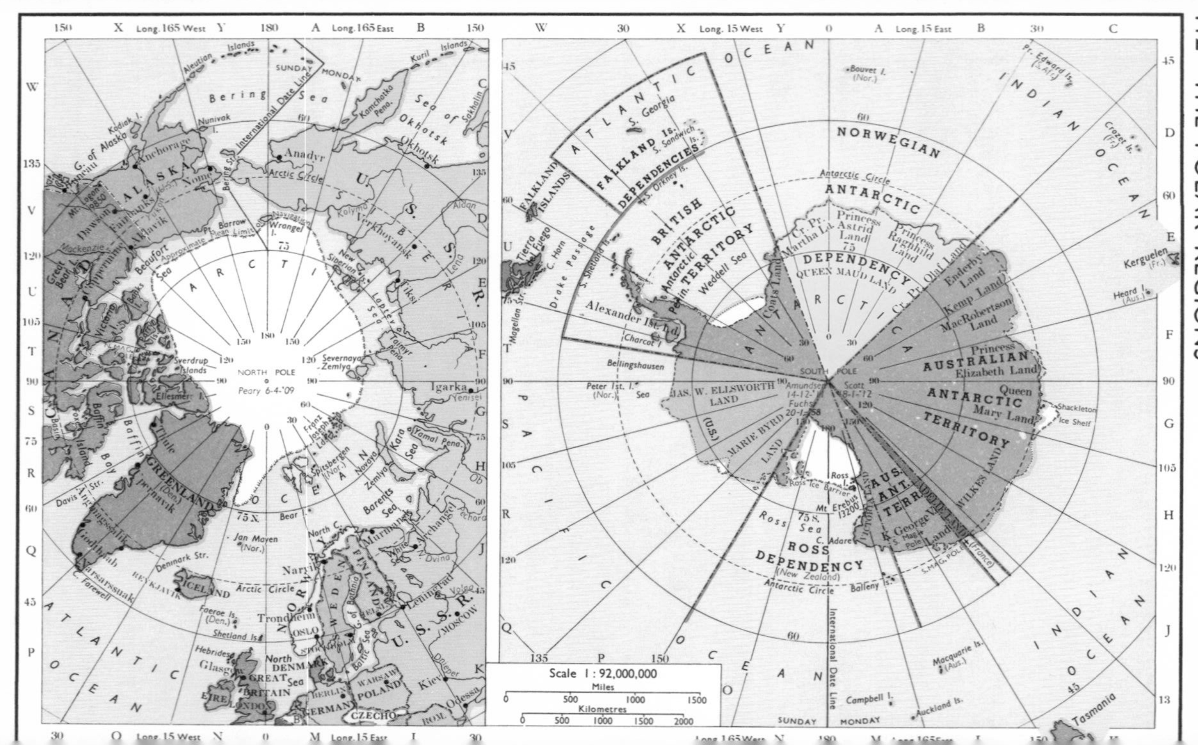
ARCTIC OCEAN
NORTH POLE
Peary 6-4-'09
Bering Sea
Sea of Okhotsk
ALASKA
U.S.S.R.
SIBERIA
GREENLAND (Den.)
Baffin Bay
Barents Sea
Kara Sea
Laptev Sea
ICELAND
FINLAND
ATLANTIC OCEAN
INDIAN OCEAN
PACIFIC OCEAN
ATLANTIC
NORWEGIAN ANTARCTIC DEPENDENCY
QUEEN MAUD LAND
ANTARCTICA
AUSTRALIAN ANTARCTIC TERRITORY
BRITISH ANTARCTIC TERRITORY
FALKLAND IS. DEPENDENCIES
FALKLAND ISLANDS
ROSS DEPENDENCY
(New Zealand)
MARIE BYRD LAND
W. ELLSWORTH LAND
(U.S.)
SOUTH POLE
Amundsen 14-12-'11
Scott 18-1-'12
Fuchs 20-1-'58
Weddell Sea
Ross Sea
Bellingshausen Sea
Drake Passage
Antarctic Circle
Arctic Circle
International Date Line
SUNDAY
MONDAY
Tasmania
Kerguelen (Fr.)
Heard I. (Aus.)
Crozet Is. (Fr.)
Bouvet I. (Nor.)
Macquarie Is. (Aus.)
Campbell I.
Auckland Is.
Alexander Ist. Ld.
Peter Ist. I. (Nor.)
Scale 1 : 92,000,000
Miles
Kilometres

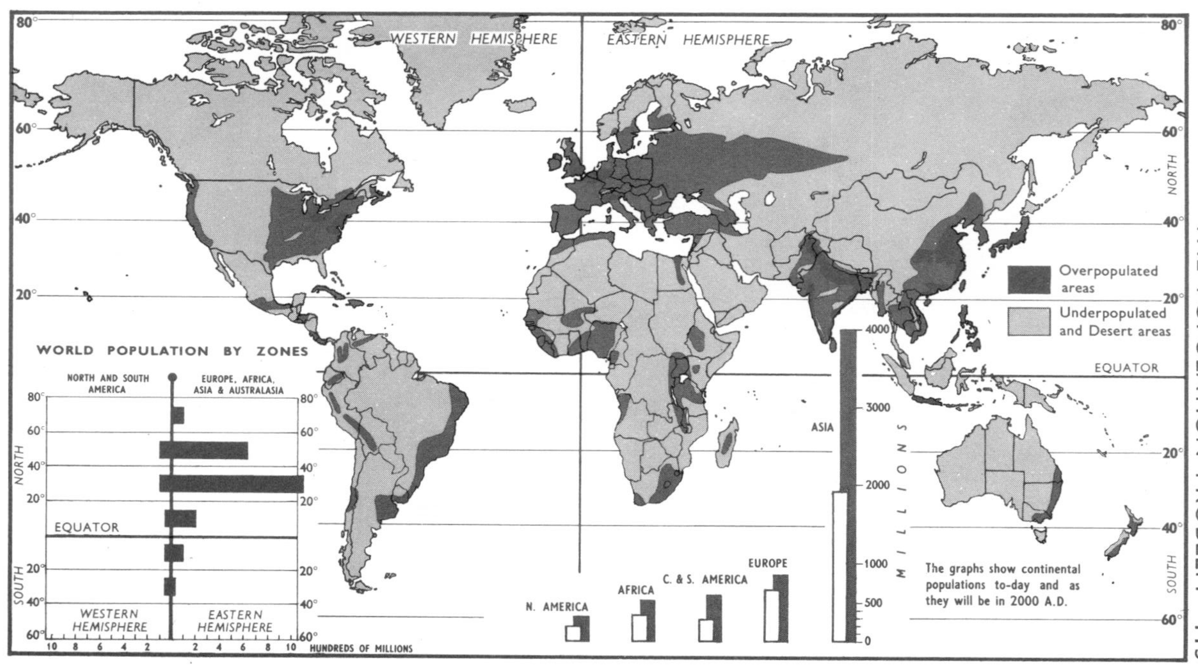
WESTERN HEMISPHERE
EASTERN HEMISPHERE
80°
60°
40°
20°
NORTH
SOUTH
EQUATOR
Overpopulated areas
Underpopulated and Desert areas
WORLD POPULATION BY ZONES
NORTH AND SOUTH AMERICA
EUROPE, AFRICA, ASIA & AUSTRALASIA
WESTERN HEMISPHERE
EASTERN HEMISPHERE
10 8 6 4 2 2 4 6 8 10
HUNDREDS OF MILLIONS
N. AMERICA
AFRICA
C. & S. AMERICA
EUROPE
ASIA
4000
3000
2000
1000
500
0
M I L L I O N S
The graphs show continental populations to-day and as they will be in 2000 A.D.

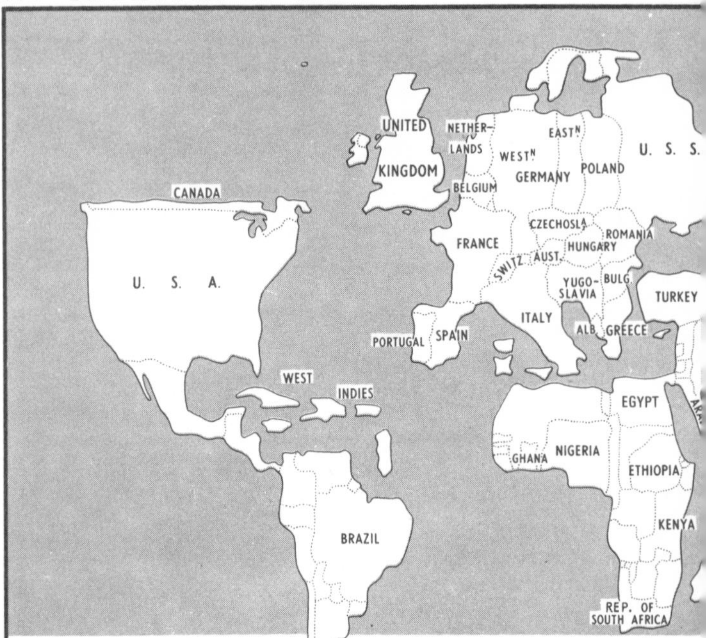

UNITED KINGDOM
NETHER- LANDS
EASTN
WESTN GERMANY
U. S. S.
POLAND
BELGIUM
CANADA
CZECHOSLA
ROMANIA
FRANCE
HUNGARY
SWITZ
AUST.
U. S. A.
YUGO- SLAVIA
BULG.
TURKEY
ITALY
PORTUGAL
SPAIN
ALB.
GREECE
WEST INDIES
EGYPT
GHANA
NIGERIA
ETHIOPIA
KENYA
BRAZIL
REP. OF SOUTH AFRICA

On this map the areas of the various countries are proportional to their *populations* and not to their actu geographical areas as on a conventional map of the world. Comparison with the latter will show up (a) thos countries such as the U.S.A. and China which are very large in both area and population, (b) those countries suc as Java and the U.K. which are small in area but relatively large in population, and (c) those countries which are larg in area but small in population - such as Arabia and Australia. The most important and significant countries a named. The small maps below are on the same basis but the outline has been 'skewed' for convenience. The illustrate aspects of Standards of Living throughout the world.

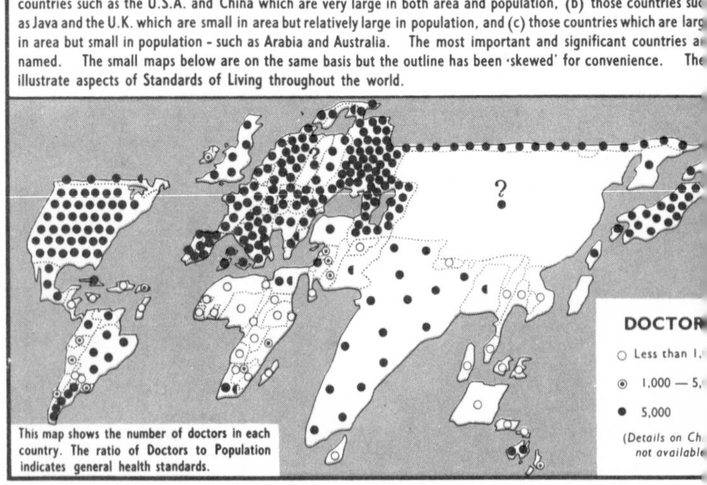

This map shows the number of doctors in each country. The ratio of Doctors to Population indicates general health standards.

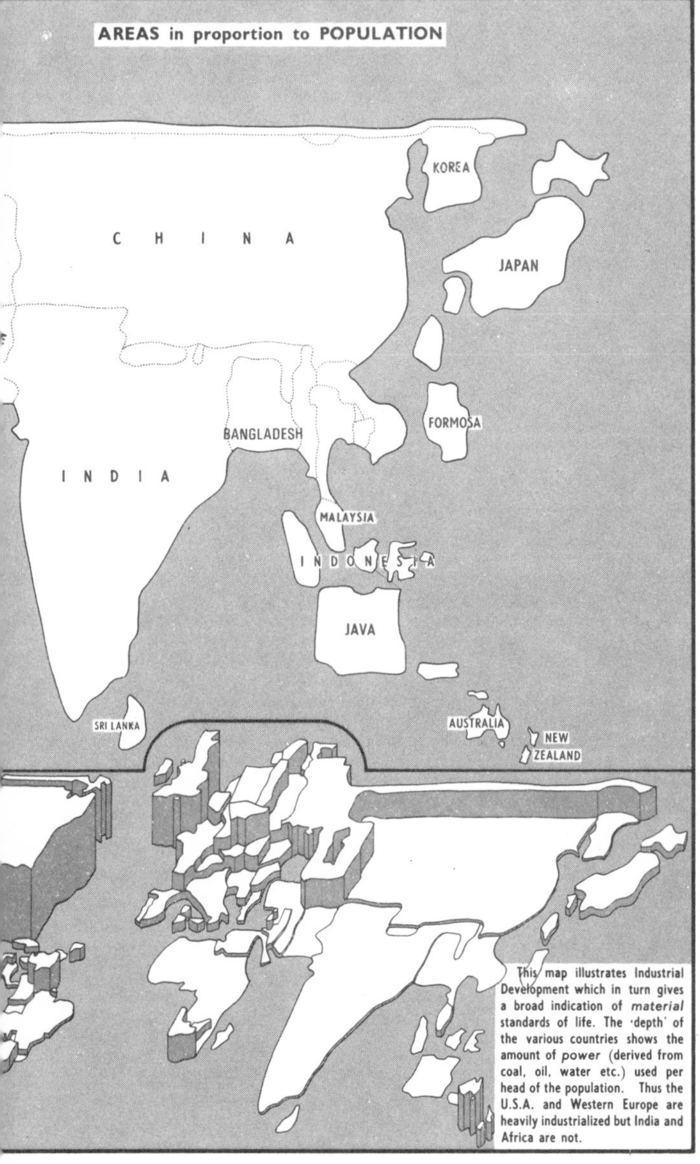

This map illustrates Industrial Development which in turn gives a broad indication of *material* standards of life. The 'depth' of the various countries shows the amount of *power* (derived from coal, oil, water etc.) used per head of the population. Thus the U.S.A. and Western Europe are heavily industrialized but India and Africa are not.

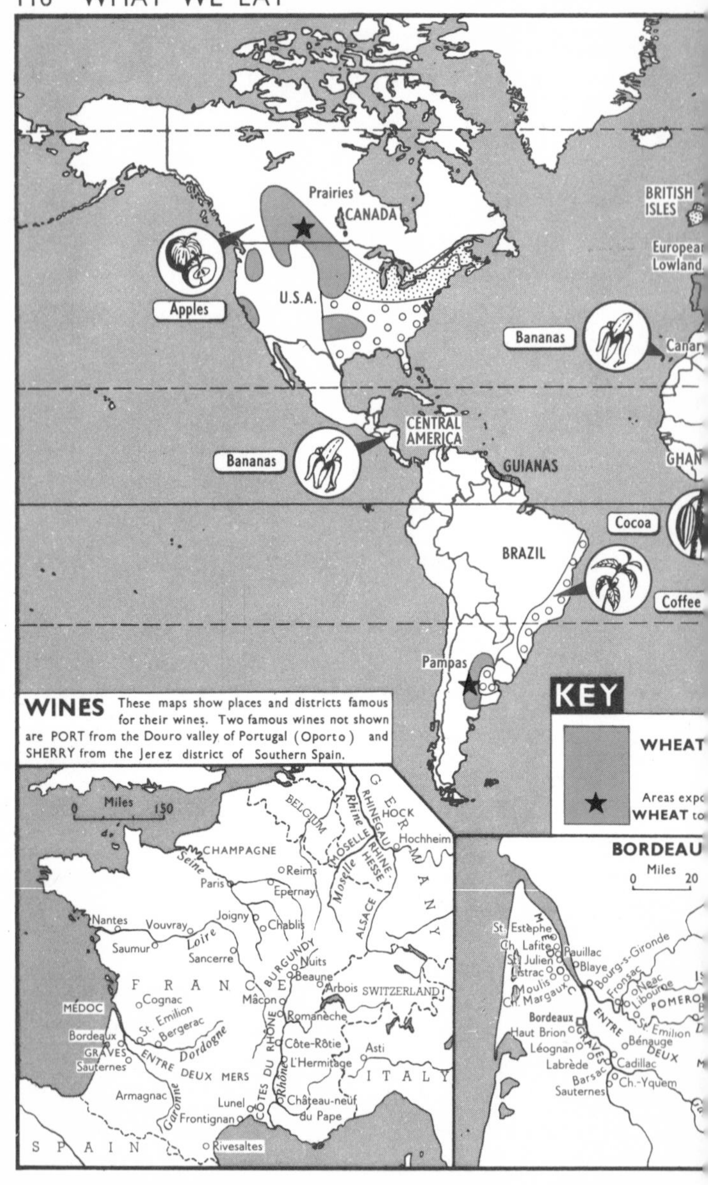

WINES These maps show places and districts famous for their wines. Two famous wines not shown are PORT from the Douro valley of Portugal (Oporto) and SHERRY from the Jerez district of Southern Spain.

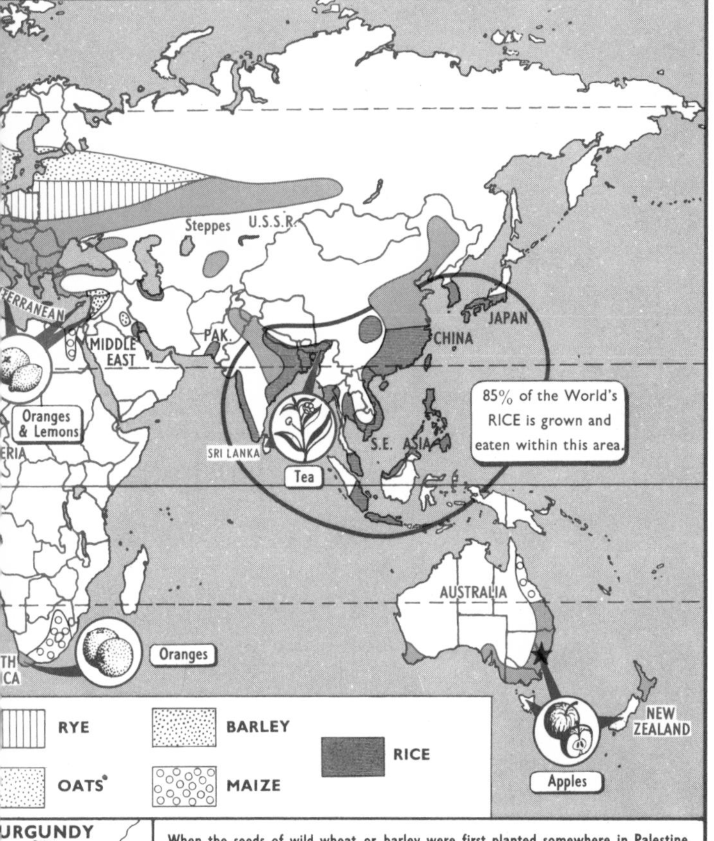

URGUNDY
Dijon
CÔTES DE NUITS
Gevry-Chambertin
Clos-Vougeot
Nuits St. George
Beaune
Volnay
hagny
Chalon-s-Saône
Miles 0 20
Saône
Mâcon
Fuissé
Moulin-à-Vent
Beaujeu
Villefranche
yons

When the seeds of wild wheat or barley were first planted somewhere in Palestine about 10,000 years ago, the foundations of modern civilization were laid. Nomadic hunters now settled down and built villages and developed arts and crafts.

Today, cereals are a basic food throughout the world, soil and climatic conditions deciding which is grown - wheat wherever possible in the temperate zones with rye and oats on the colder and wetter fringes; barley in the hotter, drier lands of the Middle East etc.; and maize and rice in the tropics and sub-tropics.

Wheat is a very important item of world trade; exports from U.S.A., Canada, Australia and Argentina followed the opening up of the great interior plains in the 1880's. Britain is the world's largest importer. Home-produced (soft) wheat is used for biscuits and cakes whilst imports supply flour for bread.

Rice, on the other hand, hardly enters into world trade although it has easily the greatest production of all cereals. It is grown in standing water and has a very high yield per acre.

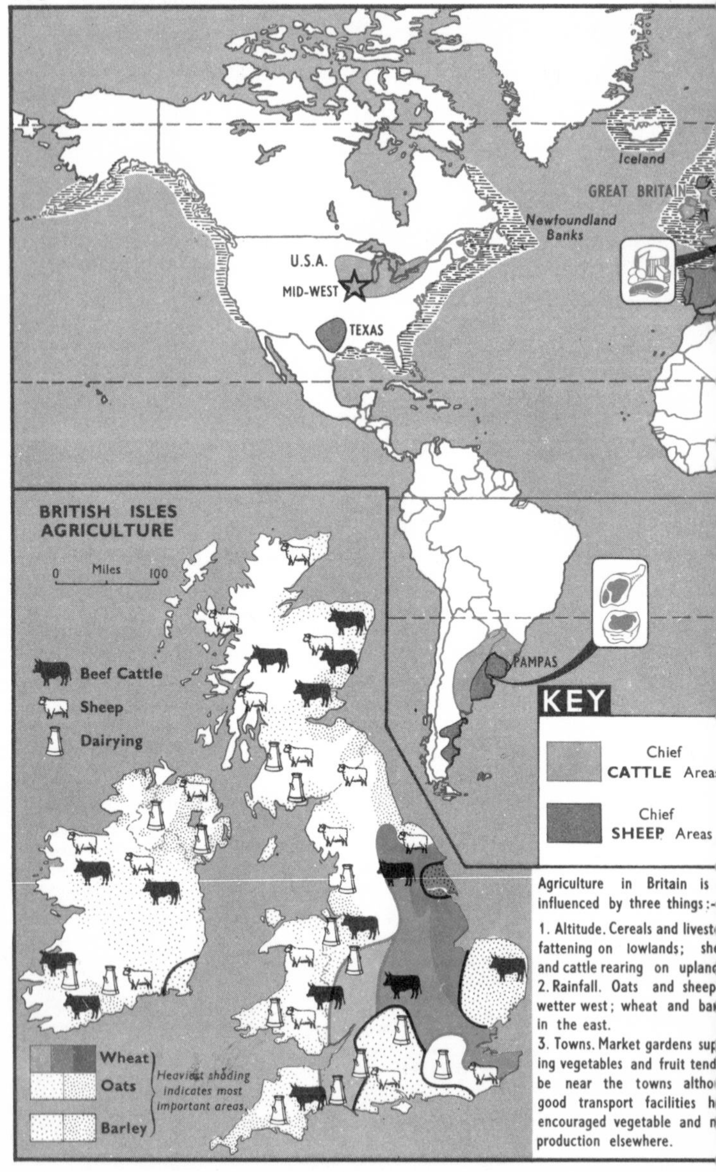

Agriculture in Britain is influenced by three things:-

1. Altitude. Cereals and livest[ock] fattening on lowlands; she[ep] and cattle rearing on upland[s].
2. Rainfall. Oats and sheep [in the] wetter west; wheat and ba[rley] in the east.
3. Towns. Market gardens sup[ply]ing vegetables and fruit tend [to] be near the towns altho[ugh] good transport facilities h[ave] encouraged vegetable and m[ilk] production elsewhere.

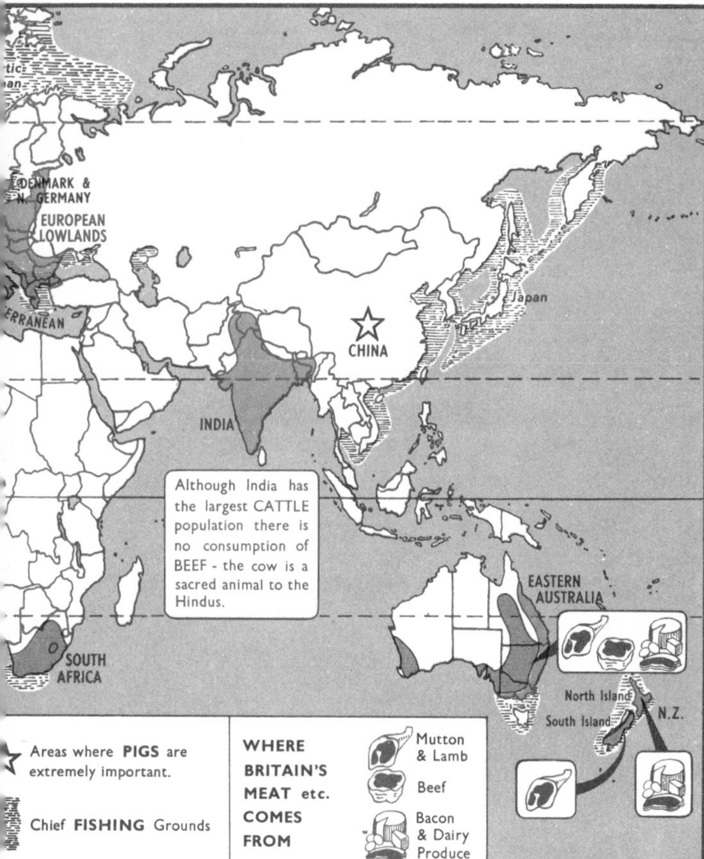

r at least 500,000 years men lived by fishing, hunting, and collecting wild plants. This lasted in the Middle st until about 8000 B.C. when crops were first cultivated and it was also in this area that wild animals were st domesticated - the ancestors of our present day pigs, sheep, and cattle.

ıce then farming has developed and spread, adapting itself to local needs and conditions. Livestock farming ıs brought to a fine art in 18th Century Britain by careful breeding and the discovery of better fodder crops, t the greatest development on the world scale came with the opening up of the great plains of the Americas, stralia and New Zealand in the 1870's and 1880's and the simultaneous invention of refrigeration ships.

day, meat consumption varies greatly throughout the world being lowest in the poor countries of Asia and ica. This is due to a variety of reasons - poverty and ignorance, unsuitability of climates and vegetation, the evalence of diseases such as those caused throughout Africa by the tse-tse fly. Also it should be noted that od from livestock is much more expensive to produce than food from crops. Finally there are religious jections to the eating of beef in India and to the keeping of pigs in Moslem countries.

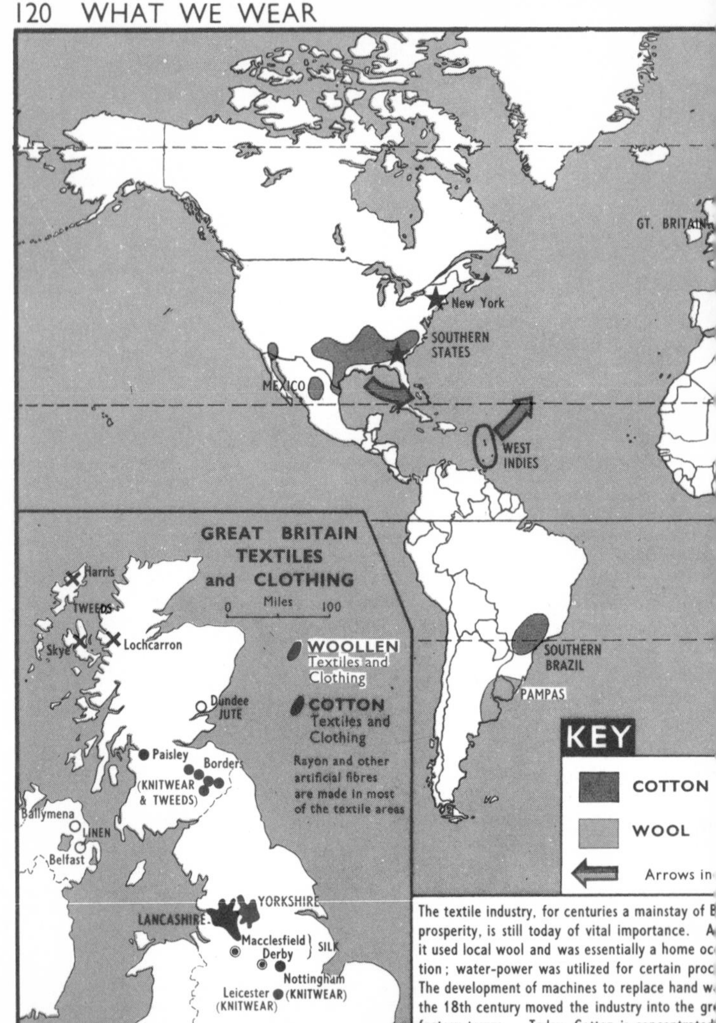

The textile industry, for centuries a mainstay of B
prosperity, is still today of vital importance. A
it used local wool and was essentially a home oc
tion; water-power was utilized for certain proc
The development of machines to replace hand w
the 18th century moved the industry into the gr
factory towns. Today, Cotton is concentrated
Lancashire and has surpassed in importance the
scattered Woollen industry. Almost all raw mat
are now imported. The newer textiles (e.g. N
have attached themselves to the older areas be
of the supply of skilled labour. The making of c
is also carried on in these areas and in London

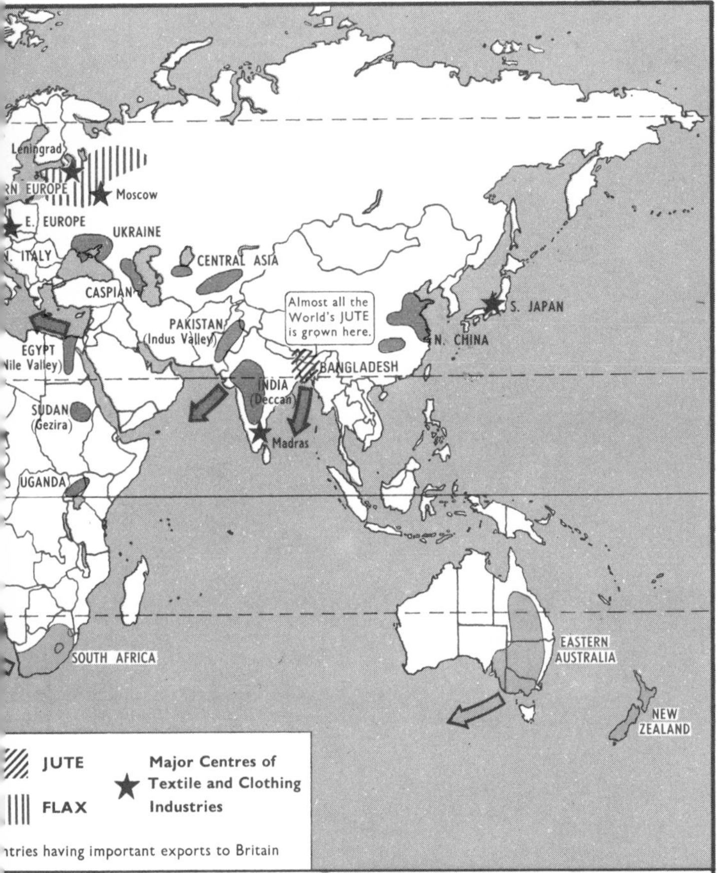

The making of textiles from natural fibres - cotton, wool, etc. or from man-made fibres - rayon, nylon, etc. is one of the world's major industries. Artificial fibres are increasing in importance and already account for a quarter of the total consumption. Production of cotton exceeds that of all other fibres and it is also the most versatile - clothing, household goods, and many industrial uses. For its growth it needs a long hot growing season and rich well-drained soils. The leading producers are U.S.A., U.S.S.R., India and China; Egypt and the West Indies export the finest cotton. Except in the U.S. and India, cotton textile industries are usually found in industrialized countries far from the growing areas - Western Europe, especially Britain, and Japan. The industry is also developing modestly in some countries such as Egypt and Mexico which are not otherwise industrialized.

Two-thirds of the world's wool is produced in the southern hemisphere but manufacturing is carried out almost entirely in the northern. Australia is the largest producer, and the U.S. and Britain the largest manufacturer.

Flax is used for clothing and industrially ; jute for sacks and carpets ; whilst hemp (for canvas) and sisal (for ropes) are also important.

Man-made fibres are produced from materials available in the industrialized countries of Europe and America; they are often associated with the chemical industries.

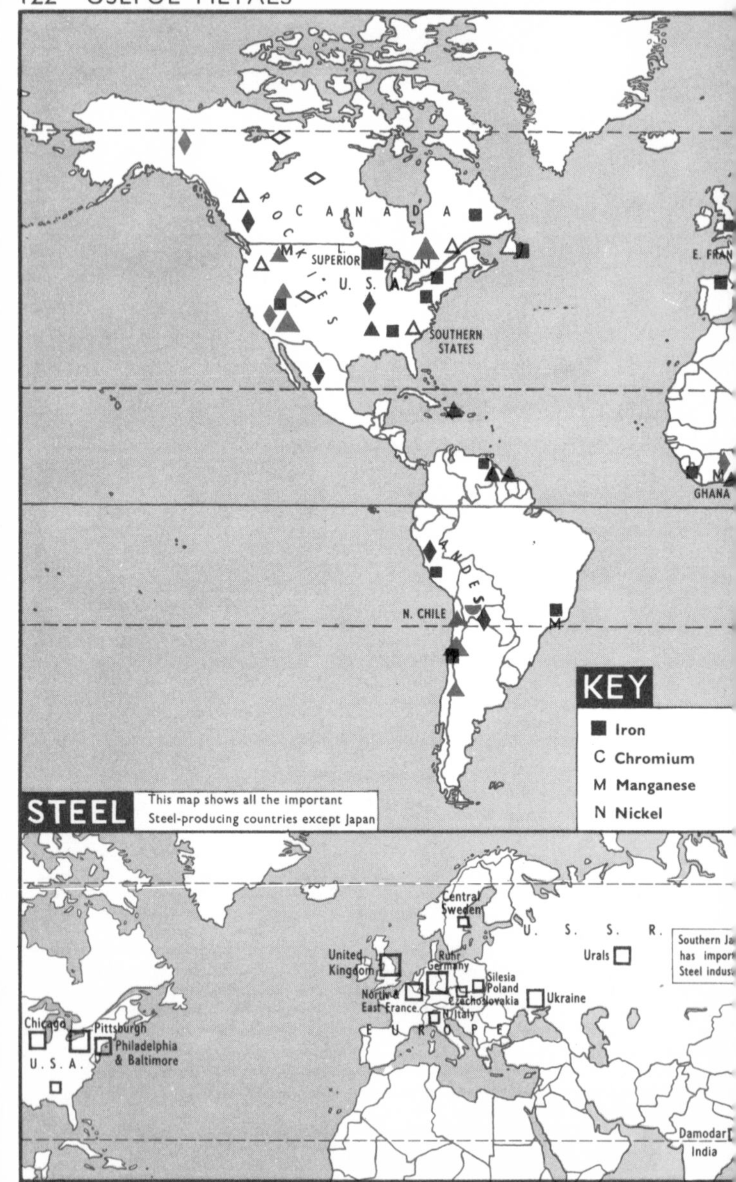
CANADA
ROCKIES
L. SUPERIOR
U. S. A.
SOUTHERN STATES
E. FRAN
GHANA
ANDES
N. CHILE
KEY
Iron
C Chromium
M Manganese
N Nickel
STEEL
This map shows all the important Steel-producing countries except Japan
Central Sweden
U. S. S. R.
Urals
United Kingdom
Ruhr Germany
Silesia Poland
North & East France
Czechoslovakia
Ukraine
N. Italy
EUROPE
Chicago
Pittsburgh
Philadelphia & Baltimore
U. S. A.
Damodar India

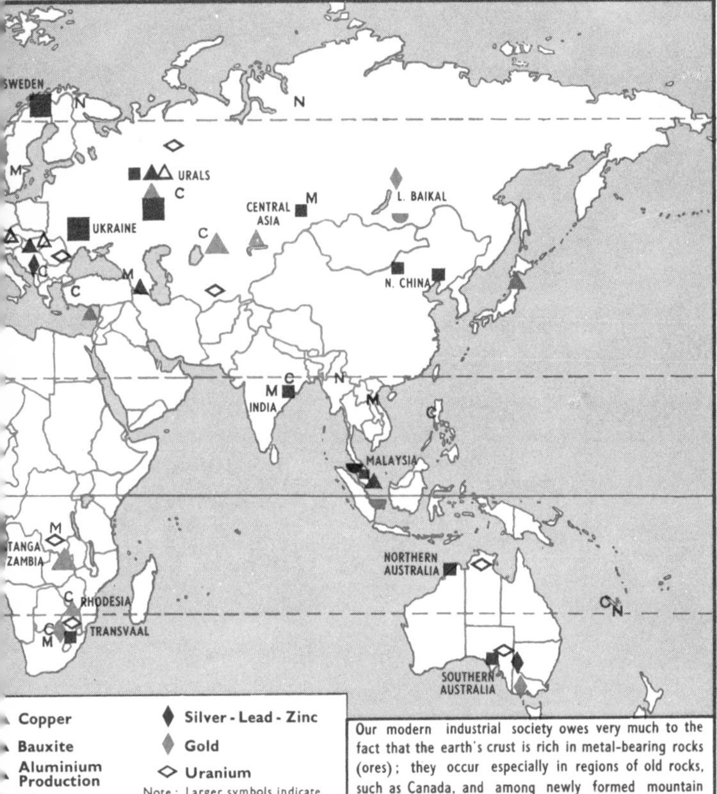

Our modern industrial society owes very much to the fact that the earth's crust is rich in metal-bearing rocks (ores); they occur especially in regions of old rocks, such as Canada, and among newly formed mountain chains such as the Andes.

Some metals, such as gold and copper, occur as solid fragments mixed with other materials and are obtained by crushing and sorting the ore. For various reasons the concentration of metal in the ore varies considerably, the very low concentrations being worked only when profitable, as for example in the South African goldfields. Other metals, such as iron, occur in chemical combination with other materials and these compounds themselves are often mixed with worthless rock. The compounds have first to be separated from the rock and then smelted or reduced to obtain the metal.

IRON is the cheapest and most useful of the metals; most iron-ores that are used contain 30-65% iron. It is smelted to make pig-iron. Where rich iron ores occur close to coalfields heavy industries based on steel manufacturing develop. STEEL is made by treating pig-iron so that it contains the exact amounts of carbon and such other metals as manganese, nickel, chromium, etc. ("alloys") as are necessary for particular purposes. COPPER being an excellent conductor of electricity is widely used in electrical engineering; it is also used to make brass. BAUXITE is the ore of ALUMINIUM, one of the most important materials used in the aircraft and car industries. Since in this case the smelting process requires large amounts of electric power, aluminium manufacturing is commonly found in areas with large hydro-electric installations such as the Pyrenees.

TIN is mainly used in the manufacture of cans and also for bronze. Silver, lead, and zinc are usually found together. SILVER is used industrially and in coins; LEAD for batteries, cables, pipes, and paints; ZINC as a coating for iron (galvanizing). GOLD is chiefly important as security for currency, and URANIUM is the most important source of atomic power.

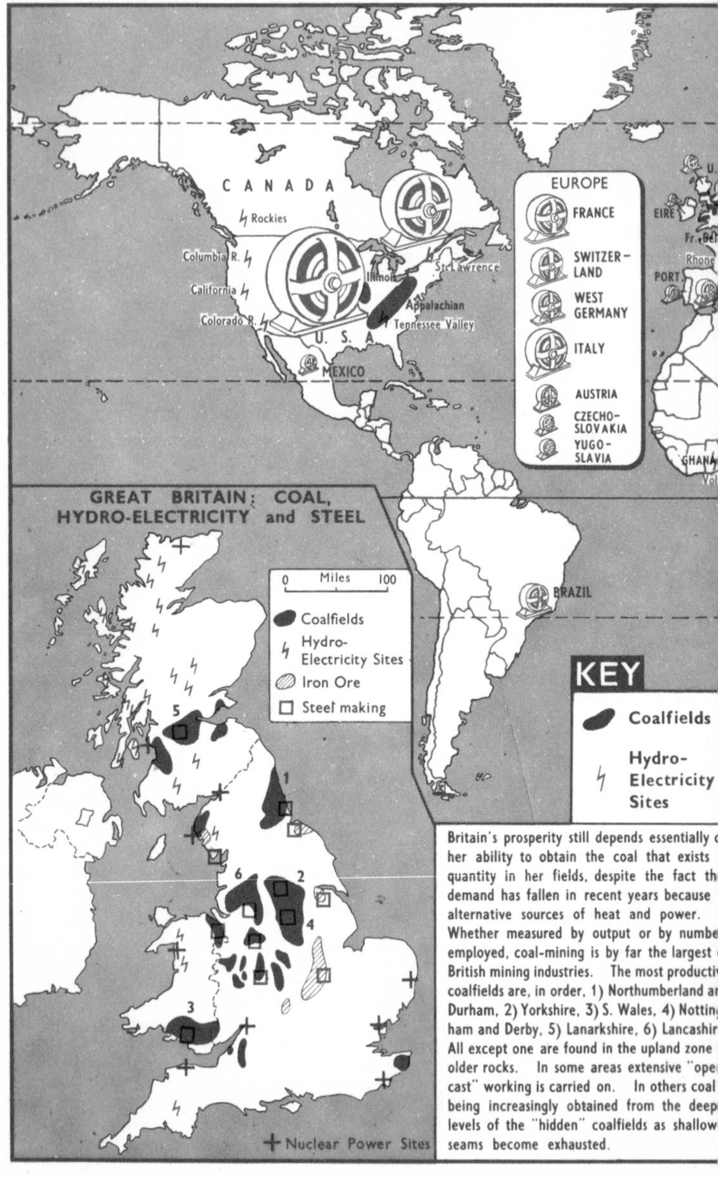

Britain's prosperity still depends essentially on her ability to obtain the coal that exists in quantity in her fields, despite the fact that demand has fallen in recent years because of alternative sources of heat and power. Whether measured by output or by numbers employed, coal-mining is by far the largest of British mining industries. The most productive coalfields are, in order, 1) Northumberland and Durham, 2) Yorkshire, 3) S. Wales, 4) Nottingham and Derby, 5) Lanarkshire, 6) Lancashire. All except one are found in the upland zone of older rocks. In some areas extensive "open-cast" working is carried on. In others coal is being increasingly obtained from the deeper levels of the "hidden" coalfields as shallower seams become exhausted.

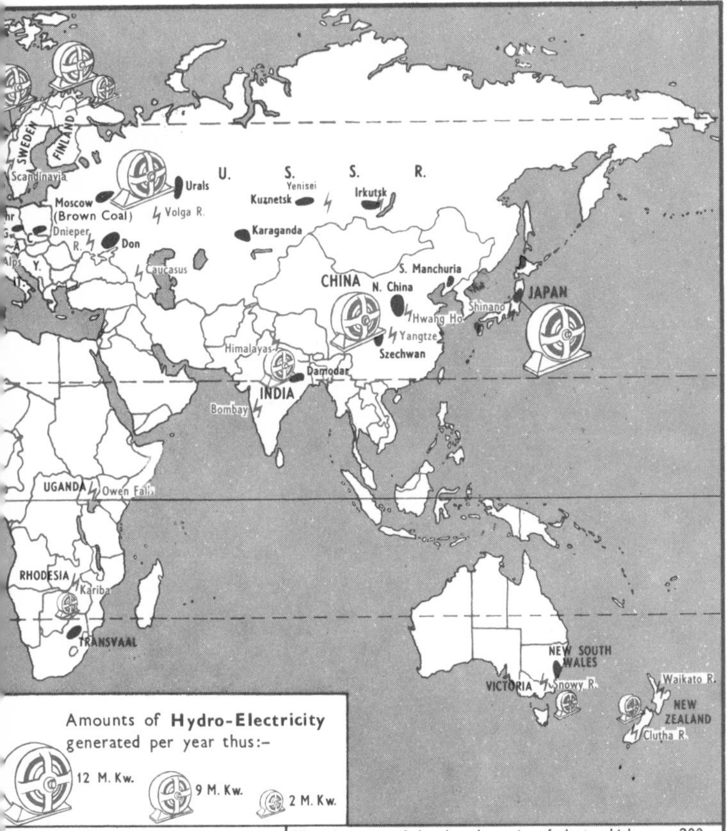

bout half of the iron consumed in Britain is ome-produced and the remainder imported, nainly from Sweden, North Africa, and Spain. ritain pioneered the modern Steel industry in he 18th Century with a series of brilliant in- entions and discoveries and today she remains ne of the great steel producers although far ehind the U.S. and U.S.S.R. Steel is the oundation of almost all heavy and much light ngineering and manufacturing.

ydro-electric installations are located in the reas of heavy rainfall and of steep valleys. uclear sites tend to be coastal for security and ecause of the need for plentiful water upplies for cooling.

All coal consists of the altered remains of plants which grew 200 - 300 million years ago.

Coalfields are unevenly distributed and coal itself varies in quality; seams also vary from the thick, undisturbed, and easily-worked to the thin and broken. Production within a country depends on demand rather than reserves; thus Western Germany produces far more than South Africa which has larger reserves. In the U.S., and to some extent Western Europe, demand is falling off owing to competition from oil and gas.

Coal is used directly as fuel, and for the production of electricity and gas. Coke is a vital raw material for the Steel industry, and other by-products are important to the chemical industries.

Many countries such as those of Scandinavia are deficient in coal and have to import their needs and or develop other sources of power. This has led in the last 50 years to the considerable development of hydro-electric power, especially in North America and Europe: Much remains to be developed however, especially in the other continents.

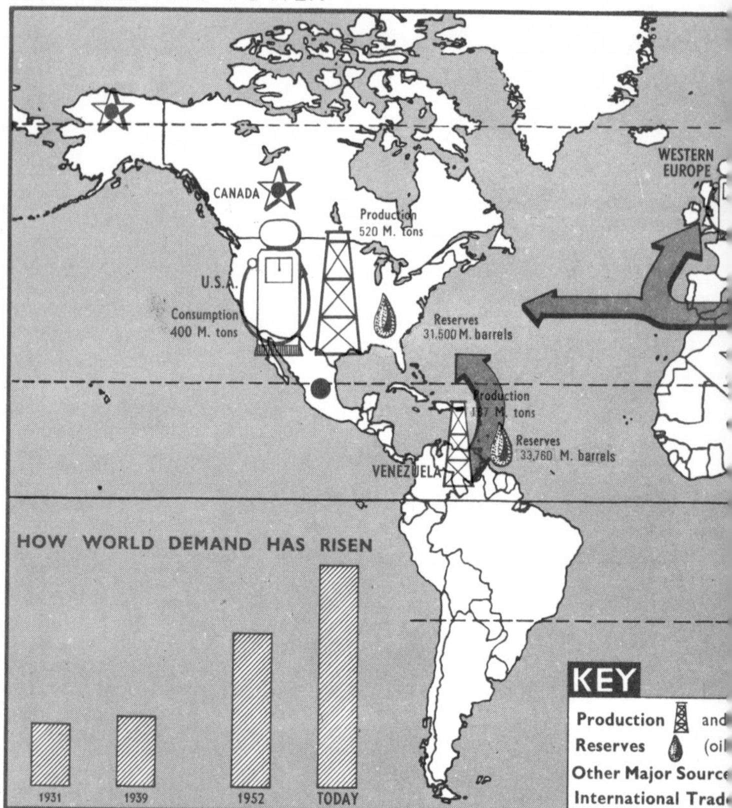

Oil, or Petroleum, supplies half the power needed in the world today, and it will be many years before it is replaced by newer sources such as atomic energy. In fact it is predicted that the dramatic rise in world demand over the past 30 years will continue until, by the end of the century, the world will require nearly four times as much oil as it is using today.

The U.S.A. is easily the world's largest consumer but does not produce enough for her increasing needs and must import (at present mainly from Venezuela) to make up the difference. Her reserves are relatively small and dwindling.

The Middle East on the other hand has enormous reserves; most of the present production of the area is imported by Britain and Western Europe but the U.S. is also undoubtedly looking to the area for future supplies. Venezuèla, the world's biggest exporter and third producer has relatively small reserves. It is not possible to estimate accurately the oil reserves of the U.S.S.R. for various reasons, but it is certain that she will need to increase her production greatly in the next few years to serve her general programme of industrial expansion.

Reserves, known and unknown, are thus the key to future developments in the oil industry. Much is hoped of the newly discovered and undeveloped fields in Western Canada, the Sahara, Siberia, Northern China, Nigeria and the North Sea. It is also very likely that new methods of extraction will make available vast reserves known to be locked up in sand and shale deposits in the U.S. and Canada.

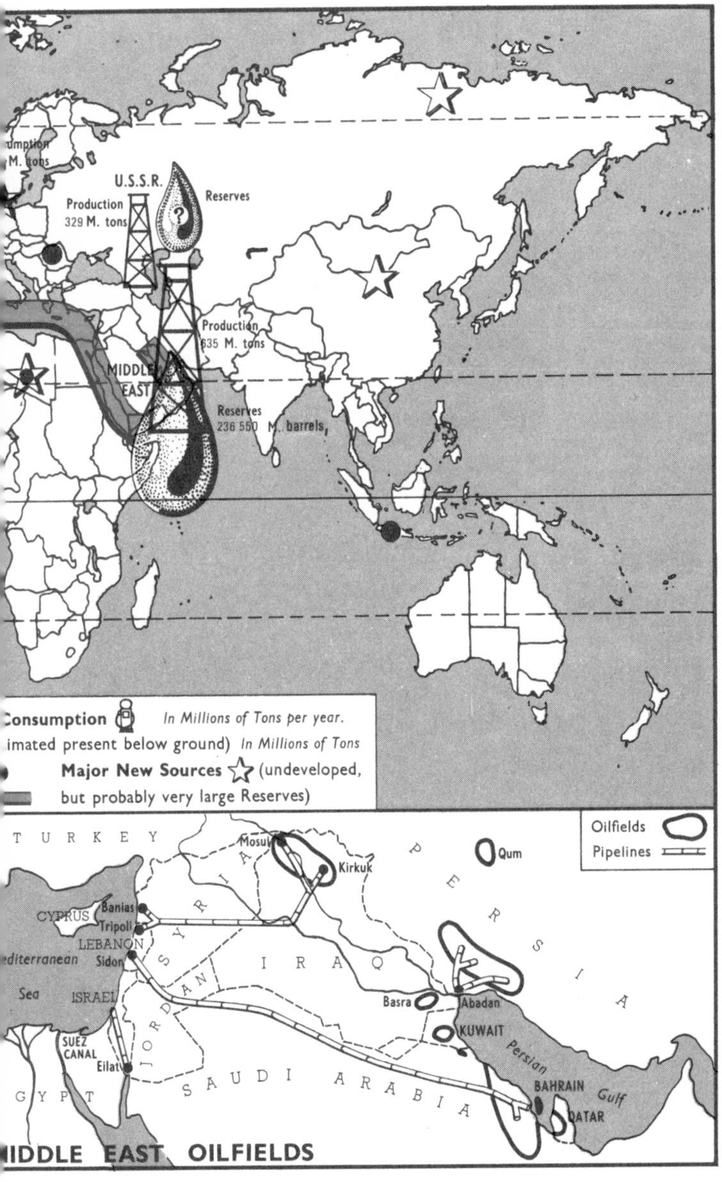

umption
M. tons
U.S.S.R.
Production
329 M. tons
Reserves
Production
635 M. tons
MIDDLE
EAST
Reserves
236 550 M. barrels
Consumption In Millions of Tons per year.
imated present below ground) In Millions of Tons
Major New Sources (undeveloped, but probably very large Reserves)
Oilfields
Pipelines
TURKEY
Mosul
Kirkuk
Qum
PERSIA
SYRIA
CYPRUS
Banias
Tripoli
LEBANON
Sidon
editerranean
Sea
ISRAEL
IRAQ
JORDAN
Basra
Abadan
KUWAIT
Persian Gulf
SUEZ CANAL
Eilat
SAUDI ARABIA
BAHRAIN
QATAR
GYPT

IDDLE EAST OILFIELDS

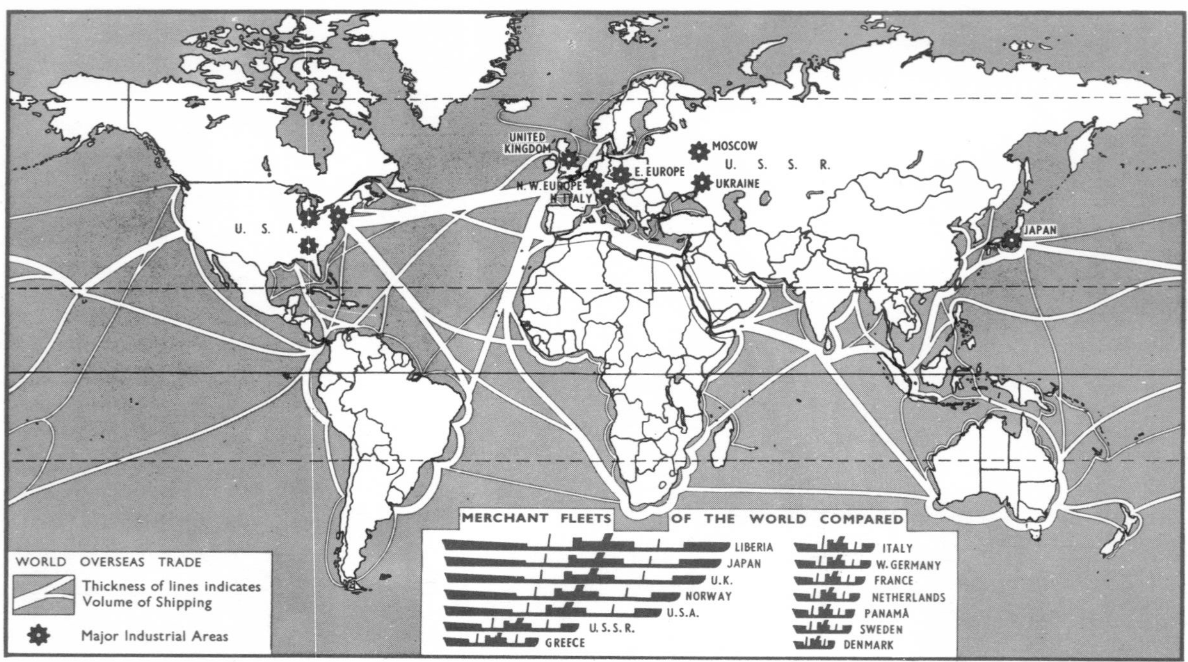
UNITED KINGDOM
MOSCOW
U. S. S. R.
E. EUROPE
N. W. EUROPE
UKRAINE
N. ITALY
U. S. A.
JAPAN
MERCHANT FLEETS OF THE WORLD COMPARED
LIBERIA
JAPAN
U.K.
NORWAY
U.S.A.
U.S.S.R.
GREECE
ITALY
W. GERMANY
FRANCE
NETHERLANDS
PANAMÁ
SWEDEN
DENMARK
WORLD OVERSEAS TRADE
Thickness of lines indicates Volume of Shipping
Major Industrial Areas

INDEX TO MAPS

The figures and letters indicate the situation of the places on the Maps; thus, Aalborg 55Ad appears on page 55 in the square Ad. In the case of the polar map p. 112, the triangles are lettered clockwise and N or S indicates whether the North or South Pole map is to be consulted. In some of the 5,000 entries common abbreviations, such as *N* for North, *Arg.* for Argentine have been used

Delgado, C. 95Kf
Delhi 74Bb
Demavend, Mt. 66Ed
Den Helder 56Ca
Denbigh, Co. 39Ed
Deniliquin 82Bc
DENMARK 64Ba
Denmark Str. 98Ha
Denny 44Ca
Denver 102Cc
Derby, & Co. 46Cb
Derevaragh, L. 48Dc
Derg, L. 49Cd
Derna 63Dc
Derrynasaggart Mts. 49Be
Derwent, R. (Derby) 46Ca
Derwent, R. (Yorks) 42Da
Des Moines 103Db
Dessau 64Cb
Detroit 104Cc
Devon, Co. 39Ee
Devon I. 101Ha
Devon, R. 44Ca
Dewsbury 46Ca
Dhahran 73Cc
Dhaulagiri 75Cb
Diamantina 110Ed
Diamantina, R. 81Db
Diego Suarez 91Gg
Dieppe 58Cb
Dijon 58Db
Dili 79Dc
Dimboola 82Bc
Dinant 57Cb
Dinaric Alps 60Cb
Dingle 51Ad
Dingle B. 51Ad
Dingwall 40Bb
Dirk Hartog I. 80Ab
Disko I. 101Lb
Diu 74Bb
Diwaniya 72Cb
Dixmude 56Bb
Diyarbakir 72Bb
Djakarta (*see* Jakarta)
Djelfa 62Bc
Dnepropetrovsk 63Eb
Dnieper, R. 63Eb
Dniester, R. 63Db
Dobruja 61Eb
Dodecanese Is. 61Ec
Dogger Bank 36Gc
Dolgelley 42Cb
Dollar 44Ca
Dolomites 64Bc
DOMINICAN REP. 107Dc
Don, R. (Eng.) 46Ca
Don, R. (Scot.) 41Cb
Don, R. (U.S.S.R.) 66Dc
Donaghadee 50Fb
Doncaster 46Ca
Donegal B. 48Cb
Donegal, & Co. 50Cb
Donegal Mts. 48Cb
Donets, R. 66Dc
Donetsk 66Dc
Dorchester 42Cc
Dordrecht 56Cb
Dorking 47Gd
Dornoch Firth 40Cb
Dorset, Co. 39Ee
Dortmund 65In
Douai 57Bb
Douglas 42Ba
Doune 44Ba
Douro, R. 59Ac
Dove, R. 46Cb
Dover (Eng.) 47Jd
Dover (U.S.) 105Dd
Dover, Straits of 47Jd
Dowlais 45Bc
Down, Co. 50Eb
DownhamMarket 46Eb
Downpatrick 50Fb
Downs, The 47Gd
Drakensberg 93Ce
Drammen 55Bd
Drava, R. 60Ca
Dresden 64Cb
Drogheda 50Ec
Drogheda B. 48Ec
Duala 94Cc
Dubawnt, L. 100Fb
Dubawnt, R. 100Fb
Dubbo 83Cb
Dublin 51Ec
Dublin B. 49Ec
Dublin, Co. 51Ec
Dubrovnik 61Cb
Dubuque 104Ac
Dudinka 67Gb
Dudley 46Bb
Duisburg 65In
Duluth 104Ab
Dumbarton 44Ab
Dumfries, & Co. 38Ec
Dunany Pt. 48Ec
Dunbar 41Cb
Dunbarton, Co. 44Aa
Dunblane 44Ca
Duncansby Hd. 40Ca
Dundalk 50Eb
Dundalk B. 48Ec
Dundee 44Ea
Dundrum B. 48Fb
Dunedin 85Cf
Dunfermline 44Da
Dungannon 50Eb
Dungarvan 48Dd
Dungarvan Hr. 49Dd
Dungeness 47He
Dunkirk 56Bb
Dun Laoghaire 51Ec
Dunmanus B. 49Be
Dunmanway 51Be
Dunmow 47Hd
Dunoon 44Ab
Duns 38Ec
Dunstable 47Gd
Durazzo 61Cb
Durban 93De
Durham, & Co. 38Fc
Durrow 51Dd
Dursey I. 49Ae
Dushanbe 66Fd
Dusseldorf 65In
D'Urville I. 84Ed
Dvina, R. 55Ed
Dysart 44Da
Dzungarian Gate 66Gc

Ealing 47Gd
Earn, L. 44Ba
Easington 45Ed
East Anglian Hts. 43Eb
East C. (N.Z.) 84Gb
East C. (U.S.S.R.) 67Ob
East China Sea 77Db
East Grinstead 47Gd
East Indies 69Gd
East Kilbride 44Bb
Eastleigh 47Fe
East Linton 44Eb
East London 93Cf
East Lothian, Co. 44Eb
East Retford 46Da
East Riding 46Da
Eastbourne 47He
Eastmain, R. 101Ic
Ebbw Vale 45Bc
Ebro R. 59Bc
Echuca 82Bc

Kaiserslautern 57Dc
Kajaani 54Ec
Kakinada 75Cc
Kalahari Desert 93Bd
Kalamata 61Dc
Kalamazoo 104Bc
Kalat 74Ab
Kalemie 95Ge
Kalgoorlie 80Bc
Kalimantan 78Cb
Kalinin 66Dc
Kaliningrad 65Ea
Kalisz 65Db
Kalkfontein 93Ae
Kalmar 55Cd
Kaluga 31Gb
Kama, R. 66Ec
Kambove 92Cb
Kamchatka Pen. 67Mc
Kamloops 100Dc
Kampala 95Hc
Kampen 56Ca
Kanazawa 77Eb
Kandahar 74Aa
Kandalaksha 54Fb
Kandavu, I. 87Hf
Kandy 74In
Kangaroo I. 82Ac
Kano 94Ca
Kanpur 74Cb
Kansas City 103Dc
Kansu, Prov. 76Bb
Kapunda 82Ab
Kara Sea 66Fb
Karachi 74Ab
Karaganda 66Fc
Karakorum Ra. 74Ba
Karasburg 93Ae
Kariba 92Cc
Karikal 74Bc
Karisimbi, Mt. 95Gd
Karl Marx Stadt 64Cb
Karlovy Vary 64Cb
Karlskrona 55Cd
Karlsruhe 64Bb
Karlstad 55Bd
Karonga 92Da
Karoo, Gt. & L. 93Bf
Karsakpay 66Fc
Kasai, R. 94Ed
Kashgar 70Ec
Kashmir, State 74Ba
Kasongo 95Gd
Kassel 64Bb
Kastrop-Rauxel 65In
Katanga 95Ge
Katmandu 75Cb
Katowice 65Db
Katrine, L. 44Aa
Katrineholm 55Cd
Kattegat 55Bd
Kaunas 55De
Kaura Namoda 94Ca
Kavalla 63Db
Kawhia Har. 84Ec
Kawthoolei 75Dc
Kayes 90Ad
Kayseri 72Bb
Kazakhstan 66Fc
Kazan 66Ec
Kazvin 72Cb
Keelung 77Dc
Keetmanshoop 93Ae
Keewatin, Dist. 100Gb
Kei Is. 79Ec
Keighley 46Ca
Kells (Ceanannus Mor)
Kemerovo 66Gc
Kempsey 83Db
Kendal 42Ca
Kenmare 51Be
Kennet, R. 47Fd
Kent, Co. 47Hd
Kentucky State, 103Ec
KENYA 95Jc
Kerala, State 74Bd
Kerch 72Ba
Kerch, Str. of 29Fc
Kerguelen I. 112SE
Kermadec Is. 87Ih
Kerman 72Db
Kermanshah 72Cb
Kerry, Co. 51Bd
Kerry Hd. 49Bd
Kerulen, R. 67Ic
Kesteven (Lincs.) 46Db
Keswick 40Cc
Kettering 46Db
Key, L. 48Cc
Key West 103Ed
Khabarovsk 67Lc
Khanka, L. 77Ea
Khanty Mansiysk 66Fb
Kharkov 66Dc
Khartoum 73Bd
Kherson 72Ba
Khingan Mts. 67Kc
Khiva 72Ea
Khorramshah 72Cb
Khyber Pass 74Ba
Kiakhta 67Ic
Kiangsi 76Ce
Kiangsu, Prov. 77Cb
Kidderminster 46Bb
Kidsgrove 46Ba
Kiel 64Ba
Kielce 65Eb
Kiev 66Dc
Kigoma 95Gd
Kildare 51Ec
Kilimanjaro, Mt. 95Jd
Kilkee 51Bd
Kilkenny, Co. 51Dd
Kilkieran B. 49Bc
Killala 50Bb
Killala B. 48Bb
Killaloe 51Cd
Killarney 51Bd
Killarney, L. of 49Bd
Killin 44Ba
Killybeg 50Cb
Kilmallock 51Cd
Kilmarnock 44Bb
Kilombero R. 95Je
Kilosa 95Je
Kilrush 51Bd
Kilsyth 44Bb
Kilwinning 44Ab
Kimberley 93Be
Kinabalu Mt. 78Cb
Kincardine, Co. 38Eb
Kinchinjunga, Mt. 75Cb
Kindu 94Gd
King I. 81Dc
King George V. Ld. 112SL
King Sd. 80Ba
King's Lynn 46Eb
Kingston (Aus.) 81Cc
Kingston (Can.) 105Dc
Kingston (Eng.) 47Gd
Kingston (W.I.) 106In.I
King William I. 100Gb
King William's Town 93Cf
Kinnairds Hd. 41Db
Kinross, & Co. 44Da
Kinsale 51Ce
Kinsale Har. 49Ce
Kinshasa 94Ed
Kintyre 40Bc
Kintyre, Mull of 40Bc
Kioga, L. 95Hc
Kippure 49Ec
Kirgiz 66Fd
Kirgiz Steppes 66Ec
Kirin, Prov. 77Da
Kirkcaldy 44Da

Las Vegas 102Bc
Lashio 75Db
Latakia 72Bb
Latium 60Bb
Latvia 55Dd
Lauder 44Eb
Launceston 81In
Lausanne 64Ac
Lea, R. 47Gd
Leamington 43Db
LEBANON 63Ec
Lee, R. 49Ce
Leeds 46Ca
Leek 46Ba
Leeuwarden 56Ca
Leeuwin, C. 80Ac
Leeward Is. 107Fc
Legaspi 79Da
Leghorn 60Bb
Legnica 65Db
Leicester, & Co. 46Cb
Leiden 56Ca
Leinster, Mt. 49Ed
Leinster, Prov. 51Dc
Leipzig 64Cb
Leith 44Db
Leith Hill 47Gd
Leitrim, Co. 50Cb
Le Mans 58Cb
Lemnos, I. 61Ec
Lena, R. 67Kb
Leningrad 55Fd
Lennox Hills 44Ba
Leon (Spain) 59Ac
Leon (Nic.) 106Ad
Leon (Mexico) 99Dc
Leonora 80Bb
Lerida 59Cc
Lerwick 41In
Leslie 44Da
LESOTHO 93Ce
Lesser Antilles 107Fc
Lethbridge 100Ec
Letterkenny 50Db
Leuchars 44Ea
Leven 44Ea
Leven, L. 44Da
Lewes 47Ge
Lewis, Butt of 40Aa
Lewis I. 40Aa
Lewiston 105Ec
Lexington 104Cd
Leyte I. 79Da
Lhasa 75Db
Liaoning Prov. 77Da
Liard, R. 100Db
Liberec 65Cb
LIBERIA 90Be
Libreville 91Ce
LIBYA 90Dc
Libyan Desert 88Ec
Lichfield 46Cb
LIECHTENSTEIN 64Bc
Liege 57Cb
Liepaja 55Dd
Liffey, R. 49Ec
Lifford 50Db
Lifu Is. 86Gg
Liguria 60Ab
Likasi 95Gf
Lille 58Ca
Lillehammer 55Bc
Lilongwe 92Db
Lim Fiord 55Ad
Lima 110Bd
Limassol 63Ec
Limavady 50Ea
Limerick, & Co. 51Bd
Limoges 58Cb
Limpopo, R. 93Cd
Linares 59Bd
Lincoln, & Co. 46Da
Lincoln (U.S.A.) 102Db
Lincoln Edge 46Da
Lincoln Wolds 46Da
Lindesnes 55Ad
Lindi 95Je
Lindsay, Mt. 83Da
Lindsey, Co. 39Fd
Linfen 76Cb
Lingen 64Aa
Lingga Is. 78Bc
Linkoping 55Cd
Linlithgow 44Cb
Linnhe, L. 40Bb
Linz 60Ba
Lions, G. of 59Cc
Lisbon 59Ad
Lisburn 50Eb
Lisdoonvarna 51Bc
Lismore 51Dd
Listowel 51Bd
Lithgow 83Db
Lithuania 55Dd
Littlehampton 47Ge
Little Minch 40Ab
Little Rock 103Dc
Liverpool 46Ba
Liverpool Ra. 83Db
Livingston 44Cb
Lizard Hd. 42Bc
Ljubljana 60Ba
Ljusnan, R. 55Cc
Llandaff 45Bd
LlandrindodWells 42Cb
Llanelly 42Bc
Llangollen 46Ab
Llantrisant 45Bc
Lleyn, Pen. 42Bb
Loanda 94De
Loanhead 44Db
Lobatse 93Ce
Lobito 91Dg
Lochalsh, Kyle of 40Bb
Lochearnhead 44Ba
Lochgelly 44Da
Lodz 65Db
Lofoten Is. 54Bb
Logan, Mt. 100Bb
Loire, R. 58Cb
Lokoja 94Cb
Lomami, R. 94Gd
Lombardy 60Aa
Lombok 78Cc
Lome 94Bb
Lomond Hills 44Da
Lomond, L. 44Aa
Lomza 65Ea
London (Can.) 104Cc
London (Eng.) 47Gd
Londonderry 50Db
Londonderry, C. 80Ba
Long I. (Bahamas) 106Db
Long, I. (U.S.) 105Ec
Long, L. 44Aa
Long Beach 102Bc
Long Eaton 46Cb
Longford, & Co. 50Dc
Longreach 81Db
Long's Peak 102Cb
Loop Hd. 49Bd
Lopez, C. 89Cf
Lop Nor, L. 67Hd
Lord Howe, I. 86Fh
L'Orient 58Bb
Lorne, Firth of 40Bb
Lorraine 57Cc
Los Angeles 102Bc
Loughrea 51Cc
Loughborough 46Cb
Louisiana, State 103Dc
Louis Trichardt 93Cd
Louisville 104Bd
Lourenco Marques 93De

Louth (Eire) 50Ec
Louth (Eng.) 46Ea
Louvain 56Cb
Lowell 105Ec
Lowestoft 43Eb
Lower Tunguska R. 67Hb
Lualaba, R. 94Gd
Luang Prabang 76Bd
Luangwa, R. 92Db
Luanshya 92Cb
Luapula, R. 95Gf
Lubeck 64Ba
Lubec B. 64Ba
Lublin 63Da
Lubumbashi 95Gf
Luce B. 40Bc
Lucerne (*see* Luzern)
Lucknow (*see* Lakhnau)
Luderitz 93Ae
Ludhiana 74Ba
Ludlow 46Bb
Ludwigshaven 64Bb
Lugansk 31Gc
Lukolela 94Ed
Lukow 65Eb
Lule, R. 54Db
Lulea 54Db
Luluabourg 94Fe
Lundy, I. 42Bc
Luneburg 64Ba
Luneville 57Dc
Lungkiang 77Da
Luni, R. 74Bb
Lurgan 50Eb
Lusaka 92Cc
Lusambo 94Fd
Lüta 77Db
Luton 47Gd
Lutterworth 46Cb
Luvua, R. 95Ge
LUXEMBOURG 57Dc
Luzern 64Bc
Luzern L. of 64Bc
Luzon 79Da
Lvov 63Db
Lydenburg 93De
Lyme Bay 42Cc
Lymington 47Fe
Lyne Water 44Db
Lyons 58Cb
Lys, R. 56Bb
Lytham 46Ba
Lyttelton 85De

Ma'an 72Bb
Maas R. 64Ab
Maastricht 56Cb
Mablethorpe 46Ea
Macau 76Cc
Macassar 79Cc
Macassar Str. 79Cc
Macclesfield 46Ba
MacDonnell Ra. 80Cb
Macedonia 61Db
Maceio 110Fc
Macgillicuddy's Reeks 49Ae
Macintyre, R. 83Ca
Mackay 81Db
Mackenzie Mts. 100Cb
Mackenzie, R. 100Db
Mackinnon Road 95Jd
Maclear 93Cf
McClintock Chan. 100Fa
McClure Str. 100Da
McKinley, Mt. 100Ab
Macquarie Is. 112SL
Macquarie, R. 83Cb
MADAGASCAR (MALAGASY REP.) 89Gg
Madeira Is. 90Ab
Madeira, R. 108Cc
Madhya Pradesh 74Cb
Madison 104Bc
Madras 74Cc
Madre de Dios, Archipelago 109Bh
Madrid 59Bc
Madurai 74Bd
Maesteg 45Ac
Mafeking 93Ce
Magadan 67Mc
Magadi 95Jd
Magdalena, R. 108Bb
Magdeburg 64Ba
Magellan, Str. of 109Ch
Maggiore, L. 64Bc
Maghera 50Eb
Magnetic North Pole 112NT
Magnetic South Pole 112SK
Magnitogorsk 66Ec
Mahalapye 93Cd
Mahalla el Kubra 91In
Mahanadi, R. 75Cb
Maharashtra 74Bb

Mahe 74Bc
Maidenhead 47Gd
Maidstone 47Hp
Maiduguri 94Da
Main, R. (Germany) 64Bb
Main, R. (N. Ireland) 48Eb
Maine, State 105Fc
Mainland, Orkneys & Shetlands 41In
Mainz 58Db
Maitland 83Db
Majorca, I. 59Cd
Majunga 91Gg
Makhachkala 72Ca
Makurdi 94Cb
Mal Bay 49Bd
Malabar Coast 74Bc
Malacca 78Bb
Malacca, Str. of 78Bb
Maladetta, Mt. 59Cc
Malaga 59Bd
Malaita I. 86Ge
Malakal 95Hb
Malange 94Ee
Malaren L. 55Cd
MALAWI 92Db
Malawi L. 92Db
MALAYSIA, EAST 78Cb
MALAYSIA, WEST 78Bb
Malden I. 87Le
MALDIVE IS. 68Ed
Maldon 47Hd
Malekula 86Gf
MALI 90Bd
Malin Hd. 48Da
Malines 56Cb
Mallaig 40Bb
Mallow 51Cd
Malmedy 57Db
Malmo 55Bd
Malpas 46Ba
Malta, I. 60Bc
Manado 79Db
Man, Isle of 42Ba
Manaar, G. of 74Bd
Managua 106Ad
Managua, L. 106Ad
Manaos 110Cc
Manchester 46Ba
Manchuria 67Kc
Manda 95Hf
Mandalay 75Db
Mangalore 74Bc
Mangoche 92Eb

Naturaliste, C. 80Ac
Navarre 59Bc
NAURU 86Ge
Naze, The (Eng.) 43Ec
Ndola 92Cb
Neagh, L. 48Eb
Neath 45Ac
Nebraska, State 102Cb
Neckar, R. 64Bb
Needles, The 47Fe
Nefud Desert 72Cc
Negro, Rio 109Cf
Negros, I. 79Db
Neisse, R. 64Cb
Neiva 110Bb
Nejd, District 73Cc
Nellore 74Cc
Nelson (Eng.) 46Ba
Nelson (N.Z.) 85Dd
Nelson, R. 100Gc
Nene, R. 43Db
NEPAL 75Cb
Nephin, Mt. 48Bc
Nephin Beg 48Bb
Ness, L. 40Bb
NETHERLANDS 56Ca
Neubrandenburg 64Ca
Neuchatel, L. of 64Ac
Neufchateau 57Cc
Neusiedler See 65Dc
Neustrelitz 64Ca
Neva, R. 29Fb
Nevada, State 102Bc
Nevis, Ben 40Bb
NewAmsterdam 110Db
Newark (Eng.) 46Da
Newark (U.S.A.) 105Ec
New Bedford 105Ec
Newbiggin 45Dc
Newbury 47Fd
New Britain 86Fe
New Brunswick 101Kd
Newburgh 44Da
New Caledonia, I. 86Gg
Newcastle (Aus.) 83Db
Newcastle (N. Ireland) 50Fb
Newcastle (Natal) 93Ce
Newcastle-under-Lyme 46Ba
Newcastle-upon-Tyne 45Dd
New Forest 47Fe
Newfoundland 101Lc
New Guinea 86Ee
New Hampshire 105Ec
Newhaven 47He
New Haven 105Ec
New Hebrides, Is. 86Gf
New Ireland I. 86Fe
New Jersey 105Ec
New Mexico 102Cc
New Orleans 99Ec
New Plymouth 84Ec
Newport (Eire) 50Bc
Newport (I. of W.) 47Fe
Newport (Salop) 46Bb
Newport (Mon.) 45Cc
Newport News 105Dd
Newquay 42Bc
New Providence I. 106Ca
New Romney 47He
New Ross 51Ed
Newry 50Eb
New Siberian Is. 67Lb
New South Wales 81Dc
Newtownards 50Fb
New York City 105Ec
New York, State 105Dc
NEW ZEALAND 84
Ngami, L. 92Bd
Nguru 94Da
Nhill 82Bc
Niagara Falls 105Dc
Niamey 90Cd
Nias I. 78Ab
NICARAGUA 106Ad
Nicaragua, L. 106Ad
Nice 58Dc
Nicobar Is. 75Dd
Nicosia 72Bb
Nicoya Pen. 106Ad
Nidd, R. 43Da
Niemen, R. 65Ea
Nieuport 56Bb
Niger, R. 88Cd
NIGER 90Cd
NIGERIA 94Cb
Niigata 77Eb
Nijmegen 56Cb
Nikolaev 63Eb
Nikolaevsk 67Lc
Nile, R. 88Fc
Nilgiri Hills 74Bc
Nimule 95Hc
Ninety Mile B. 83Cc
Nineveh 72Cb
Ningpo 77Dc
Nipigon, L. 101Hd
Nis 61Db
Nisa 65Db
Niteroi 111Ee
Nith, R. 40Ce
Niue I. 87Kf
Nkhotakota 92Db
Nogent 57Bc
Nome 98Aa
Nore, R. 49Dd
Nore, The 47Hd
Norfolk, Co. 39Gd
Norfolk (U.S.) 103Fc
Norfolk I. 86Gg
Norman Cross 46Db
Normandy 58Cb
Normanton 81Da
Norrköping 55Cd
Northam 80Ac
Northallerton 43Da
Northampton 39Fd
North Berwick 44Ea
North Beveland 56Bb
North, C. (Eur.) 54Ea
North, C. (N.Z.) 84Da
North Carolina 103Fc
North Channel 40Bc
North Dakota 102Cb
NORTHERN IRELAND 50
Northern Territory 80Ca
North Island 84Db
North Pole 112
North Riding 45De
North Sea 28Cb
Northumberland 38Ec
North-West Cape 80Ab
North-West Territories 100Gb
Northwich 46Ba
NORWAY 54Bc
Norwich 43Eb
Notek, R. 65Da
Nottingham 46Cb
Noumea 86Gg
Nova Lisboa 91Dg
Nova Scotia 101Kd
Novaya Zemlya I. 66Eb
Novi Sad 61Ca
Novokuznetsk 67Gc
Novo Redondo 94Df
Novorossiysk 31Gc
Novosibirsk 66Gc
Novy Port 66Fb
Nubian Desert 73Bc
Nullarbor Plain 80Bc
Nuneaton 46Cb
Nurnberg 62Cb
Nykoping 55Cd

Nylstroom 93Cd

Oahu I. 87Lb
Oakham 46Db
Oakland 102Ac
Oamaru 85Cf
Ob, G. of 66Fb
Ob, R. 66Fb
Oban 40Bb
Oberhausen 65In
Obidos 110Dc
Ocean I. 86Ge
Ochil Hills 44Ca
Odendaalsrus 93Ce
Odense 55Bd
Oder, R. 64Ca
Odessa 63Eb
Offaly, Co. 51Dc
Ogbomosho 94Bb
Ohio, R. 103Ec
Ohio, State 104Cc
Oise, R. 57Bc
Oka, R. 66Dc
Okahandja 93Ad
Okeechobee, L. 103Ed
Okhotsk 67Lc
Okhotsk, Sea of 67Lc
Okiep 93Ae
Okinawa, I. 77Dc
Oklahoma, State 102Dc
Okovango, R. 92Ac
Öland 55Cd
Olbia 60Ab
Oldcastle 50Dc
Oldenburg 64Aa
Oldham 46Ba
Olenek, R. 67Ib
Olifants, R. 93Dd
Ollerton 46Ca
Olomouc 65Db
Olympia 100Dd
Olympus, Mt. 61Db
Omagh 50Db
Omaha 103Db
OMAN 73Dc
Oman, G. of 73Dc
Omaruru 92Ad
Omdurman 73Bd
Omsk 66Fc
Onega, L. 66Db
Ongar 47Hd
Onitsha 94Cb
Onslow 80Ab
Ontario, Prov. 101Hc
Ontario, L. 105Dc
Oodnadatta 81Cb
Opole 65Db
Oporto 59Ac
Oran 59Bd
Orange Free State 93Ce
Orange, R. 93Be
Orange (Aust.) 83Cb
Orbost 83Cc
Ord, R. 80Ba
Orebro 55Cd
Oregon, State 102Ab
Orel 66Dc
Ore Mts. 64Cb
Orenburg 31Jb
Orford Ness 47Jc
Orinoco, R. 108Cb
Orissa, State 75Cb
Oristano 60Ac
Orkney Is. 41In
Orleans 58Cb
Ormskirk 46Ba
Ortegal, C. 58Ac
Oruro 110Cd
Orwell, R. 47Jd
Osaka 77Eb
Oshogbo 90Ce
Oslo 55Bd
Osnabruck 64Ba
Ostend 56Bb
Oster Dal, R. 55Bc
Ostersund 54Cc
Ostrow 65Db
Oswego 105Dc
Oswestry 46Ab
Otago, Distr. 85Bf
Otaru 77Fa
Otavi 92Ac
Otranto, Str. of 61Cb
Ottawa 101Jd
Ottawa, R. 101Jd
Otway, C. 82Bc
Ouagadougou 94Aa
Ouargla 62Bc
Oudtshoorn 93Bf
Oughter, L. 48Db
Oulu 54Eb
Oundle 46Db
Ourthe, R. 57Cb
Ouse, Great, R. 43Eb
Ouse, R. (Kent) 47He
Ouse, R. (Yorks) 46Ca
Over Flakkee 56Bb
Oviedo 58Ac
Owel, L. 48Dc
Owen Sound 105Cc
Ox Mts. 48Cb
Oxford, & Co. 47Fd
Oxus R. (*see* Amu Darya)
Oyo 94Bb
Ozark Plat. 103Dc

Paarl 93Af
Pacific Ocean 86
Padang 78Bc
Paijanne, L. 55Ec
Paisley 44Bb
PAKISTAN, 74Ab
Palapye Road 93Cd
Palau Is. 86Dd
Palawan, I. 79Ca
Paldiski 55Dd
Palembang 78Bc
Palermo 60Bc
Palk Str. 74Bd
Palliser, C. 85Ed
Palma 59Cd
Palmas, C. 89Be
Palmerston N. 84Ed
Palmyra I. 87Kd
Palmyras Pt. 75Cb
Pampas 109Cf
PANAMA 106Ce
Panama Canal 99In
Panama, Gulf of 106Ce
Pan American Highway 99Ed
Panay I. 79Da
Pantelleria 60Bc
Paotow 76Ba
Papa 65Dc
Papua 86Ee
PARAGUAY 111De
Paraguay, R. 108Dd
Parakou 94Bb
Paramaribo 110Db
Parana, R. 109De
Paria, G. of 107Fd
Parinas Pt. 108Ac
Paris 58Cb
Parkersburg 104Cd
Parkes 83Cb
Parma 60Bb
Parnaiba 110Ec
Parnaiba, R. 110Ec
Parnu 55Dd
Paroo, R. 82Ba
Parramatta 83Db
Parrett, R. 42Cc
Parry Is. 96Da
Partry Mts. 48Bc